German Tanks of World War II 'In Action'

German Tanks
of World War II
'In Action'

George Forty

Blandford Press
London · New York · Sydney

First published in the UK 1988 by Blandford Press
Artillery House, Artillery Row, London SWIP 1RT

Copyright © 1987 George Forty

Distributed in the United States by
Sterling Publishing Co, Inc,
2 Park Avenue, New York, NY 10016

Distributed in Australia by
Capricorn Link (Australia) Pty Ltd
PO Box 665, Lane Cove, NSW 2066

CIP Data

ISBN 0 7137 1634 7

Series editor: M. G. Burns

Typeset by Graphicraft Ltd., Hong Kong
Printed in Great Britain by Bath Press, Avon

**Propaganda pictures being taken of the new
might of the Panzers bursting through a
smokescreen on training at Wunsdorf, 29
November 1938. They are early PzKpfw IIs.**

Contents

Introduction and Acknowledgements

During World War 1, Germany showed little or no interest in the revolutionary new battlefield weapon called the tank. They built a mere handful of their own cumbersome machines and made minimal use of the small number of British and French tanks they captured. However, the true impact which the new weapon would have on future warfare was not lost to all those in authority, some influential officers being convinced that when Germany rose again — and there was not the slightest doubt in their minds that the Fatherland had only suffered a temporary setback — the tank would be given a major role to play.

The Treaty of Versailles banned all armament production in postwar Germany, so the early development of the Panzers had to be carried out in secret. It is amazing to discover to what lengths the soldiers and arms manufacturers were prepared to go in order to maintain this secrecy, not that the rest of Europe or America really took the matter very seriously. They were only too willing to believe the cover stories that the

Tractoren were truly just the farm tractors they pretended to be; indeed, the amount of assistance given to the Germans by such countries as 'neutral' Sweden and Communist Russia makes startling reading. The Germans were also actively helped by some of their erstwhile enemies in their clandestine re-armament plans, thus ensuring that the emergence of the *Panzerwaffe* was a foregone conclusion.

It is, however, very easy to be wise after the event. Most people in the 1920s and '30s just wanted to be left alone to rebuild their shattered lives and be allowed to live in peace — the horrors of World War 1 had touched practically every home in Belgium, France and Great Britain — so they were very easily persuaded to believe the lies. Behind this smokescreen Germany was not just re-arming, it was building a formidable fighting machine that would conquer almost the entire continent of Europe, with the Panzer divisions as the main striking force of the land army.

Once Hitler and his Nazi Party came to

power, all pretence was thrown aside and open re-armament grew apace. In fact it was now policy to try to make the rest of the world believe that the burgeoning German armoured forces were far stronger and better equipped than they were, and once again the subterfuge worked.

The rapid build-up of the Panzer divisions, and their training, were remarkable achievements. The Germans used to advantage the ideas of British tank pioneers such as Liddell Hart and Fuller, moulding them into a *Blitzkrieg* technique that was to prove hugely successful and was to earn their Panzer forces a battle reputation, far exceeding their wildest expectations, that would last throughout the war. Following their triumphal conquest of Poland, while the British and French dithered, the Panzer divisions sliced through them with laughable ease, despite the fact that the French on their own had more tanks, many of which were heavier and better armed than those of their fast-thinking, fast-moving opponents. It was the superior tactical handling of the German armour that won the day in 1940 and again in 1941 as it swept into Russia. With the possible exception of the fighter pilot, the Panzer commander in his dashing black uniform, death's head badges and floppy black beret was the nation's new superhero.

Once America and Russia had entered the war on the Allied side Germany had no real hope of winning. German tank production, for example, could not compare with the vast tank-building machine which swung into action all over the USA. While sheer numbers do not always make up for quality, the mere fact that the Americans *alone* could produce four times as many tanks as Germany, had to have a major effect upon the outcome of the war. Hitler's greatest mistake was, of course, his invasion of Russia and,

This is a well-known picture but it just had to be included! It shows both Axis dictators Adolf Hitler and Benito Mussolini, watching the Panzers march past, led by a *kleiner Befehlswagen*

although the Panzers destroyed countless thousands of inferior Russian tanks at the start of BARBAROSSA, they received their greatest setback when the hated *Untermenschen* suddenly produced battle winners like the T-34. Notwithstanding the eventual outcome of the land battle, the Panzer divisions showed themselves to be a formidable enemy on every battlefield. Tanks like the Tiger and Panther became legends in their own lifetime, as did Panzer Generals such as Heinz Guderian and Erwin Rommel.

Of the three basic characteristics of any tank — firepower, protection and mobility — the German tank designers favoured firepower above the other two, arguing that the gun would always be able to penetrate an enemy tank somewhere, because it was quite impossible to build an AFV with thick enough armour all over its frame. The whole history of German tank design was thus a continual search for bigger and better tank guns, followed then by the design of a vehicle to carry them. Although the machine-gun was retained as a secondary weapon to ensure against the needless expenditure of main armament rounds, the tank gun had to be of large enough calibre to be dual-purpose, namely, capable of dealing with both the enemy tank and the enemy anti-tank gun. The armour-piercing round was thus complemented by high explosive, a balanced load being carried by every tank.

While favouring firepower, German tank designers still did not neglect either protection or mobility. In general terms German tanks were invariably well-protected although up to and including Tiger I their

design featured a very square-looking profile, with armour plate at right angles. The tank hull contained the engine and transmission, the suspension and tracks, the ammunition and fuel, etc, with a bolted-on superstructure which included the turret, turret-ring and main armament. Extra protection was gained by bolting-on additional armour plate, until such time as extra thickness could be included at the building stage. From 1942, the shape of the German tank changed radically, sloping armour becoming the norm. The tremendous influence which the T-34 had on German tank design cannot be overestimated, and is reflected in such excellent tanks as the Panther and Tiger II.

As one might expect, German engines, transmissions and suspensions, etc, were normally first class, carefully made and beautifully finished. In a way this militated against increased production as it took far longer to build a German tank and many needless man hours were wasted in the finishing, whereas the Sherman and T-34 were far more suited to mass production by relatively unskilled workers. German tanks always used a front driving sprocket, so the drive had to be taken through the tank, under the turret basket, from the rear-mounted engine. After the PzKpfw I, Maybach engines were fitted to all tanks up to but not including the Maus. They were well-made engines, if complicated and difficult to maintain. Later models lacked power and were continually asked to do more and more work — the same engine for example, was put into Panther, Tiger II and Jagdtiger (the Maybach HL 230 P30) despite the fact

that the weight of the first named was 45.5 tons, the second 68 tons and the third over 70 tons.

As Germany went more and more on to the defensive their tanks became larger, heavier and more like mobile pill-boxes than the fast moving AFVs of the *Blitzkrieg* days. Hitler, who continually meddled in tank design and manufacture, had a definite 'hang-up' on size, so much German design and production effort was needlessly squandered on such bizarre projects as Maus. If all this effort had been directed towards producing more Panthers and PzKpfw IVs, then Allied casualties would have been considerably heavier, although it is doubtful if the eventual outcome would have been any different.

In this book I have deliberately tried to keep things simple and at a low level, to deal with the individual tank and its crew, rather than the Panzer formation, to endeavour to describe how the various types of German tanks evolved, came into service and were used in battle. I have done this through my usual 'In Action' mix of basic technical descriptions, backed up with first-hand accounts from Panzer crewmen, plus plenty of photographs, as many as possible coming from private collections. So much has already been written about the Panzers that it is not easy to find new facts or to discover interesting new stories about them over 45 years after they ceased to exist. However, the excellence of such tanks as the Panther and Tiger, together with the courage and efficiency of their crews, has ensured them a permanent place in military history and has made them a continual source of interest to all tank enthusiasts.

Tank designations

Before 1938, tanks under construction in Germany were described at various times by codenames to disguise their true identity — for example, as tractors: *Leichtetraktor* (light tractor), *Grosstraktor* (heavy tractor) or *Landwirtschaftlicher Schleper* (agricultural tractor) and *Bataillonführerswagen* (battalion commander's vehicle).

Experimental machines were given an identifying serial number, the first two figures indicating the vehicle weight, while the last two indicated the prototype number. A prefix VK — short for *Volkettenfahrzeuge* (fully tracked vehicle) — was added together, in some cases, with a letter or letters in brackets after the number, such as (DB) for Daimler-Benz or (H) for Henschel. Thus, VK 3002(P) would indicate that the vehicle in question was an experimental tank, weighing 30 tons, was the second prototype and was built by Porsche. In 1943 the VK nomenclature was to be replaced by the E series (*Entwicklung*, or Project). For example, E100 was the 100-plus ton tank built at the end of the war.

Once a tank entered service it was desig-nated as a *PanzerKampfwagen* (armoured fighting vehicle) which was abbreviated to PzKpfw or PzKw, plus a figure in Roman numerals from I to VI, for the various classes of light, medium and heavy tanks. Within each class, the first model (*Ausführung*) took the letter A, the second B and so on (eg: PzKpfw III Ausf C). Each AFV, when accepted into service, received an Ord-nance Inventory Number (*Sonderkraftfahr-zeugs*, or special vehicle number, usually abbreviated to SdKfz). For example, SdKfz 101 was the Ordnance Inventory Number allocated to the PzKpfw I. In addition, certain AFVs were also given nicknames in much the same way as some British and American tanks, the most famous being Tiger for PzKpfw VI and Panther for PzKpfw V.

There are so many possible different weights that can be quoted for any tank, depending upon whether they are unstowed, fully stowed, combat loaded, etc. I have tried to quote the combat weight, in imperial tons.

Acknowledgements

As always I have many people to thank for their kind assistance in the preparation of this book. Collecting material is never an easy task, particularly when so many ref-erences are in a foreign language. My Ger-man, never brilliant, was being taxed to its utmost limits until I managed to obtain the invaluable assistance of three people, firstly Oberstleutnant Manfred Blume, FRG Liaison Officer at the Royal Armoured Corps Centre, then Max Flemming, ex-Fallschirmpanzerkorps HG, who now lives in England, and finally Mrs Ingrid Randle, who was born in Germany and works as one of our Secretaries at the Tank Museum. Between them they have managed to trans-late all the material I have been sent and I am very grateful. In this context, I must thank Walter Spielberger for permission to trans-late and quote reports from his book *Die Panzerkampfwagen 35(t) and 38(t)*, and Hilary Doyle for the *translation*. Next I must thank David Fletcher, Edwin Bartholomew and the rest of the Tank Museum Library staff, from whom I have been able to obtain access to all the many British reports and papers, mainly built up during the war years by such organisations as the School of Tank Technology, which now reside in our ever-growing archives. I must also thank Roland Groom, resident photographer at the Tank Museum, for his help. As the reader will see, I have used many of the Tank Museum's splendid collection of photographs.

I have also had a great deal of invaluable assistance from both serving and retired officers and soldiers of the American, British and German armies, who have sent me photographs, reminiscences and other material, a great deal of which I have been able to include in the book. In this connec-tion I must thank: Colonel Paul Adair, Heinz-Dietrich Aberger, John Batchelor, Oberst aD Albert von Boxberg[1], Ernst J. Dohany, OTL aD Rolf Due, Curt Ehle, Frau Everth, Herbert Elsner, OTL aD Ger-hard Fischer, Mrs Sandra Forty, Hans-Harold Grahn, Major Peter Gudgin, OTL Reimar Grundies, Oberst aD Wolfgang Hartelt, Georg Heymer, Alfred Johnson, Charles K. Kliment, Hans-Ritter Klippert, Nick Mashlonik, 'Dusty' Miller, Justus Wil-helm von Oechelhauser, Oberst aD Fabian von Bonin von Ostau, Alfred Otte, Bryan Perrett, OTL Sievert Paulsen, Jeff Pavey, Horst Riebenstahl, Gerhard Remmel, Oberst aD Helmut Ritgen, Oberst aD Her-mann Rothe, Oberst aD Alfred Rubbel, OTL aD Rolf Stoves, Gerd Schroeder, Dr Heinz Spathe, Hans Teske, Lieutenant Colonel David Treasure, Emil Thran, Karl Wilhelm, Oberst aD Gerhardt Witte, Dr Kurt Wolff, Rudolf Wulff and the Kamer-adschaft of various Panzer units, who have all sent me material, or published my re-quests for help. I must also thank Herr Berwald, the Redakteur of *Alte Kameraden*, for publishing my appeal for information.

Finally, as always, I must thank my ever-patient wife, Anne, for typing my manu-script. My grateful thanks to everyone. I hope all will feel that the end result has been worth all their efforts.

George Forty
Bryantspuddle,
October 1986

1
Building the Panzers

Setting the scene

The foundation of a large tank-producing industry in Germany prior to the start of World War 2 was but a part of the overall rebirth of German industrial military might, which probably owed its beginnings to a nationwide determination to resist the draconian provisions of the Versailles Treaty which Germany had been forced to sign on 28 June 1919. Of course, major re-armament did not begin until after Adolf Hitler abrogated the Treaty in 1935 and put some 240,000 German factories on to the production of weapons of war. However, the scene had been set many years before, almost from the moment when the Armistice was signed and the victorious Allies set about ensuring that Germany would remain de-militarised for ever. The national determination to survive as a military power was perhaps personified by the giant industrial empire of Krupp which, on the face of it, cheerfully accepted the severe arms production limitations, adopted a new company slogan '*Wir Machen Alles!*' (We make everything!) and ostensibly turned their factories to producing such everyday items as typewriters and baby carriages. And yet, behind the scenes, they were quietly and methodically carrying on planning and designing weapons for the next war, moving their skilled engineers to subsidiary plants all over the world, just waiting for the day when they could return to the full production of armaments in the Ruhr. The assistance given knowingly to this subterfuge by some of the Allied and neutral countries of Europe makes disturbing reading even this long after the events. A cynic might well conclude that Europe got exactly what it deserved when war finally came in 1939, while such revelations should be an object lesson to all those who advocate appeasement as the solution to such problems in the future.

During World War 1, Germany had shown little interest in the building or employment of tanks, producing under 20 of their cumbersome 30 tonne (29.5 UK/33 US tons) A7V *Sturmpanzerwagen*,[2] as compared with nearly 3,000 British and 4,000 French tanks. Although the Kaiser's military advisors were slow at first to recognise the potential of these new vehicles, the realisation that they were the battle-winning weapon of the future had at least been accepted by some senior officers by the end of the war. General Ludendorff, for example, when reporting to the German Parliament in October 1918, said '...there is no longer any prospect or possibility of compelling the enemy to peace. Above all two factors have been decisive for this issue; first, the tanks...'. Germany was, of course, prohibited from having any tanks by the Treaty of Versailles, and, apart from limited police use, also denied armoured cars. However, this was not entirely bad news as, while Britain and France had vast numbers of obsolescent armoured fighting vehicles they could not afford to scrap, Germany could start with a clean slate — even if their start would have to be a covert one, including secret foreign assistance. The one tank designer of any merit in Germany during World War 1 had been Joseph Vollmer. In addition to designing the A7V, the only

German-built tank actually to see action, Vollmer had been working on a much lighter model, the *Leichte Kampfwagen 1*, which reached prototype stage in mid-1918. This 7 tonne (6.9 UK/7.7 US tons) model was followed by the LK II, some two tonnes heavier, with a limited traverse 57 mm gun. Vollmer completed two prototype LK IIs and had parts for a further eight (the production order had been for 580) when the war ended. He was, however, able to dismantle his tanks and slip abroad into neutral Sweden, taking all ten tank kits with him. Arriving there, he re-assembled the tanks and sold them to the obliging Swedes, who renamed them M-21s. These tanks formed the very first tank company of the Swedish Army. Vollmer did not stay long in Sweden, moving on to Czechoslovakia, where he became chief designer for the Adamov firm. From 1925, his models were produced by the Czech firms Skoda and Tatra. When

The 30 tonne A7V *Sturmpanzerwagen* was the only German-built tank to see service in the Great War. For the most part, German tank forces used captured British heavy tanks. The photograph shows a pair of A7Vs moving into action on the Western Front, June 1918.

Germany marched into Czechoslovakia in 1938, the German Army reaped the rewards of Vollmer's efforts, absorbing into German service all the excellent Czech-built tanks.

The Swedish connection

In his book *Covert German Re-armament 1919–1939*, Bart Whalley explains how Krupp acquired another dummy company in Sweden: '...Because Sweden had proved a safe and discreet haven for German re-armament, Krupp acquired a second dummy company there in addition to its Bofors cannon subsidiary. The new Krupp affiliate was the old machinery firm of AB Landswerk, located at Landskrona, in southern Sweden. It produced its first tank design in 1929, and its first production tank, the fine L-10 light tank with a 37 mm gun, appeared in 1931, and entered Swedish service in 1934. A succession of excellent tank and armoured car models flowed from Landswerk, which now dominated Sweden's armored vehicle industry. These models foreshadowed several features that would later appear in the tanks of Germany and Russia, a clear proof of the fruitful collaborative German-Russo-Swedish cross-fertilisation.'

Withdrawal of inspectors

In January 1927 the Inter-Allied Control Commission inspectors, who had been appointed to see that the provisions of the Versailles Treaty were obeyed by the Germans, were withdrawn, and there followed a period of clandestine re-armament, albeit still with some slight pretence at cover stories, although very little was needed to convince the rest of Europe that Germany was still obeying the rules, because it was exactly what most politicians *wanted* to believe. The great Krupp empire launched into a period of *schwarze Produktion* (black production), tanks being included from about 1928 onwards. One wartime inter-office memo stated that '...of all the guns which were being used in 1939–41, the most important were already fully developed by 1933.'[5] Then, in 1933, Adolf Hitler was appointed Chancellor and the National Socialists came fully into power. Two years later Hitler abrogated the Versailles Treaty and all pretence was thrown aside, or rather, put into high reverse! Indeed, the Nazis went out of their way to exaggerate the strength of the German armed forces, in order to bluff their erstwhile conquerors into believing that Germany was now invincible. Again, it is remarkable to see how easily they were able to fool the rest of the world.

Back home in Germany, tank design was being carried on covertly, while the *Truppenamt*[3] had established an Inspectorate of Motorised Troops to co-ordinate and direct all mechanised units, including shadow tank units. An early member of this organisation was Heinz Guderian, destined to become the most famous German tank officer and the true 'Father of the Panzers'. 1926 saw orders being placed with German industry for the building, in secret, of both tank and armoured car prototypes. The tanks were given cover names to disguise their true purposes, for example, the 20 ton *Grosstraktor I* (heavy tractor) was built by Daimler-Benz in 1928–29. It was one of three test vehicles ordered, Rheinmetall producing the *Grosstraktor II* and Krupp the *Grosstraktor III*. Each company made two 'tractors', all built of mild steel, all designed to mount a 7.5 cm gun and all secretly tested at the Red Army's tank testing centre at Kazan in Russia.[4] German technicians were stationed in Kazan from 1926, under the secret Rapallo Treaty signed between Russia and Germany in 1926. Sweden also collaborated in secret tank development with the Germans,

The *Grosstraktor* was built in the late 1920s under its cover name to disguise its true purpose.

The Rheinmetall version of the *Grosstraktor* had a 7.5 cm gun as its main armament and after secret testing in Russia saw service with 1st Panzer Division. It ended its days, like the other five built (two from each manufacturer), as a plinthed vehicle on the parade ground of one of the first Panzer regiments.

Guderian driving his first tank as a guest of the Swedes — fittingly, it was one of Vollmer's smuggled models! Rheinmetall and Krupp also produced three prototype light tractors, the *Leichtetraktor*, which weighed some 9.5 tonnes (9.4 UK/10.5 US tons) and mounted a 3.7 cm gun.

Allied generals must have looked on with great amusement at the odd-looking dummy tanks which 'Heinz Hothead (*Brauseweter*)' Guderian, now a full Colonel, brought on to the summer military exercises in 1929. Some were *ad hoc* push-along vehicles, but these were soon replaced by motorised dummies, with canvas and wood bodies mounted on NSU 'Dixi' and Adler cars. The Germans quickly realised the value of cheap, easily-produced dummies for training and there-after incorporated the dummy tank on their ordnance inventory. Some of these dummies were even said to have been deployed in action towards the end of the war when equipment was in short supply.

Preparing for war

From the early 1930s, German industry had begun war production in earnest. Hitler, for example, placed an order with Krupp for 100 new light tanks, to be delivered by March 1934, with 650 more to follow a year later. Krupp recalled his engineers from Sweden and began tank production on his home ground. Rapidly the wood and canvas dummy tanks were replaced with real AFVs, as Guderian put it in *Achtung Panzer*:

'German tanks underwent a radical transformation. Their formerly wooden cannon suddenly spouted fire and their erstwhile make-believe armour gave way to steel.' By 1935 the first three Panzer divisions had been formed and had received their new weapons. Neither the *Leichte* nor *Grosstraktoren* were considered suitable for battle or even training, so, while better models were being designed, two light, small tanks were rushed into production to meet the Führer's orders. The 5 ton *Landwirtschaftlicher Schlepper* (agricultural tractor), the prototype for the smaller of the two, was built in 1933, and went on to become the PanzerKampfwagen (PzKpfw I). The PzKpfw II was nearly twice its weight and evolved from the Krupp-built LKA II and the MAN-designed PzKpfw II Ausf al, the latter being chosen for production. These tanks, like their British equivalents, were only of limited use on the battlefield, although they did provide excellent training vehicles. Two other tanks were also being designed for the burgeoning Panzer divisions, a light model and a medium model. As usual, they were given cover names to disguise their true purpose, the lighter one being called the '*Zugführerswagen (ZW)*' (company commander's vehicle), while the heavier was known as the '*Bataillonführers-wagen (BW)*' (battalion commander's vehicle). From 1939, they were called PanzerKampfwagen III and IV respectively, and rapidly became the backbone of the Panzer divisions' order of battle.

The first factories to enter the field of tank production were Krupp (Essen), Rheinmetall-Borsig (Berlin-Tegel), Daimler-Benz (Berlin-Marienfelde) and Henschel (Kassel). These were all large concerns which had the in-house capacity to manu-facture most of the major components them-selves. This was particularly true of Krupp and Rheinmetall who, as big armament

works, could design, test and produce the necessary armament, armour, forgings and other main parts, while Daimler-Benz, as heavy lorry builders, and Henschel, who were locomotive and lorry producers, also had plenty of experience in heavy vehicle production. They were joined in the course of the next four years by others, such as the heavy engineering works of Krupp Gruson-werk (Magdeburg), which was by 1937 beginning to develop parallel capacity with Essen, for tank assembly and for the manu-facture of some tank components. Another such firm was the Nuremberg branch of Maschinenfabrik Augsburg-Nürnberg (MAN), also an old and well-established engineering concern with the necessary facilities and technical experience. There were cases of conversion of existing plant, plus some expansion on to adjacent sites. In a few exceptional cases, however, completely new tank assembly factories were built and grafted on to, but remained largely inde-pendent of, existing businesses. Examples of these were MIAG (Brunswick) and Al-kett (Berlin-Borsigwalde). In 1939/40, tank building increased through the incorpora-tion into the Reich industry of plants in Austria (Steyr-Daimler-Puch), Czechoslo-vakia (B-M Kolben-Danek) and Poland (Waverma). As production and demand grew, an even greater proportion of the work on component manufacture had to be sub-contracted. Indeed, many of the new as-sembly plants were entirely dependent upon getting their major components from outside

Heinz Guderian, 'Father of the Panzers', in his command half-track, watching operators work an *Enigma* code machine.

specialist firms. This required a high degree of co-ordination between the Wehrmacht and industry, between the designer and production engineer, and between all the sub-contractors, working to the laid-down standard specifications. The organisational machinery of this part of the armaments industry was based on a system of inter-locking industrial commissions. The main commission — Hauptausschuss für Panzer-wagen und Zugmaschinen — was divided into eight special commissions, covering armour production, armour development, tank production, tracked vehicle production,

The canvas and wood 'tanks' which were used so successfully for training by the emerging Panzer forces.

light armoured vehicle production, track production, engine production and trans-mission gear production. Tank armament production was dealt with by the *Waffen-hauptausschuss*, through either the special commission for light anti-tank and tank weapons, or that for heavy anti-tank and tank weapons. Many of the minor require-ments for tank production were also covered by other special commissions, representing the whole of the industry (eg, optical goods).

Production build up

The build-up of tank production was rapid as Table 1 shows. In addition to light and medium tanks some interest was also shown in designing a heavy tank to follow on from the *Grosstraktor*. This new vehicle was simp-ly called *NeubauFahrzeuge* (NbFz) (new construction vehicle) and weighed about 24 tonnes (23.6 UK/26.5 US to us). Five proto-

Wooden mock-up of the *Zugführerswagen* which later became known as the PzKpfw III.

types were built by Krupp and Rheinmetall, the former building the Model A, armed with co-axial 7.5 cm and 3.7 cm guns, and the latter the Model B (10.5 cm and 3.7 cm guns). Ordered in 1934–35, the tanks were orginally designated PzKpfw V and VI, but, as neither was put into production, these designations were passed on to the Panther and Tiger tanks. The prototype NbFzs were initially located at the tank training school at Putlos until early in 1940 when three were used in Norway. One was destroyed there and the other two returned to Germany towards the end of the year.

TABLE 1 TANK PRODUCTION 1934–39

Year	Total	Monthly average
1934	500	40
1935	700	60
1936	600	50
1937	750	60
1938	1,560	130
1939	1,680	140

Note: These figures include Czech output from 1938.
Source: Economic Survey of Germany Sect K Armaments and Munitions published by the Foreign Office & Ministry of Economic Warfare in May 1945.

On the day that Germany attacked Poland (1 September 1939), the total number of German tanks in service, but not including those recently acquired from the Czechs, was 3,195. An estimated breakdown of this total shows: PzKpfw I — 1,445; PzKpfw II — 1,226; PzKpfw III — 98; PzKpfw IV — 211; command tanks of all types — 215.[6] Most of these were involved in the short, 30-day campaign in Poland, where a total of 217 were destroyed (89 Mk Is, 83 Mk IIs, 26 Mk IIIs and 19 Mk IVs).[7] Tank production continued apace, the monthly average for 1939 being some 140, rising to 170 the

The heavy tank which followed the *Grosstraktor* was known simply as *Neubaufahrzeuge* (NbFz). The 24-ton tank was used for training and three saw service in Norway, but it was too old-fashioned to be of much use on the modern battlefield.

This fascinating parade scene was taken in the marketplace of Kamenz near Bamberg on 2 October 1936 and shows the new tanks of Panzer Regiment 3 on parade (Oberst aD von Boxberg).

following year. So, by May 1940, the total in service was 3,379. However, what was more important than sheer numbers was the fact that there were now 329 Mk IIIs and 280 Mk IVs, which would provide the trump-cards in the lightning German assault on the Western Front. As far as actual tank numbers are concerned, the Allied Order of Battle on the Western Front showed a total of over 3,000 tanks, mostly French, with under 400 British and a few Belgian, as compared with 2,574 German. Moreover, many of the French tanks were heavier and better armed, but they could not match the superior tactical handling of the Panzer divisions.

Barbarossa

When, in June 1941, the Germans launched their invasion of Russia, they had 5,264 tanks of all types, including the Czech contingent, but not counting their latest trophies of war captured from the French. There were a fair number of these and they would be mainly confined to second-line units in places like the Channel Islands, or be converted into other forms of AFV, such as self-propelled guns. Some 3,350 German tanks took part in BARBAROSSA, including the majority of the Mk IIIs and IVs then in service. Ranged against them the Russians had 20,000 tanks, although nothing like that vast number were actually with front-line units. As in France, the *Blitzkrieg* sliced its way through the opposition and the Panzer divisions quickly cut deep into Russian ter-

ritory, destroying in the process huge numbers of Russian tanks — some 17,000 as compared with German losses of 2,700. However, as the months dragged on without the expected total surrender of the enemy, and the weather conditions deteriorated, then the inherent problems of German tank design and production manifested themselves. Overcomplicated engines, narrow gauge tracks, difficult transmissions and running gear that required a large amount of maintenance, a lack of spare parts and of trained mechanics — the list was seemingly endless. In addition, while the standard PzKpfw IIIs and IVs were vastly superior to the mass of Russian tanks, they were being outclassed by the appearance of a new, powerful, Russian medium tank, the T-34, and also by the heavy KV I. Knowledge of the new tanks had come as early as November 1941, but little notice was taken until the T-34 had entered full production. There was clearly an urgent requirement for a more powerful tank to deal with these new AFVs. Heavier tanks than the Mk IV had, of course, been considered some years previously, Henschel having been given an order for a 30 tonne (29.5 UK/33 US tons) 'break-through' tank as far back as 1937. One chassis had been built and trialled, when the firm was ordered to stop work on it and to build a 65 ton tank instead. Two prototype VK 6501s were produced, but after more trials, they were told to go back to the 30-ton model (DW1). Henschel eventually produced the DW2 but it never went into production. Other prototypes ordered and produced included a 30 ton VK 3001, 36 tonne (35.4 UK/39.7 VS tons) VK 3601 and a 45 tonne VK 4501. At this stage, Adolf Hitler intervened personally, prototypes of the 45 ton version being shown to him on his birthday in April 1942. After inspecting them he gave his personal orders that the

new tank was to mount an 8.8 cm gun instead of the specified 7.5 cm. Henschel incorporated all the best features of all the experimental models into the VK 4501 (H) and the Tiger was born, entering production in July 1942. The first models off the production line were rushed to the Leningrad area in August 1942, where, after a disappointing start — due mainly to rushing untried Tigers into a difficult situation — it soon began to acquire its formidable reputation. At about the same time two other firms which had had a part in producing the VK 3001, Daimler-Benz and MAN, had designed what must rank as the best medium tank to be built during the war by any nation, the Panther. Its design was undoubtedly influenced by the T-34, and yet again Adolf Hitler played an important part in its development by ordering that it should be armed with a more powerful long-barrelled version of the standard 7.5 cm tank gun, the KwK 42 L/70. When it came off the production line in August 1943, Panther weighed 45 tons, 15 tons more than the original medium tank limit. It was to cause as much, if not more, havoc than the Tiger. Output continued to rise through 1943 and 1944 but was never sufficient to meet the Wehrmacht's ever-growing requirements. Table 2 below shows the estimated output for 1943 by producers. (NB: It shows a total output of 5,750 which is some 333 less than the total for 1943 given in Table 3. The latter is probably more accurate having been prepared some time after the war.)

An interesting line-up of PzKpfw IIIs and IVs, which really formed the backbone of the Panzer divisions for many years, taken in March 1944. They are, from left to right: PzKpfw IV Ausf F₁ (with KwK 37 L/24 version of 7.5 cm gun), PzKpfw III Ausf L/M (with 5 cm KwK 39 L/60), PzKpfw III Ausf H (with 5 cm KwK L/42) and PzKpfw F₁ (with 7.5 cm KwK 40 L/43) (Oberst aD von Boxberg).

On manoeuvres in 1939, these PzKpfw I Ausf As must have been close to their safe fording depth (58 cm/1 ft 1 in) as they crossed this stream. Indeed, it looks as though the nearest Panzer is already in trouble as the driver is 'escaping' from his flooded vehicle.

TABLE 2 TANK OUTPUT IN 1943

Assembler	III	IV	V	VI	Remarks
Niedersachsen	—	—	700	—	A new assembly plant.
Henschel	100	—	200	650	The only producer of Tigers.
MAN	—	—	500	—	—
Daimler-Benz	—	—	300	—	
MIAG	225	—	—	—	During year turned over entirely to SP guns.
Krupp Gruson	—	200	—	—	Probably also large part of tanks unallotted.
Nibelungenwerk	—	900	—	—	—
Another producer	—	900	—	—	Identity of this producer is uncertain.
Tanks unallotted	75	700	300	—	No maker's name available.
	400	2,700	2,000	650	

(Source: as for Table 1.)

Although by the end of 1943 Tiger and Panther were well on their way to redressing the tank v tank balance in favour of the Germans, they simply could not match the quantity production which the Allies achieved. As Table 3 below shows, America alone outproduced Germany in every year except 1940, despite the fact that they had to start their tank production virtually from scratch. Even Britain, during the period of severe bombing (1940–41), produced almost as many tanks as the Germans did in 1940 and then overtook and continued to outproduce them.

TABLE 3 TANK PRODUCTION COMPARISON

Year	Germany	Britain	America
1940	1,459	1,399	331
1941	3,256	4,841	4,052
1942	4,098	8,611	24,997
1943	6,083	7,476	29,497
1944	8,466	2,476*	17,565
1945	988	NK	11,968
Totals	24,350	24,803	88,410

*First six months only.
†First three months.
(Source: US Army in World War II — The Technical Services — The Ordnance Department.)

German tank designers appeared to do little to help themselves in the bargain, and instead of concentrating their efforts on producing their proven battle-winning Tigers and Panthers, they wasted valuable capacity on projected superheavy tanks, like the 140 tonne (137.7 UK/154.4 US tons) E 100, the 188 tonne (185 UK/207 US tons) Maus and are even supposed to have been considering a land monitor weighing a preposterous 1,000 tonnes! By 1945, however, enthusiasm for these superheavy monsters had somewhat waned, although the larger version of

the Tiger, the 68 tonne (66.9 UK/75 US tons) Royal Tiger, was considered a perfectly reasonable and battleworthy weapon, despite the maintenance headaches it produced. The Panther was still proving itself to be a most satisfactory heavy medium tank, while the ubiquitous Panzer IV was still in quantity production up to March 1945. Much of the country's production effort had now been shifted to producing limited-traverse AFVs, such as the *Jagdtiger* and *Jagdpanther*. The former, at 70 tonnes (68.9 UK/ 77.2 US tons), with its 12.8 cm gun, must rank as the most powerful AFV to be used in action in the war.

Maintenance and spares problems

German tanks tended to be complicated and elaborate, rather like their British counterparts, which meant that it required not only more effort to produce them, but also to look after them, than the more straightforward, uncomplicated Sherman or T-34. Within its

limited industrial capacity Germany was unable to produce sufficient tanks and spare parts simultaneously. The German armoured forces therefore suffered a constant shortage of spare parts for most of the war. Stocks of spares fell to a critical level during the summer of 1942 and never really recovered. This was also due to the fact that some armament production officials failed to realise the importance of spares. While pressing for an increase in the production of new tanks they neglected the urgent need for spare parts until it was too late and irreparable damage had been done.

System of manufacture

The general system of tank component manufacture and assembly was by the progressive batch system. This necessitated vehicles being lifted or pulled forward through a series of stationary stages, until they were finally completed and driven away for testing. Owing to the considerations of weight and crane handling, the heavier tanks had to remain static until the suspension had been fitted to the completed hull. The next stage was to install the engine, transmission, gearbox, etc. The superstructure was then lowered and bolted on to the hull, then the turret, armament, gun platform, etc, were fitted to complete the major process of assembly. The fitting of all internal equipment such as instruments, ammunition bins, vision blocks, etc, formed the final stage. This process clearly required smooth coordination of production in both major and

A photograph taken inside the Henschel Tiger factory, showing Tiger I in construction. As the report in Annex A explains, this was the Mittelfeld works.

Jagdpanthers being built. Note also the Panther Ausf G at bottom right. This was probably therefore the MNH (Maschinenfabrik Niedersachen Hannover) factory at Hannover, which were the only producers of both these AFVs.

minor components, all of which had to be tested and fitted together as sub-assemblies in other parts of the factory, or in outside specialist firms, before reaching the main assembly hall.

Survey of German AFV plants

SHAEF carried out a preliminary survey of German AFV plants immediately after the war had ended and its main conclusions include the fact that tank production had undoubtedly received special consideration from the designers of machine tools and considerable ingenuity had been displayed in the tooling-up for large machining operations such as drilling tank hulls, turrets, etc.

Good shop-floor view of a German tank factory, where production of PzKpfw III is in progress.

In many cases this was achieved by the use of several standard machine tools incorporated into a special jig. Another good feature was the excellent power-driven welding manipulators, used for hull and turret construction, which had all been designed and built specifically for the job in hand, although the majority of specialised composite AFV machine tool rigs were made up of standard units, capable of being used in normal peace-time engineering activities. Considerable development had taken place in the plants for the profiling, hardening and fabrication of armour plate in order to achieve quantity production, while there was apparently no shortage of machine tools. To quote the report: 'There is little doubt that Germany possessed a virile machine tool industry throughout the war'.

The survey covered a sample visit to some eight plants, plus the Tank Proving Ground at Sennelager and the Tank Training School at Paderborn. An example of the type of report they produced is given in Appendix A at the end of the book. It concerns the Henschel & Sohn factory at Kassel, who were the only producers of the Tiger.

Bomb damage

Up to the middle of 1943, the tank industry had only been indirectly affected by Allied bombing, in that no substantial damage had been caused to any tank assembly plants. However, from then onwards the widespread devastation in the Ruhr and other areas undoubtedly affected the supply of essential AFV components.

From the second half of 1943, the tank assembly works themselves began to suffer from air raids, the first recorded instance being at Daimler-Benz of Marienfelde. These works continued to be hit as did other main producers like the Berlin assembly plant of Alkett at Berlin-Borsigwalde. Both these factories must also have been badly affected by the very widespread local damage to housing and transport facilities. Considerable ingenuity had to be displayed in the re-disposition of assembly operations after an air attack. The same applied equally to the dispersal of machine tools where hits had been sustained on main machine shops. Nevertheless, despite severe damage to buildings, some production was always maintained, even under extremely difficult conditions.

A woman's place

Before leaving the subject of tank production there is one other interesting difference between German and Allied war production — the workers who actually produced the weapons. As the armed forces of all the combatant nations grew in size and their armament industries expanded, so their manpower problems grew. The Allies turned to their womenfolk for help, women taking the places of men in the factories as the men left to fight. Over three million American and 2¼ million British housewives, mothers and daughters worked in the factories during wartime.

In Germany, however, such a thing was unheard of. A woman's place was in the home and the 'New Order' would see that they remained there. Only 182,000 women were ever employed in German armaments factories and even their presence was resented. It was not until 25 July 1944 that Hitler decreed that all German women from the ages of 17 to 50 must register for work. By then it was of course too late for them to be of much use and only a few hundred ever reported for work. In place of women, the Fatherland used foreign, slave labour and prisoners, to meet the Reich's manpower problem. On average, in the tank production factories about 50 per cent of the workers were foreigners and this aspect undoubtedly had to be considered in the tooling-up of plants, so that this high proportion of semi-skilled labour could be employed efficiently.

2
Panzer organisations and training

The foundations of the armoured forces of the Third Reich that were to sweep so triumphantly across Europe in 1939–40 were laid by Generaloberst Hans von Seeckt, the first Commander in Chief of the *Reichswehr* (27 March 1920 until 6 October 1926), in the years of the Weimar Republic. He was convinced that any future war would be a much more fluid affair than ever before and that successful armies would be composed of integrated mobile forces, closely supported from the air. He wrote: 'In brief, the whole future of warfare appears to me to lie in the employment of mobile armies, relatively small but of high quality and rendered distinctly more effective by the addition of aircraft...,[8] Seeckt matched his words with action, by making sure that every member of his tiny army (which contained only 4,000 officers and 96,000 men), was trained both as a leader and as an instructor, in readiness for the day when they would be able to expand once more. He also fully supported the covert re-armament programme and took every opportunity to send his officers abroad, visiting other armies to glean information and new ideas. Thus, the revolutionary new theories of mechanised warfare, expounded in Great Britain by such men as Fuller, Broad and Liddell Hart, found a far more receptive audience in the new German Army than they did in their own. Heinz Guderian,[9] for example, clearly appreciated the decisive role that the Panzer divisions would play in the future, but from the outset he saw the tanks as being just one important element of a formation of all arms, rather than being totally effective on their own or totally subservient to the infantry. He was also not too proud to make use of the ideas of others, translating Broad's first mechanised warfare pamphlet *Mechanised and Armoured Formations* (known in the British Army as 'The Purple Primer' on account of the colour of its cover) and issuing it to all Panzer forces as a basic training manual. While British tankmen laboured under such constraints as a severe lack of funding, their Imperial policing

commitments and a general dislike and distrust of mechanisation by many senior officers, the Germans were able to accept the new philosophy and thus gain a considerable advantage over their erstwhile conquerors.

In his book *The Other Side of the Hill*, Sir Basil Liddell Hart recounted a conversation he had with General Ritter von Thoma in 1945, in which he described the forming of the first properly equipped Panzer units and how wonderful it was to have real tanks after having to make do with dummies for so many years.

'In 1934 our first tank battalion was formed at Ohrdruf, under the name "Motor-Instruction Commando". I was in charge of it. It was the grandmother of all the others. It was subsequently expanded into a regiment of two battalions, while two more were established at Zossen.' General von Thoma went on to explain how the new units were equipped rather slowly with the little PzKpfw I and II, then later with PzKpfw IIIs and IVs. 'Meantime our organisation

was growing. In 1935 two tank brigades were formed — one for each of the two armoured divisions that were then created.'

The two years 1934 and 1935 were probably the most momentous in the early formation and building of the Panzer forces. With the Führer's wholehearted support, the *Panzertruppe* was created, with General Lutz at its head and Guderian as his Chief of Staff, the first tank unit — Panzer Regiment 1, being formed in October 1934. Earlier that year, at an historic meeting of the Army Weapons Branch (*Heereswaffenamt*) on 11 January 1934, the basic specifications for the

Excellent group photograph of officers of the Panzer Regiment 1. They are wearing the German equivalent of the British 'Sam Browne' belt. The use of the leather cross strap was discontinued quite early in the war. The Adjutant is also wearing his aiguilete on his right shoulder (Horst Riebenstahl).

PzKpfw II and IV were approved. Later, the need for another medium tank, PzKpfw III was recognised and by the end of 1935 not only had the PzKpfw II entered service, but the first prototype PzKpfw IV had been constructed.

The first Panzer divisions

The first three Panzer divisions were formed on 15 October 1935. Their initial basic organisation bore a close resemblance to that of the British Army's experimental armoured force of 1927. 1st Panzer Division was formed at Weimar, the 2nd at Würzburg and the 3rd at the Wunsdorf manoeuvre area, with its headquarters in Berlin, taking as its emblem the Berlin Bear. Each of the three new divisions comprised a tank (Pan-

zer) brigade, a motor rifle (Schützen) brigade, plus supporting arms and services. The Panzer brigade contained two regiments, each of two battalions (Abteilung), with four companies (Kompanie) per battalion. A company contained 32 light tanks (PzKpfw Is and IIs) while the total tank strength of the brigade, including command tanks, was 561. The Schützen brigade contained a truck-mounted regiment of two battalions, plus a motor cycle (Kradschützen) battalion. In support were a motorised artillery (Artillerie) regiment of 24 10.5 cm howitzers, an anti-tank (Panzerjäger) battalion of towed 3.7 cm anti-tank guns, an engineer (Pionier) battalion, which had started life as a company but was then expanded rapidly, a reconnaissance (Aufklärungs) battalion of armoured cars and motor cycles, together with signals (Nachrichten) and service units (Einheiten).

The Condor Legion

A proportion of the new Panzer forces gained valuable combat experience as members of the Condor Legion of 'volunteers', fighting for General Franco during the Spanish Civil War which began on 17 July 1936. Four tank battalions plus 30 anti-tank companies formed the ground element of the Legion. They were able to try out and to perfect the new tactics, including air-ground support.

Mobilisation

The next two Panzer divisions, the 4th and 5th, were formed in 1938 at Würzburg and Oppeln respectively and the 10th in Prague the following April, less than a month after the Wehrmacht had marched into Czecho-

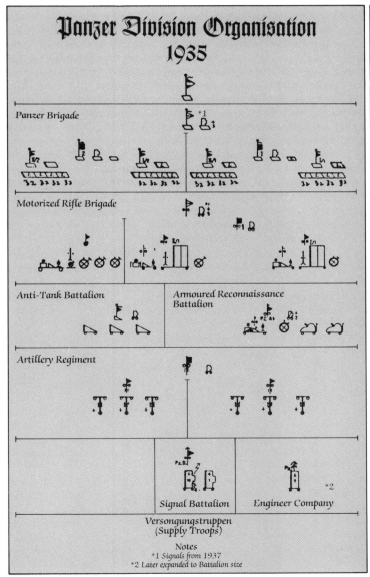

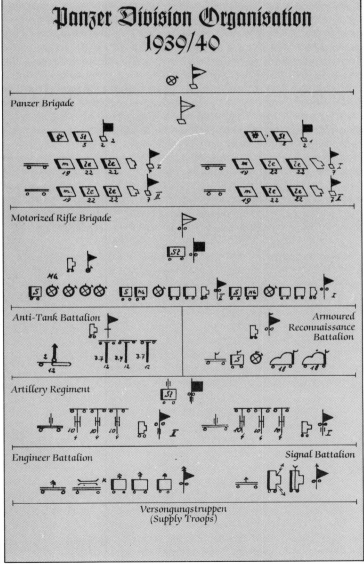

slovakia. Peacetime manoeuvres showed that the *Schützen* brigade was under-strength, so a fourth battalion was added. In the case of the 1st, 2nd and 3rd Panzer Divisions the *Schützen* regiment was expanded from two to three battalions while the *Kradschützen* battalion remained separate, but in the other three divisions the brigade was organised into two regiments each of two battalions.

There were thus a total of six Panzer divisions in being at the start of World War 2, and all were to take part in the Polish campaign. However, on mobilisation the fourth company of each Panzer battalion became the depot and reinforcement unit for the regiment, while the remainder of the battalion was re-organised into one medium and two light Panzer companies. These changes led to a reduction in the numbers of tanks in the divisions from 561 to around 300. However, as a fair proportion were by

now the more powerful PzKpfw III and IV medium tanks, their striking power was in fact far greater. Projected numbers of tanks in divisions varied. For example, just before the start of the Polish campaign 1st Panzer was meant to have 56 Mk Is, 78 Mk IIs, 112 Mk IIIs and 56 Mk IVs, making a total of 302 tanks in all, while the remainder would have 124 Mk Is, 138 Mk IIs and only 20 Mk IIIs and 24 Mk IVs, making a total of 306 tanks per division. These projected figures could not be reached in all cases, particularly for mediums, by the time the Panzer divisions took the field in Poland. The campaign in Poland confirmed the complete unsuitability of the PzKpfw I for combat, while the Mk IIs were found useful only for reconnaissance. Panzer units clearly needed to be equipped with a larger proportion of Mk III and Mk IV medium tanks. The heavier of the two, the PzKpfw IV, was singled out by

Guderian as a highly effective weapon to be produced in quantity, and indeed, it continued in production throughout the war. Although the Mk II was used for a while as a recce vehicle, eventually most of the remaining Mk I and Mk II tank chassis were utilised as gun platforms for self-propelled anti-tank guns (*Panzerjäger*). Guderian also recommended some tactical and organisational changes for Panzer units, for example, that battalion and regimental HQs should be located further forward to direct the battle, and that all HQs should be more mobile, restricted to a few armoured vehicles and well equipped with radio communications.

Light divisions

At the same time as the original Panzer

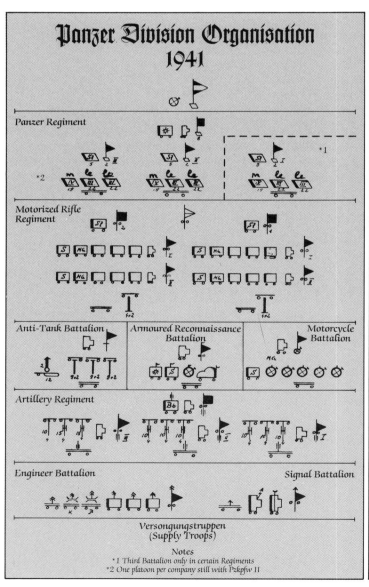

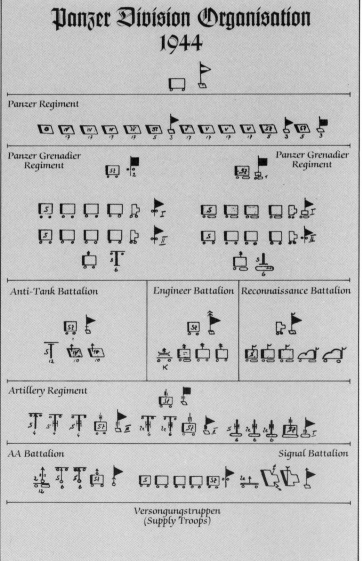

divisions were forming four light (*leichte*) divisions were raised by mechanising the German cavalry under a completely separate programme. In some ways this separate mechanisation of the cavalry had its parallel in the United States, where the newly mechanised cavalry had to call their tanks 'Combat Cars' in order not to upset the infantry who were the only arm allowed to have tanks, the US Army Tank Corps having been disbanded soon after the end of World War 1. The light divisions were small motorised formations, containing a Panzer element of one battalion with some 90 light tanks, while the motorised infantry element comprised four *Schützen* battalions. Supporting units, such as artillery, engineer and recce, etc, were all very similar to those of the Panzer divisions. In 1938, the four *Leichte* divisions passed under the control of Guderian's Inspectorate of Mobile Troops.

Later, after the Polish campaign, they became the 6th, 7th, 8th and 9th Panzer Divisions, each having its tank strength increased by the addition of a Panzer regiment of three battalions, except for 9th Panzer which received only a two-battalion regiment.

Expanding the Panzer divisions

The spectacular successes achieved by the Panzer divisions in the early part of the war firmly established their reputation for shock action out of all proportion to their actual numbers. There were, as we have already seen, more tanks on the Allied side than in the triumphant Panzer divisions that swept all before them in their lightning advance to the Channel ports. They were now considered to be the decisive element of the land

battle and a major expansion was ordered by Hitler. The number of Panzer divisions was to be doubled. However, the necessary extra tanks could not be manufactured out of thin air, although the Germans made every possible use of captured enemy AFVs, as well as the large quantity of excellent Czech tanks which they had 'acquired'. In general terms the much-vaunted expansion was achieved by the simple expedient of reducing the number of Panzer units in every Panzer division and increasing the infantry content. This had the damaging effect of dispersing and weakening the hitting power of the Panzer divisions, thus reducing their effectiveness. It was, however, a strategem which the Allies were to copy later in the war. The order authorising the establishment of the new divisions (11th to 20th Panzer Divisions inclusive) was promulgated and they came into being during the period August

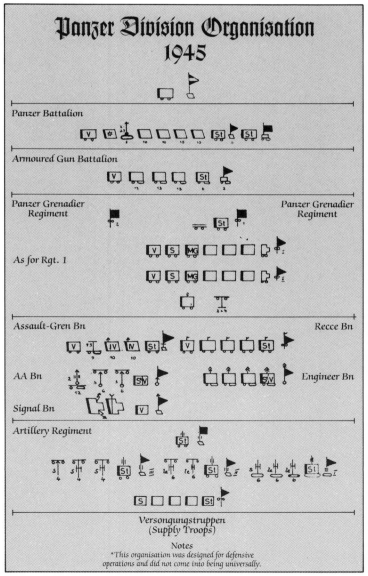

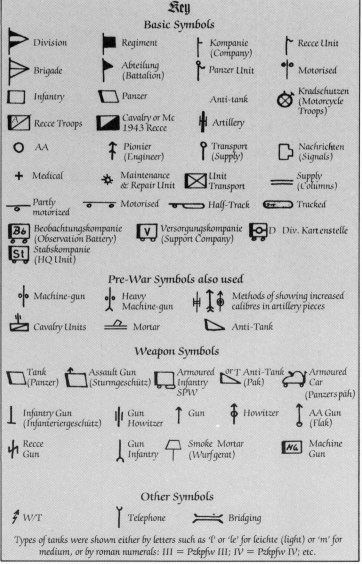

Another parade in another barracks, this time mounted. It took place on 20 April 1936 in barracks of the 2nd Battalion of Panzer Regiment 3, 2nd Panzer Division: The Regiment was mechanised the year before (Oberst aD von Boxberg).

to November 1940. They were thus quite well established and had had time to train together, before being committed to BARBAROSSA the following year.

The organisation of the Panzer division circa 1941 is shown in detail in Appendix B. However, in basic terms the tank content was now just a single regiment of two battalions although a small number of divisions did have three-battalion regiments. Numbers of tanks may have been smaller, but firepower was again increased, as each battalion now comprised a medium tank company with PzKpfw IVs and two light tank companies with PzKpfw IIIs, while the PzKpfw I and II had been relegated to other roles as has already been explained. The infantry element of the *Schützen* brigade was

Tanks of Panzer Regiment 1 on exercise, with a PzKpfw II leading some PzKpfw Is (Horst Riebenstahl).

standardised as two regiments each of two battalions, plus a motor cycle battalion, while there were other changes to the supporting arms.

Four more Panzer divisions, the 21st, 22nd, 23rd and 24th, were formed between August and November 1941, all on the 1941 organisation, so all Panzer divisions now had a tank strength of 200. There were, of course, variations between divisions, none being more marked than those of the Deutches Afrika Korps (DAK), whose commander, Erwin Rommel, was a law unto himself and operated in a theatre far enough away from Berlin to be able to run his own show. Considerable casualties on the Russian front did not help to improve matters and, although German tank-producing factories struggled hard, tank strengths did not increase above this general figure. Indeed, in many cases there were well under 200 tanks per Panzer division.

Mid-war changes

The year 1942 saw the formation of three more Panzer divisions, the 25th, 26th

and 27th. These were the last of the consecutively-numbered divisions, although there were a further 17 miscellaneous Panzer divisions formed, as the tables on pages 19 to 21 show. During 1942 a number of organisational changes also took place, the motor cycle battalion being absorbed into the reconnaissance battalion, the *Schützen* brigade HQ being removed and the two motor rifle regiments coming under direct divisional control. The infantry element also changed its title from 'Schützen' to 'Panzergrenadier'. On the tank side the change was an increase for once, a fourth tank company being added to each Panzer battalion. The tank company now contained 22 tanks (PzKpfw IIIs or IVs), the latter mounting the long 7.5 cm gun which altered its role as a fighting tank. Close support was provided by some of the PzKpfw IIIs being armed with the short-barreled 7.5 cm, thus effectively reversing the roles of the two types. In this same year the recce trops at company level were dispensed with and those at battalion and regimental level increased to seven tanks per platoon. This meant that, on paper, the number of tanks in a regiment was reduced to 164, but the number of actual fighting tanks was still maintained around 130. A few companies were also starting to be equipped with the new heavy tank the PzKpfw VI (Tiger), but these were normally not found in integral divisional units, coming under the category of 'Heerestruppen', ie, units allocated to armies, corps and divisions according to tactical requirements. By the following year, although the numbers of tanks in each regiment had not changed, yet another new tank had been introduced in the shape of the PzKpfw V (Panther). It was soon normal for one of the two battalions to be equipped with Mk IIIs and IVs, while the other had the heavy medium tank Panther. In 1944, all the motorised divisions became called Panzergrenadiers and their control was passed to the Inspectorate of Armoured Troops.

In addition, in the summer of 1944, the establishment of the Panzer division was once again altered. This time there was a reduction in tank strength within each company from 22 to 17. Finally, in March 1945, a further reduction took place, in that each regiment was reduced to one battalion containing four companies each of ten tanks — two with PzKpfw IVs and two with PzKpfw Vs . The second battalion was replaced by an armoured car battalion. Thus, throughout the war, the tank strength of a Panzer company had been consistently reduced, from a prewar total of 32 down to just ten. Despite the increased performance of the individual tanks this was a totally inadequate figure

A mounted standard bearer in his early PzKpfw II. Note he is wearing the Regimental Standard Bearer's Gorget, and carrying the pink swallowtail regimental standard (Oberst aD von Boxberg).

tactically, even before battle casualties were taken into consideration.

SS Panzer divisions

Although not strictly part of the Wehrmacht, the SS Panzer divisions of the Waffen-SS must be mentioned here. They were formed in 1942–43 and there were seven in all. Initially they were Panzergrenadier divisions, but by October 1943, all seven (1st, 2nd, 3rd, 5th, 9th, 10th and 12th) were SS Panzer divisions. Their organisa-

tion was basically the same as that of the Army Panzer divisions, except for an additional third rifle battalion in their Panzergrenadier regiments. They were also generally kept better off as far as equipment and reinforcements were concerned.

Mixed battlegroups

The organisations shown in the tables in Appendix B give what were the laid down 'norm' or official establishments. However, there were many examples of differences which were not just due to enemy action. In general terms the number of tanks in each formation was inadequate for most of the war, so the Panzergrenadiers were forced to take on more and more tasks. Mixed battlegroups, today the most favoured combat organisation in mechanised armies, were still only being tried out by both sides during World War 2. The Germans were perhaps the more successful of the combatants in this respect, and certainly the Panzer divisions gained a considerable reputation for their tactical ability, as is expressed succinctly in this quotation from one of the volumes of the official US Army history of World War 2, entitled: *The Ordnance Department, Procurement and Supply*. When discussing numbers of tanks on both sides, this says: 'These figures should demonstrate for all to see that German tank successes were due more to skilled tactical use and the employment of heavy German tanks against Allied mediums, than to any failure of American industry to produce in quantity the tanks desired by the using arms'.

Higher headquarters

Above the Panzer divisions were Panzer corps (*Panzerkorps*) and Panzer armies (*Panzerarmee*), the former controlling a

More enthusiastic crowds for this PzKpfw III as it moves through Bohemia, 1938 (Oberst aD von Boxberg).

number of divisions in which Panzer or Panzergrenadier divisions predominated, while the latter controlled some two to seven Panzer corps. There was a total of five Panzer armies in the Wehrmacht, plus one SS Panzer army and of course the unique Panzer Army Africa.

The headquarters of all German divisions, corps, armies and army groups consisted of command staff (*Kommandobehörden*) which were organised in a uniform manner. Corps and higher staffs were known as senior command staffs (*höhere Kommandobehörden*). They were headed by a chief of staff, while in divisions the first General Staff officer in charge of operations was simultaneously the head of the staff. The sections of these staffs were numbered with Roman numerals and letters, the numbers representing the sections as well as the men in charge of them. Originally the positions of I-a, I-b, I-c and I-d were all reserved for officers of the German General Staff Corps, but in 1944 the I-c at division and I-d at army and army group were frequently identified as not being General Staff officers.

The headquarters of an army group was organised similarly to that of an army, but the ranks of the officers holding corresponding positions were higher. The headquarters of a corps was also organised similarly to that of an army; however, the specialist officers more frequently took command in the field of all the units of their arm, whether organic or attached. The headquarters of divisions were organised similarly with most of the specialist officers being simultaneously in command of the units of their arms, eg, the

The Condor Legion in Spain. PzKpfw I Ausf A in the village of Grandella on the way forward to the Catalonian front.

Panzers advance into Normandy, 1940 (Rudolf Wulff).

This 15 cm siG 33 (Sf) auf PzKpfw I Ausf B passes an interesting group of roadsigns on its way through France (Rudolf Wulff).

commanding officer of the division artillery regiment (*Artillerieführer*, or *Arfü*) was also the chief artillery officer on the specialist staff of the division commander. When General Headquarters artillery units were attached to the division this *Arfü* was usually subordinated to a special artillery commander known as *Artilleriekommandeur* whose small special staff was supplemented in action by the organic staff of the division artillery regiment. While some of the designations of staff officers and sections remained unchanged in all echelons of higher headquarters, several of these titles varied in accordance with the rank and echelon in which they were functioning.

It should also be noted that the main channel of supplies flowed from the Zone of the Interior via army to division, while the army group and the corps were primarily tactical headquarters.

Panzer units in other formations

In addition to the normal organic units in Panzer or SS Panzer divisions, armoured troops (*Panzertruppen*) were integral to a wide spectrum of different types of units found in other formations. Each Panzergrenadier division contained a Panzer battalion organised similarly to the Panzer battalions in Panzer divisions. However, sometimes this battalion was replaced by an assault gun battalion. Heavy tank (Tiger) battalions, usually containing 45 PZKpfw VIs, were frequently allotted to corps as corps troops, as were similarly organised Panther battalions. Independent flamethrower battalions, consisting of three companies of flamethrower tanks (either PzKpfw IIs or IIIs), were normally found in a Panzer corps. Heavy tank companies (Tiger) (FKL) consisting of 14 Tigers and 36 remote-controlled B-IV demolition tanks, were allocated to Panzer divisions from General HQ troops. (FKL stands for Funklenk or Funklewagen: radio controlled vehicle). Finally, there were self-propelled Panzerjäger units, which were sometimes referred to as assault guns. The most powerful Panzerjäger units were equipped with such monsters as the 65 ton Elefant.

Tank crew training

The basic aims of the training given to German tank crews were summarised in a Secret wartime memo, circulated to tank units in the British Army. It explained that the basic aims of Panzer training were: rapid cross-country movement in formation by

Street fighting during the '*Blitzkrieg*' that swept through France in the summer of 1940 (Horst Riebenstahl).

day and by night; ability to open fire as soon as possible; accuracy of fire; care and maintenance of vehicles and equipment; and cultivation and maintenance of the 'Panzer spirit'. The methods by which these aims were achieved were as follows.

Driving Tank drivers were selected with great care and anyone who did not make rapid progress was given another job, such as

machine-gunner. When a tank unit had perfected driving in formation, it was then given practice in driving with other units of the Panzer division, starting with artillery and reconnaisance units. When they had mastered this stage, mixed columns formed from the various units of the Panzer division were sent on route marches lasting two or three days, the units bivouacking each night. Anyone who failed to stand up to this training was at once posted. It was also reported that course keeping was taught by navigation instructors from the German Navy.

Speed in opening fire Each gunner and loader was timed with a stopwatch and no gunner or loader was passed as efficient until he could load and fire in the laid down number of seconds.

Accuracy of fire It was reported that gunners in German tank regiments were trained by Luftwaffe instructors. It was considered essential to eliminate any man who would not make a good gunner. Gunners had to have plenty of practice and expenditure of ammunition was not to be allowed to stand in the way.

Maintenance of vehicles and equipment Maintenance was regarded as one of the most important factors in the training of tank crews. Drivers had to fully understand the servicing of their vehicles and gunners had to be able to clear all stoppages. 'A vehicle or gun which is properly serviced never breaks down', was an often repeated maxim in the Panzer divisions. Cleanliness of vehicles and equipment was carried to extreme lengths and undoubtedly contributed to the ability of German tanks to operate in all weathers and in all types of country.[10]

Development of the 'Panzer spirit' The first essential was physical fitness and crews in training began their days with cross-country runs and physical excercises. Besides determined driving in all types of country, cunning, resourcefulness and 'cool-bloodedness' were said to be part of the 'Panzer spirit'.

Horst Riebenstahl of Weilburg/Lahn served as a tank driver in Panzer Regiment 1 and drove all types of tank from the PzKpfw I to the Panther. He writes: 'During breaks on major road moves in Russia the tank

Replenishing a PzKpfw III outside Rouen, while dramatic smoke clouds rise in the background (Rudolf Wulff).

A mixed column of tanks and B vehicles crossing the River Somme at Pont Remy (Rudolf Wulff).

driver, unlike the rest of the crew, had to stay in his compartment, be it in the heat of the summer or the bitter cold of the winter. In battle, the skills of the tank driver were of outstanding importance. It was the task of the driver under the supervision of the crew commander to try and find a suitable firing position and to reach it quickly in order to ease the task of the turret crew. Quite often the fate of the entire crew depended on the driver's skills. Therefore it was absolutely essential that he had the capability to think tactically and had the technical skills. The crew formed an entity. The failure of one crew member quite often had deadly consequences for the rest of the crew.

'The killing of an enemy tank was regarded as the achievement of the entire crew. The crew commander always tried to take his driver with him in case he had to take command of another tank for whatever reason. A tank crew can only perform as well as the capabilities of each individual member.'

No doubt the sentiments he expresses would be echoed by other Panzer crewmen whatever their trade might be.

Panzers in action

What was it like to be in a Panzer division in battle? Here is an account written by Leutenant Dr Kurt Wolff of Panzer Regiment 5, which was initially part of 3rd Panzer Division, but was then used to form 5 *leichte*

The 'Desert Fox', Erwin Rommel, wearing his familiar trademark — British gas goggles — on his peaked cap (Rommel Museum, Herrlingen).

The fate of many Panzers in the desert is typified by this 'after the battle' scene, with knocked-out and burning tanks and B vehicles littering the battlefield, Libya, December 1941.

Division on its creation in August 1941 and was sent to North Africa as part of Rommel's DAK. 5 *leichte* was strengthened and retitled 21st Panzer Division on 1 October 1941. When it landed in North Africa, Panzer Regiment 5 had approximately 120 tanks, only half of which were PzKpfw IIIs and IVs. The account is quoted here with the kind permission of the *Kameradenkreis ehem Panzer Regiment 5 und Panzerbataillon 143/Stadtallendorf*. Wolff wrote: 'A Panzer regiment is a gigantic organisation. Ammunition trucks and fuel tanks move forward and often get blown up in the course of battle. Field kitchens and ration trucks search for the tracks of the Panzers of their units. However, the important movements in the dusk of the evening are the repair groups. Men who repair the engines, clean and adjust the carburettors. Springs, track rollers and track links have to be seen to and fixed. Guns and machine-guns have to be checked. You can hear the swearing of hard working men, the clanging of hammers in the wet and cold night. As soon as the sun rises through the morning mist, the regiment starts to roll forward. Thousands of other things come together before a battle is won.

'In the yellow moonlight long convoys of trucks move along the coast road, now and again attacked by English bombers. We disperse into the desert, but forward we go, 40–50 km per hour we read on our tacho. Water, fuel, ammo, bread, food and people, everything moves through the dark night which is no different from the glowing heat of the day.

'But the nicest is the attack. Oh Lord, I remember 2 July, my eyes burn! More than 100 tanks stood in our area as far as we could see, shot to pieces, on fire. Our day did not start well, we almost disappeared. Our repair shop 60 km further back had moved all immobilized Panzers on to the road to hold the breakthrough.

'But the German Panzer! Our beautiful, wide, humming Panzer. We are secretly proud that everybody needs us when danger is high! Panzer, Panzer to the fore.

'During the night New Zealanders had broken into our right-hand position. How many? Nobody knew. We pulled our defensive ring closer together. Two men stood watch by each Panzer, one by the Panzer gun, one with a Schmeisser machine-pistol outside the Panzer, listening in the night. The moon had gone down early, one could see no more than 20 metres.

'I was next to the commanding officer, with me a runner, the telephone connected to the Division. Are the New Zealanders going to attack? English fighters and bombers drop Christmas Trees [flares] to light up the landscape. Is it to guide their own troops?

'Further back on our supply lines rows of bombs fell on our transport. The artillery is silent. This is a bit wearing. In the previous night they would not let us sleep. In this spooky night only our repair teams work hard.

'At about 2.00 o'clock our listening guard returned with a prisoner. He had lost his

Blasting their way through the Russian defences, the Panzers roll on into Russia (Ernst J. Dohany).

Infantrymen being carried forward on the backs of PzKpfw IIIs in the early days of the German advance into Russia. The Panzers resemble tinkers' carts as they carry so many different things on them, in order to be self-sufficient.

way. He brought a wounded German NCO with him. The NCO was unconscious, he only moaned, that was all. A sudden order came at 3.00 o'clock. An English Rifle Brigade has broken through and must be destroyed. Our own riflemen have been over-run. Panzer the last help. The company was immediately battle-ready. The engines were running warm, orders came through the radio, the unit comes to order and is on the move. It is still dusk, the morning star stands in the east, slowly fading. The morning fog which has formed is blown away by the wind.

'Only the noise of the Panzers spreads over the yellow sandy land. Tough orders, we slowly gain the heights on the right-hand side of us. A little later our reconnaisance troops report English vehicles at 1,200 metres distance. Our gunners locate the target, the fight has started. The New Zealanders seem just to wake up and run about, as if the Germans should not have reached their position. When they at long last got their guns in position, some of their transport was already on fire. It was a quick fight, as we got

Winter begins. Panzer Regiment 31, 5th Panzer Division, advancing towards Moscow, starts to understand the hard way what a Russian winter is really like (Rudolf Wulff).

Not all fighting in Russia was in the open countryside and many hard-fought battles took place in built-up areas, such as this scene in the suburbs of Stalingrad (Ernst J. Dohany)

within 800 metres, always covering each other, because we had often in the past run into unrecognised English anti-tank positions. We could now see that also from the right, that is the left flank of the surprised enemy, German anti-tank guns, the German Panzerjäger, opened fire, the enemy's confusion was complete.

'I don't know how it came about, as I destroyed an English tracked vehicle and

HQ of 24th Panzer Division in Stalingrad (Ernst J. Dohany).

observed my hit with binoculars a shell exploded next to me, shot from an American Panzer. I managed to pull my head in. I then felt a pain in my right arm, and saw blood drip on to the shoulder of my gunner. My gunner had the first-aid box ready, he rolled up my sleeve and bandaged me up. I was lucky, just a small splinter one centimetre above my elbow joint. My Commander called through the radio asking whether his No 1 was hurt. I had ordered my driver to stop for a moment and we had fallen behind. The attack progressed with great speed, the

other AFVs had moved 400 metres in front of me. I could now move up, smilingly displaying my small bandage.

'What now happened was like a mirage. As the one Company moved forwards attacking a few enemy tanks at 1,500 metres, the rest of our unit broke into the English positions. Where before only a few artillery pieces, some anti-tank guns and tracked vehicles stood, now suddenly from holes in the ground, first ten, then fifty, in the end about six hundred Tommies emerged, waving at us. Some half-heartedly saluting, some threw their arms away, coming towards us in a line, the whole New Zealand fighting unit surrendered.

'Our Commander smiled, at last we have made another catch, after the long days of English artillery attacks, at last something to grab hold of, four burning tanks, perhaps ten self-propelled gun carriages, eight cannons, a number of tracked vehicles, machine-guns, bazookas. In the trenches we could see rifles with fixed bayonets lying about. Those dogs, we thought! But the rifle battalion following us could have sent those lads in the right direction.

'Our Commander ordered a halt, so that we could re-form our units. We then started

to attack the southerly position on the *djebel-hang* held by enemy tanks. Our forward company reported about 14 of them.

'Our shells came down in the ranks of retreating New Zealanders. At this moment in time we received a radio message from Division which confused us. South from spot Height 63 (that was approximately the area where we had rested during the night) a strong English tank brigade had broken through our lines, and the first units of them were fighting with our protective flak guns. We could now see what the English plan was. The New Zealand Brigade, which unknown to the English General no longer existed, should have attacked us from the south, the tanks coming in from the front and the right flank would have closed the ring. If that should have been successful with any possible confusion in our ranks, a large part of the German forces, at least our Panzer Division, would have been destroyed. Later we found out from captured tank crews that they had orders to break through as far as the coastal road and with more following forces, as far as Tobruk. Our Commander stood erect today, I know that this was one of his proudest moments.

'No General is with us, no anti-tank gun, no flak, no artillery, only the shrunken Panzer unit which came from the Derna area and fought forwards as far as El Alamein, more than 1,000 km. They destroyed more than 250 enemy tanks, many artillery pieces, anti-tank guns and tracked vehicles.

'Now the enemy is in front to the left and at our backs, stronger than ever before, in a better position than perhaps ever before in the campaign, they know their superiority — but whatever happens, we have to make the next move.

'We succeeded! To start with our unit made an about turn (it was easier said than done) should we bother knowing that 12 or 20 enemy tanks stood in our rear. Section by section with left and right movements, always with the enemy in the rear, uncertain, in between, urgent radio messages from Division urging us to hurry at any price. At last we rolled, while all this took place and the heavy Panzers moved from the battlefield to re-group. Then forward up on that ridge we could not believe our eyes, right in the flank, unbelievably, precisely of the advancing English Panzer brigade. No order was necessary! Our positioning was successful, steady, very steady with thought, no rushing, but with clear minds the battle can commence.

'As our tank gunner is loading for the second time, the first shell already brings smoke and fire from the enemy tanks.

'The Commander, and I standing next to

him, breathe a sigh of relief. What a picture. One has to imagine this flat ridge, running from west to east and beyond this ridge running in the same direction an approx 800 m wide depression. The English were marching in this depression and came into our fire.

'The leader of the 4th Company shot up seven tanks, another five, almost everyone could later account for two or three destroyed. We, apart from my laughable wound which only later came to mind, lost two dead and two wounded. This is meaningless compared with the 60 enemy tanks we counted later on. Most of them had burned out. The rest had to flee from an enemy they could not see and did not expect. (We stood behind a ridge with our gun barrels barely looking over the top.) They finished blowing up on a minefield, which they had managed earlier in the morning to pass along a narrow path. Now it caused their destruction. One hour later we moved slowly down the ridge and drove, shattered by the victory we saw before us, eastwards. We returned to our previous positions as if nothing had happened.

'The enemy tanks which at the beginning stood at our rear have been chased away by

Panzers and infantry get ready for a new attack in the Rostov area. This is a PzKpfw III Ausf J supporting a column of infantry.

our howitzer battery and anti-tank guns. The sweat ran down our dirty faces, it was well earned after a good job.

'The Division received report after report. We found out later that the leading units of the English brigade got shot to pieces by our flak units. Twelve Mk IIs and Mk IVs should have remained, the rest received direct fire from our flak and anti-tank guns and was finished.

'The evening came with very heavy and angry English artillery fire. Our High Command spoke of 131 AFVs destroyed.

'The next day was very hot again, very heavy, how do we bear it? Hundreds and thousands of flies crawl over our faces, our mosquito nets got lost a long time ago. We have patience, the steel on our Panzer is red hot, the water is almost undrinkable. Should we get a sandstorm at lunchtime remains our only hope...

'At the moment it is still night, we are watchful, tired, unwashed and oily. We stand watch for Germany in the African night.'

3
Pz Kpfw I and variants

Background development

It was in 1933 that the Army Weapons Branch (*Heereswaffenamt*) issued a requirement for the development of a light tank in the 5 ton class, to be armed with two machine-guns mounted in an all-round traversing turret and with sufficient armour to make it immune to small-arms fire. Five firms were invited to tender, namely Daimler-Benz AG of Berlin-Marienfelde, Henschel und Sohn of Kassel, Friedrich Krupp AG of Essen, Maschinenfabrik Augsburg-Nürnberg (MAN) of Nuremberg and Rheinmetall-Borsig of Düsseldorf. After a detailed examination the *Heereswaffenamt* chose the Krupp design (based largely upon the English Carden Lloyd tankette) and selected two of the firms to oversee final developments — Krupp for the chassis and running gear, Daimler-Benz for the superstructure and turret. Krupp had called their design the 'LKA 1' and also used the designation 'LKA/LKB' for the project, but the *Heereswaffenamt* preferred to use the codename '*Landswirtschaftlicher Schlepper (La S)*', meaning 'agricultural tractor', so as to try to disguise its true purpose. The first three prototypes were built by Henschel in late 1933 and tested in early February 1934. The La S and LKA 1 designations continued to be used until 1938 when the Wehrmacht adopted military class names

and model numbers, which in this case was *PanzerKampfwagen (MG) (SdKfz 101) I Ausf A*. The earliest versions to appear had open-topped hulls and no turrets (*ohne Aufbau*) and were as such ideally suited for driver training and basic tactical manoeuvres.

Only about 15 of the Ausf A *ohne Aufbau* were built. Quantity production of the Ausf A began at Henschel in July 1934, the complete contract being for 150 vehicles. It is difficult to determine exactly how many Ausf As were built and figures in various British and German sources range from as low as 300 to over 800. However, the authoritative Walter J. Spielberger, in his book *Die Panzer-Kampfwagen I und II*, quotes the chassis numbers for the Ausf A as running from Nr 10,001 to 10,477, which seems to indicate a total build of 477.

From the outset, the Germans appear to have fully appreciated the vulnerability of the little tankette, indeed, they were really only suitable for training purposes as *Exerzierpanzer* and probably never intended to fight in battle, yet, as we shall see, they had to fight and quickly proved their vulnerability.

The Ausf A was the first German tank ever to enter mass-production and the total build took place in 1933–34. Its first public appearance was at the *Reichsparteitag* at Nuremberg in 1935.[11]

PzKpfw I Ausf A

The Model A weighed 5.4 tonnes (5.3 UK/5.9 US tons) combat-loaded and the *ohne Aufbau* 3.5 tonnes (3.4 UK/ 3.9 US tons). It was a two-man tank (commander, who also manned the machine-guns, and a driver). It was armed with two 7.92 mm MG 13 machine-guns, for which 1,525 rounds were carried. The engine was a 57 hp Krupp M305 air-cooled, four-cylinder petrol engine. The tank had a top speed of just over 37 km/h (23 mph) and a range of some 145 km (90 miles). Fuel capacity was 145 litres (32 gal), contained in two tanks mounted in the rear corners of the driving compartment. The engine was at the rear and a shaft brought the drive forward through a dry plate clutch to the gearbox at the front of the tank and thence to the drive sprockets. There were five forward and one reverse gears. The driver, who sat forward on the left side of the tank, controlled the AFV's progress by means of two steering levers, each having two handgrips — one for normal steering, the other with a thumb plunger to act as a parking brake as no handbrake was fitted. The driver's instrument panel included an oil temperature gauge, rev counter and speedometer. The driver looked through a vision port directly to his front, which was protected by a hinged armoured flap (with two vision slits). Two

LKA 1, the Krupp prototype of the PanzerKampfwagen I.

Close-up of an Ausf A *ohne Aufbau* at a Fahrschule in 1935 (Oberst aD von Boxberg).

Similar view of an Ausf B *ohne Aufbau* (Oberst aD Hermann Rothe).

Driving instruction in progress on an Ausf B *ohne aufbau* in Panzer Regiment 5 (3rd Panzer Division) barracks in Wunsdorf (Oberst aD Hermann Rothe).

An excellent line-up of PzKpfw I Ausf As of Panzer Regiment 1 (1st Panzer Division) wait to march past in their barracks (Horst Riebenstahl).

PZKPFW I AUSF A (SDKFZ 101)

Date of origin 1934
Weight (tonnes) 5.4
Overall dimensions (m) Length 4.02
 Height 1.72
 Width 2.06
Armament/Ammunition carried
 Main 2 × 7.92 mm MG 13
 2,250 rounds
 Secondary N/A
Armour thickness (mm) Max. 13
 Min. 6
Engine Type Krupp M 304
 bhp/rpm 57/2,500
Crew 2
Max. speed (km/h) 35
Range (km) 145

more vision ports were provided both forward and rear on both sides of the hull, all with hinged armoured flaps (with single vision slits). The turret was offset to the right, with four vision ports — two at the rear and one on each side — all with armoured flaps but only those at the rear had vision slits in them. The two machine-guns[12] were mounted co-axially, but could be fired independently. The weapons elevated to +18° and depressed to −12°. Sighting was by means of a Zeiss RFZ2 telescope, which had a magnification of 2.5. Armour plate was 13 mm thick on the front of the tank, also on the sides and rear of both turret and hull, while the roof and belly were 6 mm. The suspension comprised a front driving sprocket and five roadwheels, the rear one, which was slightly larger than the others, also acting as the idler. The front roadwheel was independently sprung with a coil spring and hydraulic shock absorber, while the rest were arranged in pairs and connected together by a girder. Three return rollers were mounted above the roadwheels and the tracks contained 64 links. Wireless equipment consisted of an FuG2[13] with a short

wave receiver (27,200–33,300 kcs) which was only a listening set with a range of some two miles on voice and four miles on morse.

PzKpfw I Ausf B

The Ausf A soon proved to be underpowered, so a more powerful model, the Ausf B, was designed with a Maybach six-cylinder NL 38 TR water-cooled engine. The larger engine required a longer chassis (410 mm/16 in longer) and a modified suspension, there now being a separate idler as well as the five road wheels — all equal in size, still with the front roadwheel being independently sprung and the rest in artic-

ulated pairs. There were also now four return rollers and 100 links in each track. Track adjustment was made via the rear-mounted idler, which was on a cranked arm. It was also raised so that there was no change to the length of track actually in contact with the ground, thus the tank's manoeuverability was not affected. Combat weight went up to 6 tons, while the more powerful engine gave a better power-to-weight ratio and increased its speed despite the extra weight. The Ausf B was first issued to units in 1935 and production continued until 1939, although the manufacture of certain components, including chassis, was continued until 1941. About 1,500 vehicles were produced, including a number without turrets and superstructure (*ohne Aufbau*) for use on driver training and as tracked fitter's vehicles. However, it was found to be too small for recovery purposes and was soon mainly relegated to the training role.

A platoon of Ausf Bs on training, parade with crews front (Oberst aD von Boxberg).

PZKPFW I AUSF B (SDKFZ 101)

Date of origin 1935
Weight (tonnes) 6.0
Overall dimensions (m) Length 4.42
 Height 1.72
 Width 2.06
Armament/Ammunition carried
 Main 2 × 7.92 mm MG 13
 2,250 rounds
 Secondary N/A
Armour thickness (mm) Max. 13
 Min. 6
Engine Type Maybach NL 38 TR
 bhp/rpm 100/3,000
Crew 2
Max. speed (km/h) 40
Range (km) 140

Further developments

There were two further developments of the PzKpfw I, the Ausf C and Ausf F. The former was initially known under an experimental machine nomenclature as the VK 601. It was designed as a fast reconnaissance vehicle with improved armour protection (10–30 mm) and better armament (a 2 cm gun replacing one of the two MG 13s). The Ausf C weighed some 8 tonnes (7.9 UK/8.8 US tons), had a top speed of nearly 80 kmh (50 mph), a range of some 300 km (188 miles) and was powered by a Maybach 150hp HL 45 P engine. Its improved suspension had large interleaved roadwheels and no top rollers. An order was placed for 40 to be built by Krauss-Maffei and these were completed in 1942. A small number only were given combat evaluation, the remainder being issued to reserve units. No further production of the Ausf C took place.

In late December 1939, the *Heereswaffenamt* issued another contract for the development of a tank to be known as the VK 1801, which was later called the PzKpfw I Ausf F. It stemmed from the VK 601 development and was designed to give the little tank the thickest possible armour (up to 80 mm) so that it could be used for the close support of infantry in the attack, providing immediate machine-gun fire. The resulting AFV weighed over 20 tons, had a similar suspension to the Ausf C with interleaved roadwheels, but naturally had to be more robustly built in order to take the extra weight of armour. Powered by the same engine as the Ausf C, its top speed was greatly reduced to just over 25 kmh (15 mph) and the range was reduced to 150 km (94 miles). Krauss-Maffei produced a number of these overweight little tanks, but although two were given combat

Good view of the bottom plate, tracks and suspension of PzKpfw I.

Close-up of the driver's controls in a PzKpfw I.

evaluation in Russia, there is no evidence that they were ever issued to units.

Kleiner Panzer Befehlswagen (KL Pz Bef Wg) SdKfz 265

This light tracked armoured command vehicle used the same chassis as had been developed for the Ausf B, although a small number were built by modifying the Ausf A. Instead of the normal traversing turret, the *Kleiner Befehlswagen* had a fixed, built-up

Engine compartment PzKpfw I from rear.

superstructure which provided room for an additional radio set (FuG6 — ultra short wave receiver and a 20-watt transmitter, both on 27,200–33,300 kcs frequency band, with a range of six miles on voice and eight miles on morse), for a radio operator and a small map table. Armament was one ball-mounted MG 34 machine-gun for which 900 rounds were carried. The top of the cupola consisted of two half-flaps hinged to either side. Some 200 were built between 1935–37,

were used successfully, as the following section explains.

Battle history

The Ausf A, and its successor, the Ausf B, both saw service with the armoured portion of the 'volunteer' Condor Legion, which went to support General Franco's Nationalist forces in the Spanish Civil War. The commander of the land element was Colonel Ritter von Thoma — who later, as a General der Panzertruppe, surrendered to the British at El Alamein on 4 November 1942 — was then one of the Third Reich's most up-and-coming Panzer officers. He was required to train the Nationalist tank forces, such as they were, and to gather combat experience for the future.[14] Two tank companies were despatched from Germany in September 1936 and more followed. Although it is difficult to quantify the exact strength of the German Panzer forces in Spain, at the height of the war there appears to have been a tank force of four battalions, each with three companies and equipped with 15 tanks per company. Of the total of 180 tanks, some 120 were PzKpfw I Ausf As and Ausf Bs, while the rest were captured Russian T-26Bs. The latter, armed with a 45 mm gun, was the main tank on the Republican side. Although von Thoma's tanks achieved some successes, especially when they were used *en masse*, Spain was hardly the place to learn much more than basic troop tactics. However, it did give the panzer troops battle experience and also showed very clearly that they needed a tank with much better protection and more firepower.

The Panzers were on the move again in 1938, the year of the *Anschluss* with Austria. Although they did not have to fire a shot in anger this time they did have to travel a long way — over 640 km (400 miles) — and there were many breakdowns leading to much adverse comment. From the troops' point of view this was a very useful and necessary basic lesson to learn and led to a complete overhaul and bolstering up of the repair and recovery services needed to support the Panzer divisions. However, coupled with the lack of startling success in Spain, it did give rise to grave doubts about the effectiveness of armoured forces. These quickly disappeared with the success of the *Blitzkrieg* tactics in the campaigns in Poland and France which followed. The PzKpfw Is were used in both operations and, although

PzKpfw I Ausf F, the heavily-armoured VK 1801 infantry assault tank, was only ever built in small numbers for evaluation purposes, and never went into full production.

and issued to Panzer unit headquarters from company to brigade level. They remained in service until late 1942.

Other variants

There were a number of other variants which used either the Ausf A or Ausf B basic chassis. Based on the PzKpfw I Ausf A there was: an ammunition carrier (*Munitionsschlepper SdKfz 111*), an armoured bridgelayer (*Brukenleger*) and an armoured flamethrower (*Flammenwerfer*); while based on the Ausf B there was: a self-propelled heavy infantry gun (15 cm sIG 33(Sf)), a self-propelled anti-tank gun (4.7 cm Pak(t)(Sf)) and a demolition charge laying tank (*Ladungsleger*). These are illustrated in the accompanying photographs. The ammunition carrier and the two gun vehicles were most numerous, being an ideal way of prolonging the life of an obsolete tank chassis. Both SPs saw service until late 1943, over 200 Ausf B chassis being converted into the anti-tank gun (Panzerjaeger) and nearly 40 into the heavy infantry gun. The bridgelayer was far too light to be practical, but both the flamethrower and demolition charge laying tank

Novel use of a *Befehlswagen* as an ambulance.

they again showed their vulnerability and lack of firepower, they were well handled and did much to give rise to the myth of German tank invincibility. PzKpfw Is were used in small numbers during the invasions of both Denmark and Norway, while a few still remained in operational service after 1941, being used in both Russia and North Africa. Most of the little tanks were by then relegated to the training role, or, as has been explained already, converted to other uses.

Oberst aD Hermann Rothe joined Panzer Regiment 5 at Wunsdorf near Berlin as a cadet in 1938. He learned his soldiering on a Panzer I and recalled those early days thus: 'The passing of the military driving test in the first few months was an essential part of our training. The driving lessons were usually carried out in Panzer I as the photos show. Our teachers — regular NCOs — made it very clear that they did not like us to stall the engine or throw a track. The punishment for this was to spend some time running behind the tank over the training area! Most of us already had a civilian driv-

ing license, so it was quite difficult remembering to put your foot down on the accelerator when making a turn rather than braking. However, we all enjoyed our training and it gave us great respect for our tank drivers when we were commanding tanks later. Driving Panzers I to IV required a lot of physical strength. Conditions for drivers were very hard in the first few years of the war, bearing in mind the heat and the cold, the dust and the very bad visibility once the armoured visor was closed, both on the battlefield and during the long approach marches, in fact I would say they bordered on the limits of human endurance. This was the reason why a good driver was always highly respected and looked after by his crew. Panthers and Tigers were the first tanks to have assisted steering. These systems called for fingertip control rather than brute strength, so they took a bit of getting used to at first.'

What was it like to serve in a PzKpfw I? Oberst aD Albert von Boxberg told me: 'One of the biggest problems was that we were ordered to operate with the turret hatch closed, which made it hard for the commander to observe, having only the vision

slits to look through. The commander had then to depend upon the driver to help observe through the hull vision slits or go against the rules and leave the turret hatch open. As a means of command and control in the early years from 1935–37, we used semaphore, six flags being issued to the tank. These had to be held in different positions out of the turret to tell the commanders of the other tanks in the unit or sub-unit what they had to do next. This made flag drill on foot an important part of tank crew training. In battle the turret hatch was always left open, so injuries or head wounds were chances you had to take in order to be able to see all round.

'I remember a big mixed training excercise in 1936, which was held on a training area near Munster on the Lunebergeheide, I was given the job of being an umpire. I had a car which made it easier to see the attack of the tanks and the motorised infantry battalion. The order was to drive with all turret hatches closed so as to make the excercise as realistic as possible. The first semaphore signals were given by the platoon and company commanders, acknowledged and carried out properly. But as soon as battle was joined every semblance of control was lost, with tanks going everywhere, in all directions. Most ended up in a marsh where they got stuck! The criticisms were bad and the matter was discussed afterwards at a conference. Undoubtedly, however, it was not the command that had failed but rather the means of command, which is what many officers had thought all along would happen.'

An engineer action.

Contained in a US Army pamphlet *Small Unit Actions — German Campaign in Russia 1941–45* is an interesting account of the use of the engineer tank — the *Ladungsleger* — in an operation to capture two bridges during the German advance in 1941. According to the report the vehicles used were PzKpfw IIs fitted with special booms at the rear, for the purpose of depositing demolition charges or removing obstacles. However, the only *Ladunsleger* I have ever seen has been based upon the PzKpfw I, so I have chosen to include the account in this chapter. The first of the two bridges was a road bridge which was successfully captured after fierce hand-to-hand fighting with the Russian bridge demolition guard. The force commander then turned his full attention to the second, which was a railway bridge on which his assault detachment had run into trouble. The narrative explains: 'When the first three assault detachments, *en route* to the highway bridge, turned east at Varpas shortly after

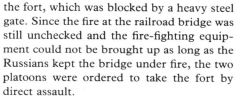

Ladungsleger auf PzKpfw I, with its demolition arm folded, negotiates a pontoon bridge.

Excellent veiw of a 15 cm heavy infantry gun, showing exactly how the gun was mounted on to the hull of the PzKpfw I Ausf B, taken on the banks of the Desna River in Russia (Rudolf Wulff).

Repairing track damage on a 15 cm siG 33(Sf) heavy infantry gun, belonging to 704 Kompanie, in France, 1940 (Rudolf Wulff).

Rear view of the Panzerjäger 4.7 cm PaK (t), taken at the School of Tank Technology.

02:00, the other truck continued north on the main highway, which led directly to the railroad bridge. Several hundred yards short of the bridge, at the intersection with the road that parallels the river, there was an old fort whose outer wall the truck had to pass. As the vehicle turned right on to the river road it received small-arms fire from the fort. In a matter of seconds the truck caught fire and was hastily abandoned. The detachment then attempted to fight its way forward to the bridge on foot, a distance of some 500 yards. However, the men were soon pinned down by the Russian fire, despite which they slowly and laboriously crawled toward the bridge. Just as the detachment had inched close enough to rush the bridge, there was a terrific explosion. Apparently aware of German intentions, the Russians had detonated charges attached to the steel piers. As the smoke cleared, it became evident that the demolition had not been very effective. The bridge was still intact. The wood planking and the rail ties had, however, caught fire, and there was danger that the fire might set off additional charges, which would normally be placed beneath certain girders of the truss sections. Quick action on the part of the assault detachment was therefore necessary if the fire was to be extinguished and the bridge saved.

'At 03:30 the 2nd and 5th Platoons of Company C arrived at the east entrance to the fort, which was blocked by a heavy steel gate. Since the fire at the railroad bridge was still unchecked and the fire-fighting equipment could not be brought up as long as the Russians kept the bridge under fire, the two platoons were ordered to take the fort by direct assault.

'The men of the 5th Platoon, who had dismounted and tried to place a demolition charge next to the gate, drew heavy Russian small-arms fire. An estimate of the situation indicated that it would be inadvisable to approach the gate without the protection of armor. Accordingly, one of the 2nd Platoon's special engineer tanks was ordered to back up the gate and lower a 110 lb [50 kg] HE charge from its boom. As soon as the charge had been deposited and the tank had moved to a safe distance, the charge was set off. The terrific explosion destroyed the gate and stunned the Russians in the immediate vicinity. However, as the German tanks advanced through the breach, they again drew fire. Their progress was further impeded by a second wall, whose gate, also of steel, was on the side facing the river. Again a special engineer tank had to be brought up with a 110 lb HE charge, which was set off with the same results as the first. At this point a few Russians surrendered. The remainder of the garrison, about 20 in number, continued to resist from the CP, which was located in a structure at the very center of the fort. While the Russians in the fort were trying desperately to repulse the German attack, Company C's fire-fighting equipment proceeded to the railroad bridge and quickly extinguished the blaze. Using shaped charges and hand grenades the 5th Platoon finally succeeded in driving the Russians from their last foothold within the fort. At 04:00 the fight for the fort came to an end. Of the company of Russians that had held the fort, 70 had been killed or wounded and 30 taken prisoner.

'The entire action had been carried out with great speed, only half an hour having elapsed between the initial assault on the fort and its capture. When interrogated, Russians captured at the fort stated that they had been ordered to hold out as long as possible, even if the bridge were demolished. They were to keep the Germans from moving up bridge equipment over the highway and to delay the German advance as long as possible.

'With both bridges firmly in German hands, Company C's mission was accomplished. In the fierce fighting which continued until evening the 8th Panzer Division captured Dvinsk and continued its northwestward advance toward Leningrad.

'The preceding example illustrates to what extent the commitment of armour in situations where speed is imperative can result in major successes. The seizure of the two bridges at Dvinsk was possible mainly because the four captured Russian trucks were sent ahead of the main body of Company C, thus taking the Russians by surprise and preventing them from demolishing the bridges before the Germans could reach them. The selection of Company C for this mission was justified because its special engineer tanks and half-tracks had sufficient firepower to pin the Russians down north of the highway bridge and pave the way for the division's advance into Dvinsk. During the fighting for the fort, the special engineer tanks once more proved invaluable in destroying the two gates. Only armor could get close enough to the gates to place the demolition charges in the face of the heavy Russian small-arms fire.'

4
Pz Kpfw II and variants

Background development

When it became clear that the production of the new medium tanks — *Zugführerswagen* and *Bataillonführerswagen* — would take longer than anticipated, it was decided to build another light training tank which, like the PzKpfw I, would be relatively inexpensive and easy to manufacture. The new tank would be heavier, have better armour and a more powerful gun than its predecessor. Accordingly, in June 1934, the *Heereswaffenamt* issued development contracts for a tank in the 10-ton class to three manufacturers: Krupp, Henschel and MAN. The Krupp solution was based upon their LKA I prototype of the PzKpfw I, but with a larger turret mounting an automatic 20 mm cannon and one machine-gun. They designated the three-man machine the 'LKA II'. The Henschel and MAN designs were very

The MAN pilot version of PzKpfw II, known as the La S 100.

similar to the LKA II, except for their suspensions. After testing, the design submitted by MAN was chosen for further development, being known thereafter under the codename '*Landwirtschaftlicher Schlepper 100 (La S 100)*'. MAN was chosen to develop the chassis and Daimler-Benz the superstructure and turret, while certain other manufacturers were brought in to help with production, namely Wegmann of Kassel in 1935, Famo of Breslau and MIAG of Brunswick in 1936.

The first production run was for 25 vehicles, produced in 1935 and known as the *1/La S 100*, which was taken into service and known (from 1938) as the PzKpfw II Ausf A1. This initial model was well within the stipulated combat weight and weighed only 7.2 tonnes (7.1 UK/7.9 US tons). It had a crew of three, with armament comprising a 2 cm KwK 30 automatic gun, plus a co-axially mounted 7.92 mm MG 34 machine-gun, which from then on became the standard Panzer machine-gun. The engine was a

PZKPFW II AUSF a1 (SDKFZ 121)		
Date of origin 1935		
Weight (tonnes) 7.2		
Overall dimensions (m)	**Length** 4.38	
	Height 1.95	
	Width 2.14	
Armament/Ammunition carried		
Main 1 × 2 cm KwK 30		
180 rounds		
Secondary 1 × 7.92 mm MG 34		
Armour thickness (mm)	**Max.** 15	
	Min. 5	
Engine **Type** Maybach HL 57 TR		
bhp/rpm 130/2,600		
Crew 3		
Max. speed (km/h) 40		
Range (km) 200		
Remarks Also known as the 1 Serie La S 100		

Maybach six-cylinder HL 57TR producing 130 bhp. There was a plate clutch and a six-speed crash gearbox. The suspension consisted of three pairs of small wheels which were sprung by leaf springs and connected by a girder-type beam to one another, while there was an adjustable idler at the rear and three return rollers at the top of the hull. Two further batches of the initial model were built, the first batch of 25 having better engine cooling and being known as the Ausf A2 while the third batch, this time of 50 tanks, was called the Ausf A3. This third model had improvements in the cooling, tracks and suspension. All three models had a rounded nose with armour plate up to a maximum thickness of 13 mm (15 mm on the mantlet).

The 2/La S 100 (PzKpfw II Ausf B) appeared in 1936, fitted with the HL 62 TR Maybach engine after the HL 57 TR was found to be insufficiently powerful. This and other minor changes put up the weight to 7.9 tonnes (7.8 UK/ 8.7 US tons). The Ausf B was also fitted with new reduction gears and wider tracks. A total of 100 Ausf bs were built. In 1937, Henschel were brought fully

into the construction programme and the Ausf c (3/La S 100) was produced. This model had major changes to the suspension, the small roadwheels and girder assembly being replaced by five medium-sized wheels, each suspended on quarter elliptic springs, while the return rollers were increased from three to four. This type of suspension was thereafter to become a main feature of the PzKpfw II and it was retained throughout all further production of the Ausf A, B and C. The Ausf c was the final development model before the tank entered mass-production. The Ausf A was the start of mass production and appeared in 1937. It was manufactured by MAN and was identical to the Ausf C. This was followed by the Ausf B and Ausf C in 1938 which had only minor differences. Over 1,100 were produced between 1937 and mid-1940, making the PzKpfw II the most numerous type of tank in the Panzer divisions at the start of the war. It was to bear the brunt of the fighting in both the Polish and French campaigns, quickly showing, like its predecessor the PzPkpfw I, that it was both under-armoured and under-gunned.

PzKpfw II Ausf A, B and C

Combat-loaded, the weight of the tank was 8.9 tons. Its three-man crew comprised a commander, who also acted as gunner, a wireless operator and a driver. Armament was one 2 cm KwK 30 automatic gun mounted on the left of the fully-traversing welded turret. The gun weighed 63 kg (139 lb), had a cyclic rate of fire of 280 rpm and was fed by ten-round magazines of which 18 were carried. Co-axially mounted on the right was an MG 34 machine-gun, which weighed 11.6 kg (25.5 lb), had a cyclic rate of fire of 8–900 rpm and was fed by a metal link belt containing 150 rounds. The belts were stowed in belt bags,[15] (of which 17 were carried). The engine was the Maybach HL 62 TR water-cooled petrol engine producing 135 hp at 2,600 rpm. PzKpfw II had a top speed of 40 km (25 mph) and a range of some 200 km (125 miles). Fuel capacity was 200 (45 gal). The engine was housed in a rear compartment offset to the right. A cardan shaft took the drive forward to the gearbox which was also offset to the right in the driver's compartment. It was a crash-type gearbox with six forward and one reverse gears.

The driver sat on the left, with one single slitted visor incorporating a removable glass block. He had an access hatch in the front glacis plate. There were two further vision ports covered by slit armoured flaps on either foward side of the superstructure. The

**PZKPFW II AUSF A, B & C
(SDKFZ 121)**
Date of origin 1937
Weight (tonnes) 8.9
Overall dimensions (m) Length 4.81
                           Height 1.99
                           Width 2.22
Armament/Ammunition carried
  Main 1 × 2 cm KwK 30
         180 rounds
  Secondary 1 × 7.92 mm MG 34
Armour thickness (mm) Max. 15
                            Min. 5
Engine Type Maybach HL 62 TR
       bhp/rpm 135/2,600
Crew 3
Max. speed (km/h) 40
Range (km) 200
Remarks From 1940 extra 20 mm
             plates bolted on front glacis

This early PzKpfw II suffered track damage in Poland, September 1939 (Rudolf Wulff).

wireless operator had a seat on the hull floor at the rear of the fighting compartment and he had a vision port in the rear of the superstructure, with an access hatch fitted alongside the engine behind the turret. The commander was housed in the turret which had no floor, so the commander's seat was suspended from the turret wall and rotated with it. There were four vision ports in the turret, two on the left, one on the right and one at the rear. On the turret roof initially there was just a split hatch which was later replaced by a commander's cupola with eight episcopes for all-round vision and a single hinged flap for access (from late 1940). There was no power traverse and the hand traverse was operated via a dog clutch which had three modes — EIN (in gear): traverse gear engaged, lock disengaged; AUS (free): traverse gear disengaged, lock also disengaged; and EST (locked): traverse gear disengaged, lock engaged. In the AUS position it was possible to traverse the turret by means of two handles on the turret ring. The commander fired the 20 mm by means of a trigger on the elevating handwheel (to his left), while the MG 34 trigger was on the traverse handwheel (to his right). Sighting was by means of a TZF 4 sighting telescope, which had a magnification of 2.5. There were two ports in the gun mantlet with bullet flaps, allowing the machine-gun to be fired over open sights. On the rear of the tank was a rack of five smoke candles which could be released by pulling a wire inside the fighting compartment, thus providing a local smoke-screen if the tank was caught in the open. The smoke candle was ejected from the rack by a strong spring.

Panzer troop training regulations issued by the German High Command in 1939 had this to say about the weapons of the PzKpfw II: 'The 2 cm KwK 30 gun is a weapon with excellent penetration and a high rate of fire. It is therefore chiefly designed as an anti-tank weapon. Enemy tanks should be engaged from static fire positions at a range of 600 m. The gun can also be used against enemy anti-tank guns at ranges of 500 m, but only if it is impossible to outflank the enemy gun and engage it with machine-guns.[16] Also, a tank platoon commander can direct the fire of his other tanks on to a target by engaging it first with his main armament. Short bursts of two or three rounds is the normal method of engaging targets from fire positions or on the move. Cannon and machine-guns can be used simultaneously against targets such as gun crews or troop concentrations. The co-axial machine-gun has a high rate of fire and is extremely accurate, so it is an ideal weapon to be used against all manner of unprotected targets, such as riflemen, machine-gun crews, anti-tank or artillery gun crews. It is particularly effective against massed infantry, but of little use against dug-in, protected targets. Such enemy positions should be outflanked. Short bursts is the normal method of engagement, whether static or on the move, while a continuous succession of well-aimed bursts will maximise the effect upon the target.'

Basic armour consisted of 15 mm plate on front, sides and rear of both turret and hull, with 10 mm top plates, except for the top front and top rear plates of the superstructure which were 15 mm. Belly plates were 5 mm. In late 1940, all three models ap-

peared with extra 20 mm plates bolted on to the front of the hull and turret, and 15 mm plates on the front glacis plate and gun mantlet. This was probably done as a result of the battle experience gained in Poland. The basic glacis, upper and lower nose plates, were made in one single piece bent round, giving the nose its early characteristic appearance. The additional plates, however, were straight, making the nose of the tank now look angular. Radio equipment comprised three wireless sets, two receivers and one transmitter, all members of the crew having speech and listening facilities. A 2 m (6 ft 6 in) rod aerial was mounted on the left rear corner of the superstructure and was dipped manually from inside the fighting compartment. When dipped the aerial rested in a wooden trough on the track guard. Intercommunication between commander and driver was via a voice tube. From the Ausf A onwards the tank was suppressed to prevent engine noise interference with the radios.

PzKpfw II Ausf D and E

Called the 'Schnellkampfwagen' (fast fighting vehicle), the 8/LaS 138 (PzKpfw II (2 cm) (SdKfz 121) Ausf D and E) was developed during 1938 by Daimler-Benz specifically for the mechanising cavalry. It had torsion bar suspension with four large double-tyred road wheels in place of the medium-sized Ausf A, B and C suspension. The engine was the Maybach HL 62 TRM

Note the reworked, strengthened hull on this
Ausf A and also the PzKpfw I in the background.

**PZKPFW II AUSF D & E
(SDKFZ 121)**
Date of origin 1938
Weight (tonnes) 10.0
Overall dimensions (m) Length 4.64
                            Height 2.02
                            Width 2.30
Armament/Ammunition carried
  Main 1 × 2 cm KwK L/55
            180 rounds
  Secondary 1 × 7.92 mm MG 34
Armour thickness (mm) Max. 30
                           Min. 5
Engine Type Maybach HL 62 TRM
          bhp/rpm 140/2,600
Crew 3
Max. speed (km/h) 55
Range (km) 200
Remarks Designed originally for the
             mechanising cavalry, some con-
             verted to flame

A PzKpfw II Ausf D/E broadside, while a
PzKpfw I is guided into position.

Good close-up of a PzKpfw II Ausf F arriving in North Africa.

and this, with the new suspension, raised the top speed to over 55 kmh (34 mph) for the 10-ton tank, but crew, armament and armour remained unchanged from the Ausf C. They were due to be issued to the tank units of the *leichte* divisions but under 50 were actually produced, some of which were later converted to flame throwing tanks.

Ausf F

This was the final model in the normal production of the series, being manufactured by FAMO between early 1941 and the end of 1942. Its late production enabled the makers to bring in modifications gained from battle experience, so the Ausf F was uparmoured

at the front to 35 mm and sides to 20 mm, raising the combat weight to 9.5 tonnes (9.3 UK/10.5 US tons), which resulted in a slight loss of speed as compared with the Ausf A, B and C of the main production run. Other changes included the fitting of a conically shaped idler and a dummy visor alongside the driver's normal visor. This appears to have been done in order to draw fire away from the real driver's visor. The dummy one was made from a one-piece aluminium casting and did not cover an aperture of any kind. The following comment was made on the Ausf F in a School of Track Technology report dated November 1943: 'The modifications have not changed the basic design, they seem hardly worth the trouble as the vehicle is becoming obsolescent. All recent reorganisa tions of the German Armoured Division show that the number of PzKpfw IIs in the Regiment continues to diminish.'

The British were, of course, unaware of Hitler's decision to expand the armoured force, which was made in July 1941. This meant that there was a demand for more and more tanks, so it was easier to keep established production lines producing than to switch to new types with the inevitable loss of production until the new lines were established. Labour shortages at the factories also did not help. The cost of building the PzKpfw II (less armament and communications equipment) was 50,000 Reichmarks[17] (£1,650/$6,650).

Further developments

A number of other models of the PzKpfw II were produced which included the following.

Ausf G This was a light reconnaissance

Gunner's telescope in a PzKpfw II.

Close-up of the suspension of a PzKpfw II.

tank initially known as the *neuer Art* VK 901. It weighed some 9.2 tonnes (9.05 UK/10.1 US tons), had yet again another completely redesigned suspension with five pairs of overlapping road wheels and torsion bar springing. Only a small number were ever built and none saw operational service although some of the turrets were later used for static pillboxes.

Ausf J With a suspension similar to the Ausf G, this model — the VK 1601 — was an attempt to put as much armour as possible on to the PzKpfw II, without altering its basic features. Front armour went up to 80 mm, sides and rear to 50 mm and top to 25 mm, the extra armour putting the tank's weight up to 18 tonnes (17.7 UK/19.85 US tons). The engine was a Maybach HL 45 p producing 150 hp, which gave the Ausf J a top speed of just under 31 kmh (20 mph). Again only a small number were produced and few saw operational service.

Ausf L The *Luchs* (Lynx) SdKfz 123 was produced using the experience gained from the construction of the Ausf G and Ausf J and its appearance was very similar to the former VK 901. Combat weight was just under 13 tons. The initial order was for some 800 vehicles, the first 100 to be armed with a 2 cm KwK 38 L/55 and co-axial MG, while the rest would have a 5 cm gun as main armament. The Ausf L had a crew of four men and a top speed of 60 km/h (37.5 mph). The first 100 *Luchs* were produced and saw action with the recce units of some Panzer divisions. Only a small number of the 5 cm version were ever built before production ceased in May 1943.

VK 1602 The Leopard, as it was called, was designed to be a heavily armoured AFV for use on battlefield reconnaissance tasks, with a weight of some 26 tons. Armament was to be a 5 cm KwK 39/1 gun. Construction of the vehicle did not actually take place, but the gun turret, which had been developed by Daimler-Benz, was later used on the Puma armoured car.

PzKpfw II Flamm (SdKfz 122)

One of the most successful uses of the PzKpfw II was as a light flame-throwing tank, using the chassis of the Ausf D and Ausf E, a number being converted while others were built from scratch. Armament

PzKpfw II Ausf G, also called the VK 901, had overlapping roadwheels and torsion bar springing.

PzKpfw II Ausf J, the VK 1601, was designed as a heavily-protected recce tank, but only a few were ever issued.

consisted of a single MG 34 mounted in a much smaller turret than normal, plus two flamethrowers each of which was mounted in a small turret externally on the front of the AFV on the track guards. Each flame-thrower had its own fuel tank (159 L/35 gal), mounted just behind it, protected by shields, while the radius of traverse of each gun was 180° and elevation from 10° to 20°. They could be fired independently by electrical means from panels in the turret, had a range of 32 m (35 yd) and a capacity for some 80 squirts of two to three seconds' duration. Fuel was projected by compressed nitrogen while ignition was by acetylene flame. The commander of the tank normally fired the flame guns which were used to deadly effect in Russia against enemy bunkers and fortifications. They were, however, quite vulnerable themselves because of the external fuel tanks.

Head-on view of the PzKpfw II Ausf L, *Luchs* (Lynx), which saw limited action with recce units of Panzer divisions.

Rear view of a PzKpfw II *Flam* during tests after being captured by the Russians. This model is based upon an Ausf E. Note rear-mounted smoke dischargers.

Self-propelled variants

As with the PzKpfw I there was an SP version which mounted a 15 cm heavy infantry gun, the sIG 33 auf Sf II, or 'Sturmpanzer II', produced in small numbers all of which served with Rommel's DAK in North Africa. Three other far more successful SPs on this chassis were as follows.

SdKfz 132 This mounted a captured Russian 7.62 cm anti-gun, over 200 being converted in 1942–43, and was known as the Marder II.

SdKfz 131 Also known as Marder II, it mounted a 7.5 cm Pak 40/2 anti-tank gun and was used by *Panzerjäger* units throughout the war.

SdKfz 124 Undoubtedly the best known

Close-up of one of the two flame projectors that were mounted on the front corners of the tank.

15 cm siG 33 self-propelled heavy infantry gun.

Mounting the captured Russian 7.62 cm gun, the SdKfz 132 used either an Ausf D or E chassis.

Miscellaneous models and variations

Other variations of the PzKpfw II included an amphibious tank (*Schwimmpanzer II*) which had flotation devices fitted to its sides and front; an armoured bridgelayer (*Brukenleger*) with a two-part sliding bridge; and a tracked carrier for the engineers (*Pionier-Kampfwagen II*) which was produced by the removal of the turrets from old PzKpfw IIs when they were overhauled.

The *Marder II* (Marten), SdKfz 131, was produced in large numbers and mounted a 7.5 cm PaK. It was used successfully throughout the war.

of the SPs on PzKpfw II chassis was the *Wespe* (Wasp), an SP light field howitzer, which mounted a 10.5 cm le FH 18 M howitzer and was built in fairly significant numbers (over 670) in 1943–44. The name *Wespe* was dropped as a result of an order from the Führer in February 1944. Combat weight was 11.8 tons, crew five, while 32 rounds were carried. In addition to the *Wespe*, some 150-plus ammunition-carrying vehicles were also built, some of which were converted into *Wespe* in the field. The *Wespe* was first used in action at Kursk in 1943.

Battle history

In its day the Pzkpfw II was a reliable tank and at the time of its construction a match for enemy tanks of similar size and weight, but it was of course vulnerable to anti-tank guns and the guns of heavier tanks. It first saw service when issued to Panzer units in the spring of 1936 and later saw action in Poland and France. Official figures showed that there were 2,009 PzKpfw IIs in service in May 1940, which included 17 Ausf Fs; a year later in May 1941 there were still 1,024 operational, including 85 Ausf Fs, while even in January 1942 there were still some 1,250 (with 89 Ausf Fs) Serving in Panzer units. It was used in all theatres and was undoubtedly the backbone of the early Panzer divisions until PzKpfw IIIs and IVs took its place.

Tactically, the PzKpfw II formed the heavier element of the light tank company of the Panzer regiment in 1939–40 and there were 160 of them in each Panzer division. In the 1940–41 reorganisation, the PzKpfw II was relegated from a fighting tank to a recce tank, and five were allocated to each company, battalion and regimental HQ for this purpose. This meant a drastic reduction in

the number of PzKpfw IIs per division — only 65 out of a total of 201 tanks. In March 1942, the numbers were even further reduced. The recce platoons at company level were abolished and those at regimental and battalion level increased from five to seven tanks. Thus, a Panzer division now had only 28 PzKpfw IIs out of a total of 164 tanks. Finally, in 1943, it was dropped completely.

Oberst aD Hermann Rothe remembers his early days in command of a PzKpfw II in Panzer Regiment 5: 'Shortly after the invasion of Poland in September 1939, I took over a section of a Panzer platoon, comprising a Panzer I and a Panzer II. I commanded the Panzer II and had a very experienced NCO driver and a young Gefreiter (Lance Corporal) as my radio operator. As commander I had to operate both the guns — the 2 cm KwK and the machine-gun. If my memory serves right the KwK had magazines of either 10 or 20 rounds.[18] It was a magnificent weapon when it was working properly, which it only did under great protest when conditions were very dusty. Then, with a good deal of cursing and swearing I had to go through the motions of loading! The machine-gun was our main weapon and proved particularly useful

against massed infantry attacks, also against cavalry, lorries and light armoured vehicles.

'Even today I still get a shiver down my spine when I recall that attack by the elite Polish cavalry brigade which took us all by surprise. They attacked us in extended line abreast with drawn sabres — probably the very last time such a classic manoeuvre was ever attempted in modern war. Our Regimental commander ordered us to fire with machine-guns only and to aim for the horses' legs. The prisoners we took after the charge kept touching our Panzers in amazement which puzzled us greatly until we discovered they had been told that the Germans only had cardboard tanks and that was why they had charged us with drawn sabres!

'With my Panzer II I covered over 2,000 km in under three weeks without a single breakdown — probably because I had an excellent driver who knew exactly how to look after his tank.'

It is difficult to find detailed battle accounts which only relate to the PzKpfw II,

but it clearly bore the brunt of the fighting in the battle for France in 1940. The history of Panzer Regiment 35, 4th Panzer Division, contains numerous accounts of actions during that campaign, such as the following about the capture of bridges over the River Seine near Romilly.

'We pushed forward past La Frère on to the River Marne near Mont St Père. The move forward was slow as there was also an infantry division on the roads and it was raining heavily. The far side of the river was deep in mud and conditions were getting worse every minute. All the armoured cars had to be dragged clear by the Panzers...

'At dawn on 13 June the Regiment finally crossed and continued southwards. Our echelon vehicles followed slowly. We passed Montmirail and headed towards Maclaunay, where we met up with the other regiment of our brigade. At 12:00 hr, our Regiment, on its own, positioned itself for an attack. The artillery followed. The attack was aimed at Sesanne. At first we moved rapidly forward, but soon enemy artillery and anti-tank guns retaliated. Our artillery observer successfully guided our own artillery on to their targets. The first prisoners, with their hands in the air, passed us marching to the rear. The 2nd Battalion's Panzers finished off five anti-tank guns. Near Les Essarts we met enemy tanks for the first time. Two were destroyed and the rest retreated in a hurry. The French infantry was almost wiped out, the remnants escaping into the distance. A short halt was ordered so as to reorganise and regroup. An artillery battalion plus one AA battery joined us and at 18:00 hr the advance forward towards Sesanne continued.

'No enemy was sighted. While the 2nd Battalion surrounded the town, regimental headquarters motored straight in, followed by the 1st Battalion. At the southern exit, near the railway station, we encountered three enemy heavy tanks. Having nothing else to shoot at them apart from our 2 cm light tank guns we could not pierce their thick armour. Ironically, however, they still fled as soon as we engaged them. The 2nd Battalion opened fire on the retreating enemy convoys and took many prisoners. At a nearby airfield we captured six aircraft intact. We took over the railway station and stopped all trains from running, putting out the fires in their boilers. Then the 36th Regiment took over from us and we continued to advance southwards.

'All round us we saw columns of enemy retreating. We opened fire and captured literally hundreds of prisoners. In St Troy alone, the light Panzer section captured 500 men. But some of the enemy still kept fighting back and we came under fire in every village. Bardonne was taken. It was already 18:30 hr when we received the orders: 'The Regiment is to advance to the Seine, capture the bridge at Marcilly and form a bridgehead in Romilly'.

'From this moment on we no longer took any notice of any enemy columns. We came under fire while overtaking them, but what the heck, we had only one aim — the Seine! We still had a long way to go and it was already evening. Near Marcilly we encountered enemy infantry but when we attacked them they threw away their weapons and fled. It was already 22:00 hr when we entered Marcilly. Here the situation changed dramatically and we came under heavy fire from the houses, from the roofs and cellars. We heard the slow "tac-tac" of the French machine-guns. Our 7.5 cm "shot us a bit of silence", but all too often the enemy fire flared up again. The 2nd Battalion reached the bridge after hard and slow progress. Immediately in front of it were several barricades and we came under both anti-tank and machine-gun fire. The situation was critical as we could not see the far bank very clearly.

The Battalion adjutant, Oberleutnant Malguth, decided to scout ahead on foot and the Regimental Adjutant, Guderian, accompanied him. One Panzer drove into position to give them covering fire.

'Our pioneers and recce sections were then moved up to the front. They cleared the houses near the bridge and occupied them, so that they could engage the enemy over the river. Suddenly three of our pioneers, together with Leutnant Stoff, rushed across the bridge in an almost suicidal attempt to capture it. The bridge was packed with explosives, but fortunately the enemy did not have enough time to set them off. Oberleutnants Malgruth and Guderian followed the pioneers. Guderian jumped off the bridge straight into a trench filled with French soldiers. The situation for him was critical, but a cleverly-thrown hand grenade gave him the opportunity to escape unharmed. The French fought a short but bitter battle and were finally forced to surrender. Oberleutnant Malguth took his Panzer across and the rest followed.

'The enemy did not counter-attack, so the Company continued to Romilly. They first captured a brand new bridgelayer section, then a 28 cm mortar. At a roadblock, however, we collided with an enemy column. We opened fire and brushed them aside. Soon we reached the town and captured two bridges, still undemolished. The enemy didn't even know we had arrived. We reached the market place and the Regimental Command section took up position there. A section of the 2nd Battalion together with the light armoured section of the Regiment tried to get some organisation into Romilly. The numbers of prisoners collecting in the marketplace grew by the minute. The 5th Company under Oberleutnant Malgruth cleared the way through the town and forward as far as the next village, finishing off another enemy convoy on their way.

'It was past midnight before the whole Regiment reached Romilly. The bridgehead over the Seine was secure. Even though the Regiment had been constantly on the go for the last 36 hours, the Panzers still had to remain on duty in case of a counter-attack. We had captured 33 aeroplanes at a nearby airfield, amongst which were seven heavy bombers. In the train station all the trains were halted, while the number of prisoners kept rising. Holiday trains were stopped and we gave the passengers a friendly welcome.

'The following morning more troops from our Division arrived and relieved us, so we could have a well-deserved break. The 2nd Company captured another Seine bridge in Sauvage on 14 June and took large numbers of prisoners. The 2nd Battalion then pushed forward to Maziere and Chatres, where the fighting was bitter. The light armoured sections were ordered to give support to the 8th Company. Hundreds of prisoners were eventually taken. Towards midday our orders had been accomplished. This success had been achieved mainly due to the initiative of the individual soldier. All of a sudden the French resistance collapsed. The afternoon remained peaceful and both battalions made themselves comfortable in the villages to the east of Romilly. Everyone hoped for a quiet and peaceful night although some had to remain at stand-to.

'Our move southwards continued on 15 June at 14:00 hr, but not before we had fought off an attempted enemy breakthrough near La Belle Etoile, where we lost one man and had two wounded by anti-tank gunfire.

'Endless columns of French soldiers passed us. Most of them just threw away their guns and asked the way to the prisoner-of-war camp. Some looked a little apprehensive, other greeted us in a friendly manner. Lots of them were drunk. The civilian population kept calm, some even smiled at us. We drove on until we ran out of fuel. We had reached the area around Chables. Replenishment should have been at a nearby road junction. Suddenly we came under fire. Leutnant von Gerdtell, Feldwebel (Sergeant Major) Janneck and Feldwebel Drew drove into a nearby wood and tried to persuade the French to give themselves up. On this occasion 40 prisoners were taken. Then, in a second machine-gun attack, the prisoners escaped and both Corporals were wounded, but Gerdtell managed to get back to his tank and rescue them. It was now 22:00 hr. Determinedly Oberleutnant Malgruth drove forward in his Panzer II, closely followed by a Panzer I. Several others tried to persuade them not to go after the French on their own, but Malgruth just laughed and waved. He successfully destroyed the enemy machine-gun nest and then called out to the French to surrender in order to prevent further bloodshed. At that moment he was hit in the head by an enemy bullet. He collapsed into Leutnant Konigstein's arms, where he died. The news quickly spread through the rest of the Regiment. He was a most hardworking and brave officer and did not deserve to die in that manner. We took his body with us and buried him the next day at Braux. The advance continued all that night until we reached Nevers. No enemy were seen. A number of prisoners were pulled out of blown-up vehicles and a machine-gun post was silenced at the entrance to the town. It was 03:00 hr when we got there and we spent the rest of the night freezing in our vehicles.'[19]

5

Pz Kpfw 35(t) and 38(t) and variants

Background development

Czechoslovakia ceased to exist as a free, independent country on 15 March 1939, when Hitler annexed Bohemia and Moravia, incorporating them into the Third Reich as a protectorate. Slovakia remained independent, in theory anyway, although closely linked to Germany. All the arms and equipment which had belonged to the well-equipped Czech Army was taken over, while the large Czech armament industry came under German control and continued to produce high quality weapons, vehicles and equipment for the German forces, including significant numbers of tanks and other AFVs. Prewar the Czechs had earned an enviable reputation for the excellence of their armaments, with such companies as Skoda and CKD (Ceskomoravska Kolben Danek) of Prague, producing armoured fighting vehicles for both home consumption and export.

The main tank in service with the Czech Army at the time of the annexation was the LT vz 35, which made up nearly three-quarters of their armoured forces of over 400 tanks. Among the prototype AFVs still to go into quantity production was the LT vz 38. These two AFVs, which became known in the German Army as the PzKpfw 35(t)[20] and PzKpfw 38(t) were among the most widely used foreign-built tanks in the Wehrmacht. In addition, Germany's Balkan allies such as Romania, Bulgaria, Hungary and, naturally, Slovakia, all had Czech tanks in service, while the Russians repaired and re-used captured 38(t)s. Before the war, the Czechs had run a thriving tank export business, with Sweden being one of their major customers. In its highly successful variant form as an SP anti-tank gun (the Panzerjäger *Hetzer*) the lifespan of the 38(t) was prolonged long after the war had ended, by the Swiss who pur-

chased over 150 *Hetzers* from the Czechs and continued to use them up until the early 1970s.

PzKpfw 35(t)

Developed by Skoda in 1934–35, the LT vz 35 light tank was of an advanced design and incorporated many innovative features

which unfortunately led to problems in its early in-service life. These had been mainly sorted out by the time it was later taken into German service, where it was used as a gun tank until 1941–42 and longer still as a tractor minus its turret. However, its poor reputation remained and it was never considered to be as good as the 38(t). When the German Army seized the Czech tanks, they redesignated them as the Panzer-

Front view of the Czech LT vz 35 with its original ochre, green and brown camouflage and licence number plate. These were retained when the tanks were later used by the Slovak Fast Division.

PZKPFW 35(T)
Date of origin 1934
Weight (tonnes) 10.5
Overall dimensions (m) Length 4.9
                       Height 2.35
                       Width 2.1
Armament/Ammunition carried
  Main 1 × 3.7 cm vs 34
      72 rounds
  Secondary 2 × 7.92 mm MG
      (vz 35 or 37)
Armour thickness (mm) Max. 35
                          Min. 8
Engine Type Skoda T11
      bhp/rpm 120/1,800
Crew 4 (in German service)
Max. speed (km/h) 40
Range (km) 200
Remarks Developed by Skoda as the
           Czech LT vz 35 light tank

Kampfwagen 35(t). Combat weight was 10.5 tonnes (10.3 UK/ 11.6 US tons), main armament a Skoda A-3 37 mm vz 34 anti-tank gun, which had an armoured cowl fitted over its recoil cylinder for protection as the cylinder stuck out of the front of the fully-traversing turret. Alongside the main gun was a ball-mounted 7.92 mm vz 35 or vz 37 machine-gun which could be disconnected, so that the two guns could be fired either simultaneously or individually. A second 7.92 mm MG was mounted in the hull in a ball socket on the

left wall in front of the driver. It could be locked into a straight position and fired by the driver when the tank was moving.

Ninety rounds of ammunition were carried for the 37 mm, which had a dial sight, hand traverse and elevation from −10° to +25°. Armour thickness was up to 35 mm on the nose and mantlet, while the sides, rear and roof were 16 mm. Armour was of a riveted and bolted construction, so suffered from 'popping' rivets when the tank was hit by a heavy enemy shell. This meant that the rivet heads were liable to sheer off when the tank was struck, leaving the shanks, which had absorbed part of the incoming round's velocity, to fly around inside the tank acting as secondary projectiles. The tank was powered by a four-cylinder Skoda T11 water-cooled petrol engine, which produced 120 bhp at 1,800 rpm. The 35(t) had a top speed of 40 km/h (25 mph) and a range of 200 km (125 miles). As the tank had rear driving sprockets there was no need for a drive shaft through the tank hull as was the case with the PzKpfw I and II. The transmission and steering were quite innovative, being pneumatic, with the aim of reducing driver fatigue. Unfortunately, this led to many problems, especially in the terrible weather conditions experienced in Russia, where a heater had to be fitted to try to prevent the steering system freezing up. The suspension had eight small bogies on each side, coupled in pairs, each set hanging from a large leaf spring which was bolted to the hull. It was a good, reliable suspension and

enabled the vehicle to carry out long road marches without breakdowns. Track life was also prolonged to 8,000 km (5,000 miles). Note also the small, separate, track tensioning wheel located just before the front idler. The crew was originally three, increased to four in German service — commander, gunner, loader/radio operator and driver.

The initial production batch was tested by the Czech Army in the summer of 1936, but had then to be returned to the makers for repairs. By November 1936 a total of 103 constructional changes had been made, but when the Army carried out further testing in 1937 they still found that the tanks could not be run for over 2,000 km (1,250 miles) without major repairs. Kliment and Doyle[21] say that there were 297 Lt vz 35 on the Czech Army list in March 1939, out of a total of 184 tanks and 75 armoured cars. Of these, 79 Lt vz 35s were left with the Slovak forces and used in the 3rd 'Fast' Division, which was then stationed in Slovakia and went on to fight alongside the German Panzer divisions in Russia. The remaining 218 were taken into German service. Oberst aD Helmut Ritgen explains in his history of the 6th Panzer Division how, in mid-April 1939, 1st *leichte* Division (which later became 6th Panzer Division) received 130 Skoda LT vz 35 light tanks for the 11th Panzer Regiment and 65th Panzer Battalion. He talks about

Side view of the LT vz 35, showing its very distinctive suspension of eight small bogies coupled in pairs and 37 mm gun with the armoured cowl over its recoil cylinder, sticking out in front of the tank.

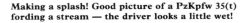

Making a splash! Good picture of a PzKpfw 35(t) fording a stream — the driver looks a little wet!

them as the 'fine and reliable offspring of the Vickers six-ton tank which was designed as an infantry support vehicle with a three man crew', then he goes on to explain how the OC of 11th Panzer ordered that they should be manned by four men by the addition of a loader (without seat or observation ports) and that German radios should be fitted. Despite the lack of Czech instructors and a shortage of technical manuals, training progressed very well and by July it had been decided to discard all the division's PzKpfw Is and some of the PzKpfw IIs and to re-equip with the Czech tanks.

'The division, together with the 11th Panzer Regiment, now fielded a tank regiment of three battalions each with an HQ, one medium and two light tank companies, totalling 65 PzKpfw II, 114 PzKpfw 35(t) and 42 PzKpfw IV — 221 tanks in all. No other panzer regiment of that date could match this number of guns.'[22]

Oberst (Colonel) aD Dipl Ing Icken was the head of the governmental planning department at that time and recalls the following: 'On 15 March 1939, the 3rd Panzer Division, to which Panzer Regiment 6 belonged, marched into the "Golden City" of Prague. As I was the regimental technical adjutant of Pz Regt 6 I had the task of supervising the investigation of the Czech battle tanks LT vz 35, which were located at Milowitz, a military training area nearby. These tanks later received the German designation "PanzerKampfwagen 35(t)". Together with other tank commanders I carried out tests on several vehicles on the area around Milowitz and on an obstacle course. Czech soldiers provided us with much useful information on the tanks as they were new to us. The Czech officers believed that they would be recruited by the German armed forces, but this was something we could not confirm. They were therefore very interested in this possibility and pointed out that such an arrangement had existed in the Austria-Hungary empire. It must be said that our co-operation with the Czechs was excellent and showed hardly any restraint. There was never any friction, acts of sabotage or any resistance. The 35(t)s were useful, manoeuvrable vehicles which, for the level of development at the time, had considerable firepower (3.7 cm cannon and two MG), also technically interesting transmission and steering. The riveted tank hulls were a disadvantage because of their high sensitivity to

PzKpfw 35(t) moving through light snow, 8 March 1940.

A 'Skoda' being used for a spot of recovery work on the Russian front in 1941. Note the considerable external stowage which was required by tank crews to live and fight while moving over long distances through inhospitable surroundings (Charles Kliment).

shelling. Accordingly, my report was made known to the 3rd Panzer Division.'[23]

Battle history

The PzKpfw 35(t) saw its first action in Poland in September 1939, 1 *leichte* Division playing a vital part in the defeat of the gallant Polish Army. Few tanks were lost and the reliable Czech-built tanks became the backbone of the division. They again proved their worth when the division with artillery and air support burst through the Maginot Line defences then spearheaded the German advance across the Meuse. After the French campaign had been successfully concluded there was a further reorganisation which left 11th Panzer Regiment with three battalions of two light tank companies, each of 22 PzKpfw 35(t)s, and a medium company of 14 PzKpfw IVs and five PzKpfw IIs.

Despite the fact that the 35(t)s were beginning to show their age and had actually been declared no longer suitable for combat in the spring of 1941, they were not replaced and were in action again in June 1941, as part of 4th Panzergruppe, operating on the far northern flank of the German invasion of Russia, driving towards Leningrad. As the weather got colder the 35(t)s were hampered by their pneumatic clutch, brakes and steer-

ing, which froze up. The Soviet T-34 and KV 1 made short work of the lightly-armoured Czech-built tanks. 'The very last tank of 6th Panzer, named "Anthony the Last" broke down on 10 December near Klin, which was given up a few days later.'[24]

Variants

A small number of PzKpfw 35(t)s were converted into command vehicles for use in 6th Panzer Division, by adding extra radio sets and fitting them with a collapsible frame aerial which could be erected over the back

decks. When the tank was replaced as a first-line piece of equipment a small number of remaining chassis were converted into mortar tractors (*Mörserzugmittel*) or tractors (*Zugkraftwagen*) with a trailer capacity of 12 tons, for use in the maintenance sections of tank formations. Both conversions had a crew of two, no turret and a canvas cover over the open hull.

PzKpfw 38(t)

When the Czech Army was modernising in the mid-1930s they had allocated considerable funds towards the purchase of large numbers of light tanks. As has been explained, the poor in-service reputation of the Skoda-produced Lt vz 35 was such as to preclude the purchase of any more of this type of tank. Instead, a tank evaluation board was established to carry out thorough testing of all available new designs from which the best would then be chosen. Skoda produced two models, CKD four. The outright winner of the trial was the TNHP-S tank, which CKD had built for the export market. During 3½ months' testing, it logged 5,584 km (3,490 miles) of which 1,533 km (958 miles) were in heavy terrain, without a single serious defect.[25] In addition, the new tank was very easy to maintain, needing under 30 minutes' maintenance daily. It was decided to adopt the TNHP-S as the standard light tank for the Czech Army and it was given the nomenclature 'LT vz 38'. In

These PzKpfw 35(t)s are the command version (*PzBefWg*). Note the large external frame aerial over the back decks, and absence of bow MGs (Charles Kliment).

First prototype of the Czech TNHP, showing the dish-shaped suspension wheels. Armament was a Skoda A 7 37 mm gun and two heavy ZB vz 37 machine-guns.

July 1938 an order was placed for 150, the first 20 being due to be delivered by the end of that year. The international situation, however, forced a slowdown in production, so that none of the new tanks had been delivered before the Germans invaded the country. It was not until May 1939 that the first new tanks were ready. The Germans took over the first nine off the assembly lines on 22 May 1939. They were extremely impressed. The light tank was clearly far superior to their own PzKpfw I and II, both in armour and firepower. Not only did they instruct CKD — now known as Bohmisch-Mahrische-Maschinenfabrik (BMM) under new German management — to complete the 150 order as quickly as possible, but also placed more orders for a further 325 tanks. They renamed the tank the PanzerKampfwagen 38(t).

Oberst Icken had this to say about the PzKpfw 38(t): 'The Czech officers at Milowitz revealed to me at the time that the series production of a newly developed tank was imminent. This vehicle, which later became known as the PzKpfw 38(t), had a battle weight of 9.7 tons and the same weaponry as the 35(t) tank. The German armed forces were unaware of this fact. Following our trip to Milowitz, which we had made lightly armed and in uniform, driving a light open car, we visited the firm of Ceskomoravska Kolben Danek (CKD) in Prague. This was the old renowned first Bohemian-Moravian machine factory, which took on the manufacture of motor vehicles as early as 1907, under the name of the Prague Automobile Factory. This firm built cars, heavy goods vehicles and tractors for the Austro-Hungarian army up to 1918. The factory

buildings gave the impression of being solid but old fashioned, even if a lot of work had gone on in them.

'The porter told us in broken German that no work was being done there now and that the factory was closed. However, as we were on the premises he was prepared to call some engineers on the telephone who were working in the drawing office. Although we had no official authorisation, they showed us all over the plant, where machine parts of all types could be assembled and explained to us about the newly developed tank, just released for series production. During this visit I established that delivery could take place of a tank with a well formed, simple leaf spring running gear and four large road wheels, newly developed Wilson transmission gears with forward gear shift, steering gears as well as an effective cannon. These vehicles were produced under tough conditions. After I had given Major

Thomale, a tank expert in the OKH AHA AgK Ing6, a good assessment of the newly developed Czech tank, a commission of the OKH, made up of members of the Ing6 of the army weaponry office, the WA Pruf 6 (development) and WA B6 (procurement), came to Prague.

'The procurement office WA B6 again issued in April 1939 a German annexation treaty to the firm CKD (German name was Bohmisch-Mahrische Maschinenfabrik) which was drawn up in accordance to schedule and without complaint. From April 1939 approximately 100 newly produced

Good shot of a column of PzKpfw 38(t)s replenishing during the advance through France in 1940 (Charles Kliment).

Typical scene at the end of the Slovak uprising in 1944, with abandoned vehicles littering the roads, including this Slovak PzKpfw 38(t). The Germans crushed the uprising in two months and by late October 1944 the survivors had retreated into the Tatia mountains. One of the original 38(t) Ausf S is kept as a memorial in the town at the centre of the uprising, Banska Bystrica (Charles Kliment).

38(t) tanks were delivered to the German armed forces. The takeover of these Panzers, progressively simple and well constructed, was moreover never properly supported by Wa Pruf 6, since the development had not been directed or arranged from there. Colonel Dipl-Ing Wilhelm Philipps, head of Wa Pruf 6 and late commander of Panzer Regiment II, was responsible for German tank development from 1937, and it was his task to adapt the 35(t) tank for German service. He completed the work in an extraordinarily short time, making room for a loader and German radio equipment, as well

Good close-up shot of the turret armament of the memorial PzKpfw 38(t) Ausf S which is still kept in running order at Banska Bystrica (Charles Kliment).

Similar close-up shot of the bow machine-gun. This tank is paraded every year during the anniversary of the uprising (Charles Kliment).

Good front view of a PzKpfw 38(t) Ausf A.

Models produced

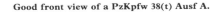

The first model, the Ausf A, was produced between May and November 1939, a total of 150 being built. To all intents and purposes the Ausf A was identical to the TNHP-S tank except for the fact that the Germans increased the crew to four men with the addition of a loader for the main armament. Space for the extra crewman was found by the removal of three six-round ammunition bins. Next came the Ausf B, C and D (325 produced between January and November 1940) which had small changes such as the addition of smoke grenades on the rear, the removal of the battle aerial (the 'pipe' aerial on the left side of the Ausf A was a good recognition feature) and the installation of German lighting. Ausf E and F followed between November 1940 and October 1941, a total of 525 being produced by BMM. They reflected the battle experience acquired in Poland with additional armour

achieved by riveting on extra 25 mm plates on all frontal surfaces and 15 mm sheets on the sides. The Ausf S was produced to fill a Swedish order placed in 1939 for 90 tanks from BMM, which was postponed while the orders for the German Army were completed. Germany then decided to keep the tanks for themselves while opening negotiations to allow Sweden to build the 38(t) under licence. The Ausf S was similar to the Ausf A, B and C, having been designed, and the build starting, at the same time as the Ausf A even though they were not completed until the Ausf F was being produced. The final version of the 38(t) to see service was the Ausf G which had more

welded armour than previous models putting the weight up to 9.5 tonnes (93.5 UK/ 10.5 US tons). Not all the chassis built were actually used for tanks, a fair number were used for SP anti-tank guns.

The total production figures for the models A to G were:

Model	No produced	Model	No produced
A	150	S	90
B	110	G	500 (but only 321 built as tanks)
C	110		
D	105		
E	275		
F	250		

(Source: Kliment and Doyle.)

Rear view of a PzKpfw 38(t) *Befehlswagen*. The 38(t) did not make a good command tank as its turret was much too small to be fitted with all the extra equipment needed (Oberst aD Hermann Rothe).

The Ausf G was the result of a demand for more protection and used basic 50 mm armour on the frontal surfaces.

tonnes (9.25 UK/ 10.4 US tons), had a crew of four (commander/gunner, radio operator, driver and the added loader as explained above), and was armed with a Skoda A-7 37 mm tank gun, the German designation being the 3.7 cm KwK 37(t). Secondary armament comprised two 7.92 mm machine-guns, one mounted in the turret and fired either co-axially or independently by the loader, the other at the front in a spherical mounting, which could be fired free by the operator or, when clamped, by the driver. Armour was 25 mm on the front, 15 mm on the sides and rear and 10 mm on top. The 15 ft long (4.6 m) tank was powered by a Praga EPA six-cylinder, water-cooled petrol engine developing

Thus the total of PzKpfw 38(t) tanks produced was 1,411 plus three prototypes. Finally, a small number of a new recce tank, the PzKpfw 38(t) *neuer Art*, were built in early 1942. These followed the layout of the 38(t) but incorporated mainly welded armour up to 35 mm thick and were powered by a Praga V-8 engine. The tank weighed just under 15 tons yet had a top speed of nearly 62 km/h (39 mph). It did not get further than the development stage and never saw combat.

General description

The PzKpfw 38(t) Ausf A weighed 9.4

The Panzerjäger 38(t) mit 7.5 cm PaK 40/3 Ausf M, or *Marder III* for short, was the result of Hitler's order that all 38(t) production was to be used for SP guns from mid-1942 onwards. Here *Marder III*s are loading aboard a troop train for the Eastern Front.
The *Marder III* served on all fronts from about May 1943 onwards. This one was photographed in the Liri valley, Italy, near Aquino in May 1944.

The 15 cm SP heavy infantry gun was known as *Grille* (Cricket), of which 282 were produced in 1943–44 (Some sources call it the *Bison*, possibly in error.) The 15 cm SP heavy infantry gun was mounted in both PzKpfw 38(t) Ausf H chassis and on the special new Ausf K chassis.
This Cricket was captured by men of the US First Army in Belgium, following the Allied drive to stem the German Ardennes offensive (US Army).

125 bhp at 2,200 rpm. Top speed was about 40 km/h (25 mph) while the range was about 250 km (126 miles). The suspension consisted of four large rubber-tyred wheels on either side, mounted on stub axles, with each pair of wheels being sprung by semi-elliptical leaf springs. A front driving sprocket, rear mounted idler and two small return rollers carried the manganese steel tracks which were 293 mm (11.55 in) wide. A Praga-Wilson pre-selector five-speed gear-box drove the sprockets by means of two-stage epicyclic steering gear. Detachable spuds were available for the tracks to increase grip on snow and ice. Ninety rounds of 37 mm ammunition were carried for the main gun, plus 2,400 rounds for the machine-guns.

The turret had hand traverse which could be disengaged and the turret then moved by the commander/gunner using a shoulder pad. He aimed the gun through a co-axially-mounted telescopic sight, and elevated or depressed it with his shoulder pad between −10° and +25°. There was no turret basket. The commander's cupola was fixed, with a single lid and fitted with four periscopes. The radio (FuG 37(t)) was carried in the left front side of the hull and made the radio operator's position very cramped indeed. A 3 m (10 ft) rod aerial gave the set a range of 5 km (3 miles), while there was also a fixed pipe battle aerial along the left-hand side of the tank which had a range of under 1 km (600 yd). There was no intercom as such, but the commander could pass some commands to the driver by a system of coloured lights (red, yellow and blue, with three bell pushes; the latter were appropriately painted and carved in different ways so that they could be felt in the dark).

British trial

In February 1939, CKD endeavoured to interest the British Army in the TNHP and one mild steel prototype was shipped to the UK for testing in March 1939. The detailed report on this trial is now held in the Tank Museum library and contains many interesting comments, some of which are quoted below. In general terms the British appear not to have been very impressed by the TNHP, despite the fact that it was undoubtedly superior in firepower and performance to the then in-service British light tanks and compared favourably with the A-9 cruiser.

'This vehicle was subjected to trials between 17.3.39 and 29.3.39 and covered 291 miles including 103 across country. The commander's field of view is not ideal and it is hard to judge distance through the episcope and the three periscopes. His position is satisfactory except that the sling provided precludes a comfortable position behind the gun. The hull gunner's field of view covers the field of fire. The wireless set renders his position uncomfortable and the headroom is inadequate. The driver's vision is adequate except for driving in traffic, when a member of the crew must sit outside the hull to act as pilot. The position is comfortable and the controls are well placed but headroom is inadequate. The vehicle is inadequately ventilated and the fumes given off by the steering gear soon become objectionable. Care is necessary in steering on roads as the action of the epicyclic handbrake is rapid. The vehicle does not skid under normal conditions and is safe up to its maximum speed. It is easy to handle on side slopes and does not suffer from reverse steering, but when descending hills the steering is heavy and insensitive. The power is adequate, whether the vehicle is opened up or closed down.

The *Hetzer* (Baiter) was one of the most successful tank destroyers ever produced. Its lifespan was considerably lengthened by the Swiss, who kept over 150 of them in service until the early 1970s.

'The suspension of the vehicle renders it unsuitable as a gunnery platform. It has a short juddering motion of about 2-inch amplitude. Otherwise the springing is good and the vehicle rides across country in a manner similar to that of a Tank Cruiser A9 Mark I, although on roads the juddering motion occasionally mars the performance. The maximum permissible speed on Course No 12 was 10 mph [16 km/h]. The capacity of this vehicle for negotiating natural obstacles is not adequate to its role. It will cross a 5-feet stream, and probably a 7-feet trench with hard sides, but will not climb a 4-feet sandbank. A height of 2 feet 10 inches is the maximum vertical obstacle which can be surmounted safely. The exhaust is very quiet

This *Hetzer* was not so lucky, as it met up with sharpshooting GI armed with a bazooka in Oberhoffen. Private Kenneth C. Walker proudly stands beside his 'bag', rather like a prewar big game hunter! (US Army).

and across country the vehicle is quiet, but on roads the tracks are very noisy. The tracks were not new when the vehicle was received but they do not appear to have worn appreciably and the rate of wear appears low. They are of robust design and exhibited no tendency to be thrown during any of the tests.

'The traversing gear can be thrown out of action and the turret can then be pushed round by the gunner. It is doubtful, however, whether the turret is so accurately balanced that this could be done on severe inclines... It is extremely difficult for the tank commander to load the turret machine-gun or to get at it to clear stoppages; on the other hand if the third man is used for this purpose his position is remarkably cramped. A convenient action position is provided for a case of 8 rounds of ammunition for the 37 mm gun. The belt of the turret machine-gun gets in the way of the driver when the turret is trained forward or to the left front.

'The workmanship and detail design appear to be generally good, but not extravagant, and the cost per ton should be less than that of British tanks. Comfort of crew and ease of evacuation of wounded are inferior.

'On the whole the machine is almost equivalent to our Cruiser Tanks, but little experience or experiment has gone into the design of the fighting arrangements, and performance had been obtained at the expense of the crew and general "fightability". Apparently the positions of the crew are as follows:

gunner and loader. Owing to the judder set up by the suspension the gun platform is much inferior to our light tanks... A single handed turret gunner is at a disadvantage and although the bulk of the 37 mm ammunition is in the turret bulge, his max rates of fire (stationary) are probably: HE — 6 rpm AP — 8 rpm. He cannot load the co-axial MG. If the hull gunner acts as loader the rate of fire is increased, but the latter's position is far too cramped. With a separate loader, there is less need for ammunition in the bulge and the more constant weight of the wireless set may be substituted for it.

'The tank was comfortable to ride in and judging by the way it took jumps there is very little chance of the crew being injured when travelling over unknown country. The stiffness of the suspension, however, set up a judder or wobble in the turret (which seemed loose laterally), making it impossible to lay the guns when travelling at over 5 mph. Even at this speed shooting was poor. Other factors which added to the difficulties of firing on the move were: poor and non-instinctive elevating and traversing gears (free gun control was impossible); poor firing gear; looseness of mounting; absence of brow-pad; inferior telescope; lack of observation of strike of shots; gun and turret incorrectly balanced. On the whole this machine offers a gun platform very much inferior to that of our Light Tanks Marks V to VIB.' (Sour grapes perhaps when one remembers that the British light tanks were only armed with machine-guns!)

total of 59 PzKpfw 38(t)s were used of which seven were damaged and later repaired.[27] A small number of 38(t)s were later used for Operation *Wesserübung Nord* — the invasion of Norway — in April 1940 but were then brought back to take part in the attack on France. 7th and 8th Panzer Divisions both contained the Czech-built tanks, 229 being used in this campaign. Casualties were heavier than in Poland, but again most vehicles were recovered and repaired, so the actual total losses were really very small. Not so in Russia, where large numbers of 38(t)s were knocked out — Kliment and Doyle put the losses of PzKpfw 38(t) as 796 in the first six months of operations, when Czech-built tanks made up more than a quarter of the total strength of the Panzer formations. Like the 35(t) it was now clear that the 38(t) was not viable for tank v tank operations, so other uses had to be found for its very reliable chassis and components. Some of the light tanks were handed on to Germany's allies, or used for internal security duties in occupied areas such as anti-partisan work, policing, etc, so significant numbers of PzKpfw 38(t)s still remained on the active list until much later in the war.

Colonel aD Dipl-Ing Heinrich Wust had this to say about his experiences with the PzKpfw 38(t): '*Armoured march from Prague to Eisenach*. In the autumn of 1939 following the Polish campaign, the good old PzKpfw I "Krupp-Sport" had had its day, and therefore we were to use the Czech PzKpfw 38(t) in addition to the PzKpfw II and IV. To familiarise ourselves with the new tanks we had first to collect some vehicles from the factory in Prague. We had calculated that the 350 km road march would take some four-five days going on our previous tank experience, so we decided to allow a week, including an allowance for unusual occurrences. However, we were totally speechless when only two and a half days after the departure of the tank collecting party, we suddenly heard the noise of tanks. The column of PzKpfw 38(t)s came into the barracks in elegant turns, coming to a halt bang on time. The commander said that as the tanks had run so smoothly there had been no need for long maintenance halts and they had covered the distance in one almost non-stop march. The tank division was naturally delighted to hear this and continued to have a high regard for the tank's mobility.

	On the move	At the halt
Commander-Gunner:	In cupola commanding.	Manning turret gun.
Operator-hull gnr:	Manning hull gun.	Loading.
Driver:	Driving position.	Driving position.

'From the above it is easy to see that the tank will be outgunned when moving or out-manoeuvred when stationary. One man cannot command and shoot at the same time. Two suggested re-arrangements, both involving a somewhat larger turret and a crew of four are:

I
Comd/loader (cupola on right)
Gnr/op (wireless in bulge)
Hull gnr
Driver

II
Comd (cupola at left rear)
Gnr (moved forward)
Loader/op (wireless in bulge, no hull gun)
Dvr

'If the sprockets were placed at the rear and the propellor-shaft removed from the fighting chamber, a rotating floor could be fitted. The floor of the present fighting chamber offers a poor foothold for both

Battle history

PzKpfw 38(t) saw its first operational service with Panzer *Abteilung* 67 of 3 *leichte* Division in Poland during the summer of 1939. A

'Compared with PzKpfw II and IV, the 38(t) was weaker and badly protected. However, overall it was on a par with contemporary German tanks, because of its better mobility and more effective armament. The road performance was so excellent that

The *leichter Einheitswaffentrager* (light weapons carriage) was produced in prototype only, in early 1945. It was designed to carry either a 10.5 cm or, as seen here, an 8.8 cm gun.

several effective variants were produced later to prolong its lifespan — such as the Marder and Hetzer. The individual components of the 38(t) chassis were optionally matched and the unusually good mobility of the PzKpfw 38(t) can be traced back to this. The engine, steering and running gear worked as a unified whole. The accommodating nature of the tank as far as servicing and repairs must also be emphasised. Long technical breakdowns were virtually unknown.

'*Somme breakthrough*. Part of the 7th Panzer Division won a bridgehead 3 km [1.9 miles] deep on the south bank of the Somme on 5 June 1940, and at 16:00 hrs the bulk of the division began attacking to the south with Panzer Regiment 25 leading, three battalions up. The deceptive flat looking slope was actually quite steep and had to be negotiated at an angle when going into the attack. The light companies with their 38(t)s negotiated the slope without any difficulty, but the IVDs of the heavy company were not so lucky and most tanks lost tracks during the journey. This caused a delay in the breakthrough. Scarcely any situation, even driver training in sandpits, presented a serious problem for the 38(t)s, as evidenced by their superiority on the banks of the Somme, where the PzKpfw 38(t)s swept effortlessly past the slow moving PzKpfw IVs.

'*Phantom Division*. After breaking through the Weygand Line, the town of St Vàléry on the Channel coast was taken on 12 June. During the surrender, one of the French Generals asked General (later Field Marshal) Rommel what was the division that had beaten them. When Rommel proudly replied "the 7th Division", the Frenchman was heard to say: "Damn: The Phantom Division again! First in Belgium, then on the Somme, now here, we have come across this division, wandering like ghosts all over France." The name Phantom Division was thereafter taken as a name of honour for the

59

7th Panzer Division. It was certain that nobody would regard the use of the PzKpfw 38(t) as the sole cause of this honour but they did a great job. For example, in the mornings shortly after breakfast, General Rommel would climb aboard a 38(t) with the crew and set off on a recce with Colonel Rothenburg, commander of the 25 Panzer Regiment. They often went 20 to 30 km beyond the front line and let the rest of the division follow on behind. Certainly Rommel would not have undertaken these "outings" into enemy territory in either a Panzer III or IV, because they were too slow and likely to break down. On the other hand, the quick, manoeuvrable, and dependable PzKpfw 38(t) was eminently suited for such brilliant coups.[28]

Variants

Marder III The first of the highly successful Panzerjäger to use the 38(t) chassis came into being quite early on in the Russian campaign, when it was found that the in-service German anti-tank guns were ineffective against the heavier Russian tanks. The only gun that did the job was the captured Russian 7.62 cm field gun. In late December 1941, the Weapons Department was ordered to produce an interim SP anti-tank gun, which consisted of the complete Russian gun carriage fixed to the top of the tank chassis (minus turret). The gun crew had a measure of protection to their front and sides by means of fixed armour plate. Another variation of this *ad hoc* type of SP anti-tank gun on the 38(t) chassis used the German 7.5 cm Pak 40/3, while a heavy infantry SP gun, the sIG 33, which mounted a 15 cm gun, was also produced in some quantity (90 built in early 1943). Late production models of the Marder III had the engine repositioned centrally in the chassis, allowing the crew compartment to be positioned further back on the hull, giving a much better level of protection. A large number of this type of SP was produced in 1943–44 and became the early 'backbone' of the *Panzerjäger* forces under the designation Panzerjäger 38(t) mit 7.5 cm Pak 40/3 (Sd Kfz 138).

Hetzer Marder III was, however, only an interim solution to the problem, but led to the production of one of the most successful *Panzerjäger* of the war. This used the well-proven components of the PzKpfw 38(t), but was of a completely new design, with a wide, low profile, 60 mm of frontal armour and plenty of room for the four-man crew, together with 41 rounds of ammunition for the main gun plus 1,200 rounds for the roof-mounted MG 34.

A better version of the Praga engine was installed giving the AFV a top speed of over 42 kmh (26 mph). Hetzer was first used in action in May 1944 and thereafter was used in large numbers — 2,584 were built up to March 1945. Hetzer conversions included both a recovery vehicle (*Bergepanzer 38(t) Hetzer*) and flamethrowing tank (*Flammpanzer 38(t) Hetzer*), while there were other AFVs based upon the 38(t) chassis including tracked ammunition carriers, an SP anti-aircraft gun, and even an ingenious driver training vehicle, which was powered with a wood-burning gas generator in order to save using precious petrol!

Postscript

The true value of the Czech tanks to the German Army was very succinctly summed up by Oberst (Colonel) aD Helmut Ritgen in Walter J. Spielberger's book *Die PanzerKampfwagen 35(t) und 38(t) und ihre Abarten* when he said: 'Until the moment that I started to help to write this book I did not realise, that — if I am correct — all the 1940–41 newly organised Tank Regiments, namely 29, 39, 27 and 21, were equipped with PzKpfw 38(t). Which means, that without the 38(t) and the Czech production facilities, we would have had four less Panzer Divisions at our disposal and without them an attack on the Soviet Union would have been impossible.'

6
Pz Kpfw III and variants

Background development

By the mid-1930s German thinking on the types of tanks needed for their future Panzer formations had crystallised upon two basic models, one light and one medium. The majority of the tanks in the Panzer divisions would be of the former type, light, fast and armed with a 2 cm gun, while the slower, heavier model would have a dual-purpose armament with the main task of providing close support. At first it was visualised that the light tank with its 2 cm gun would be able to deal with most enemy tanks, as well as taking on such tasks as reconnaissance, while the heavier enemy AFVs would be dealt with by infantry-manned anti-tank guns sited in depth. However, the more that possible future battlefield scenarios were explored, then the more it was appreciated that the poorly-armed and thinly-armoured light tanks would never be able to hold their own in tank v tank battles. Clearly another type of tank was needed in a weight class somewhere between the other two, armed with a sufficiently powerful gun to deal with most types of enemy armour. Guderian and his Inspectorate of Armoured Troops wanted this new light tank to mount a 5 cm armour-piercing gun, but the *Heereswaffenamt* considered that a 3.7 cm would be sufficient, arguing on the grounds of standardisation with the infantry anti-tank gun. Although Guderian felt strongly that the thickness of armour on potential enemy tanks would require a gun of no less than 5 cm, he reluctantly agreed to accept the smaller calibre weapon, provided the new tank would be built with a wide enough turret ring to accept a larger calibre weapon in due course. It was also agreed that the new medium tank — which was known from 1936 as the *Zugführerswagen* (platoon commander's vehicle) and later as PanzerKampfwagen III (SdKfz 141) — would be very like the heavier *Bataillonführerswagen* in size, shape and layout. Both would have five-man crews, with the tank commander, loader and gunner in the turret, and the driver and radio operator in the hull.

The commander was to be in a suitably raised position in the turret, between the gunner and loader, with his own all-round viewing cupola. He would communicate with the rest of the crew via a throat microphone, which was an integral part of the tank's wireless layout. A number of firms were issued with development contracts for the new tank in 1935, some prototypes being produced the following year and trialled extensively. The Daimler-Benz design was chosen for production and the first production model, the Ausf A, was built in 1936.

Ten Ausf As (SdKfz 141), designated as the 1/ZW, were built by Daimler-Benz between 1936 and 1937. Main armament was the 3.7 cm KwK L/46.5 gun, with twin MG 34s in the turret and a further MG 34 in the hull (manned by the radio operator). While the general design of the hull and turret set the pattern for future models, the suspension was very different, with five large double bogie wheels on either side, suspended on coil springs, with a front mounted sprocket,

The MKA seen here was the Krupp prototype produced to meet the Heereswaffenamt's specification for the Zugführerswagen.

PZKPFW III AUSF A (SDKFZ 141)		
Date of origin 1937		
Weight (tonnes) 15.4		
Overall dimensions (m)	Length	5.7
	Height	2.34
	Width	2.81
Armament/Ammunition carried		
Main 1 × 3.7 cm KwK L/46.5		
150 rounds		
Secondary 3 × 7.92 mm MG 34		
(2 turret, 1 hull)		
Armour thickness (mm)	Max.	15
	Min.	5
Engine Type Maybach 108 TR		
bhp/rpm 250/3,000		
Crew 5		
Max. speed (km/h) 32		
Range (km) 165		
Remarks Ten only were built		
of the first model		

rear idler and two return rollers. It was powered by the Maybach 108TR engine and the 15.4-ton tank had a top speed of 32 km/h (20 mph). Armour was 15 mm or less. Issued in 1937, it was found unsatis-

The original Krupp turret for the PzKpfw III Ausf A mounted a 3.7 cm KwK L/46.5 with an internal mantlet. It fired 3.7 cm Pzgr 40 AP ammunition with a muzzle velocity of 1,020 m/s (3,350 fps) and could penetrate 34 mm of homogeneous armour plate at 500 m (550 yd).

factory and was withdrawn in early 1940. The Ausf B (2/ZW) was also built in small quantity (only 15 produced) by Daimler-Benz in 1937. The major change lay in the suspension, which this time comprised eight much smaller bogie wheels on each side, suspended in pairs on leaf springs, with three return rollers. Again, like the Ausf A, the 2/ZW was issued to units, saw service in Poland and was withdrawn in early 1940. The Ausf C (3a/ZW) followed, again with modifications to its suspension, extra leaf

Only ten PzKpfw III Ausf As were produced, and as this photograph shows, had the distinctive five roadwheel suspension with coil springs and just two return rollers, so unlike any other PzKpfw III suspension. They were withdrawn from service in 1940 (Oberst aD Hermann Rothe).

springs being introduced so that now each bogie was individually suspended, but it suffered the same fate as its predecessors, the 15 produced being withdrawn from service shortly before the campaign in France. The fourth model, the Ausf D (3b/ZW), had an improved suspension with angled leaf springs, new sprockets, idlers and transmission, but still kept the eight small road wheels. It also had a new cupola. Some 30 were built, issued to the Panzer units in 1938, saw service in Poland and were then withdrawn, although a few did serve on in Norway in 1940. The first model to go into anything like full-scale production (96 produced) was the Ausf E (4/ZW). It had thicker frontal armour (up to 30 mm), a better engine (Maybach HL 120TR) and an entirely new suspension design with six individually supported road wheels and a new gearbox. These changes all put the combat weight up to 19.5 tonnes (19.2 UK/21.5 US tons).

In September 1939, Army Regulations announced that the PanzerKampfwagen III

had been adopted after successful troop trials. At about the same time it was realised that Guderian had been right all along and that the 3.7 cm gun was too small, so the fitting of the 5 cm gun was authorised with the consequent loss of one of the twin MGs. However, production of the new gun would take time, so the next model, the Ausf F, still mounted the smaller gun at the beginning of its production run, although the last quarter of the 435 produced were armed with the 5 cm weapon. Some Ausf Es and Fs were also converted to take the new gun. Six hundred of the next model, the Ausf G, were built by seven different manufacturers, the main improvement being an increase in armour thickness on the hull rear to 30 mm and a new cupola (late production only). The Ausf H (308 built) had a newly-designed turret, transmission and running gear. It was also the first model to have a turret basket fitted, plus additional added-on 30 mm armour plate on the front of the tank, making it relatively impossible for contempory Allied tank and anti-tank guns to knock it out at normal engagement ranges. The add-on armour was integrated into the basic build in the next model, the Ausf J (SdKfz 141/1) which was produced in greater quantity than any other model of the PzKpfw III series — 2,616 being produced between March 1941

The PzKpfw III B, C and D all had a similar suspension, comprising eight small road wheels on either side. Some 30 Ausf Ds, as seen here, were built and served until early 1940, a few fighting in Norway.

**PZKPFW III AUSF J
(SDKFZ 141 & 141/1)**
Date of origin 1941
Weight (tonnes) 22.3
Overall dimensions (m) Length 5.52
Height 2.5
Width 2.95
Armament/Ammunition carried
Main 1 × 5 cm KwK L/42
84 rounds
Secondary 2 × 7.92 mm MG 34
Armour thickness (mm) Max. 50
Min. 10
Engine Type Maybach 120 TRM
bhp/rpm 300/3,000
Crew 5
Max. speed (km/h) 40
Range (km) 155
Remarks From end of 1941, fitted
with longer-barrelled
KwK 39 L/60 gun

PZKPFW III AUSF N (SDKFZ 141/2)
Date of origin 1942
Weight (tonnes) 23
Overall dimensions (m) Length 5.65
Height 2.5
Width 2.95
Armament/Ammunition carried
Main 1 × 7.5 cm KwK L/24
64 rounds
Secondary 2 × 7.92 mm MG 34
Armour thickness (mm) Max. 57
Min. 10
Engine Type Maybach HL 120 TRM
bhp/rpm 300/3,000
Crew 5
Max. speed (km/h) 40
Range (km) 155
Remarks Now relegated to the
support role in place of
the PzKpfw IV

96 Ausf Es were built with increased armour and a completely new suspension design of six individually supported road wheels. Many were converted to mount the 5 cm KwK L/42 gun with an external mantlet (Horst Riebenstahl).

and July 1942. Initially the Ausf J was armed with the short-barrelled 5 cm KwK L/42 gun, but this was changed to the longer-barrelled L/60 gun on Hitler's personal instructions for the last 1,000-plus produced. In addition, the tank now had thicker armour — up to 50 mm — as standard, a better visor for the driver and a new ball-mounting for the hull MG. The all-up weight was 21.5 tonnes (21.1 UK/23.7 US tons). Ausf L (650 produced in the latter half

of 1942) was yet another attempt to up-armour the PzKpfw III, by adding 20 mm thick spaced armour to the front of the superstructure and gun mantlet, increasing the tank's weight by 200 kg (441 lb). Ausf M (250 built) was only slightly different to its predecessor, but had better fording equipment. Some 100, built by MIAG, were turned over to another manufacturer, Wegmann, to be converted to flamethrower tanks (see later). By the time the Ausf N (SdKfz 141/2), the last model in the main development family, was designed, it had been found that the PzKpfw III was simply not up to the standard of its opponents and there

was no scope left for adding on more armour or improving the hitting power of its main armament. By then (mid-1942) it was clear that PzKpfw IV had taken over as the main battle tank, so their roles were reversed and the Aust N was fitted with a short-barreled close support gun — the 7.5 cm KwK L/24 howitzer. Thicker armour put the weight up to 23 tons and 663 were built.

The PzKpfw III was fitted with three radios — two receivers and one transmitter — all contained in the radio operator/hull gunner's compartment. The two receivers were mounted to the left of the operator over the gearbox. The transmitter was fitted in front of the operator under the glacis plate. All outer set cases were earthed. HT was supplied by rotary transformers fed from the tank batteries. There were three control boxes in the tank — for commander, driver and operator. The loader and gunner had no means of communicating, although from the Ausf L onwards there was a voice tube for communicating between commander and gunner. The three crew members with boxes all had throat microphones and headsets with twin earphones, the operators being slightly different from the other two. The commander had no direct control over the radios and could not change sets or switch to the tank's IC, as the operator did all the switching. There was a lamp signalling system between the commander and the operator, comprising two lamp fittings, one in the turret, one beside the operator. Each had two coloured bulbs (red and green). This was later replaced by a more effective and simpler system. The aerial rod was 2 m (6 ft 6 in) long, tapering from 28.5 mm (1⅛ in) at the bottom to 6 mm (¼ in) at the top. It was mounted at the right rear of the fighting compartment and incorporated an aerial dipping mechanism.

Basic description

With such a range of models to chose from it is impossible to give more than a general description of the basic 'norm', which identifies a PzKpfw III. The following is a description which appeared in a SHAPE confidential handout dated October 1944, entitled *A Summary of German Tanks:* 'The PzKpfw III is a tank of the cruiser class. The weight is about 22 tons and its armament now consists of a long-barreled 5 cm gun (5 cm KwK (L/60)) with a co-axial MG mounted in the turret and one hull MG mounted on the right-hand side of the front superstructure. In addition small-arms are carried, such as machine carbines, egg grenades, signal pistol, besides each member of the crew being armed with a revoler.

'The tank is divided from front to rear into three separate compartments. At the front is the driver's compartment; he sits on the left-hand side with his steering levers and foot controls immediately in front of him. The gear-box (above which is the instrument board) and the gear lever is on his right and

the parking brake on his left. The steering mechanism is either hydraulically or mechanically operated and is of the epicyclic brake type. He has a vision port, protected by a laminated glass block and an outer armoured visor, to look through forwards. When the visor is closed the driver slides an episcope into position — two holes are drilled through the front superstructure plate above the visor for this purpose. When the ordinary vision port is in use, these two apertures are covered by a plate on the inside. There is another port behind the driver's left shoulder; it is fitted with a readily removable glass block.

'The wireless operator sits next to the driver on the right-hand side of the tank. He has a hull MG in a ball mounting which is controlled by a head rest attached to the mounting. The browpad and telescope eye-piece are all fixed on the same mounting so that as he moves his head to direct the MG, his eye is always in the centre of his sight. The wireless equipment is normally situated to the left of the operator, over the gear-box, although sometimes a small set may be found

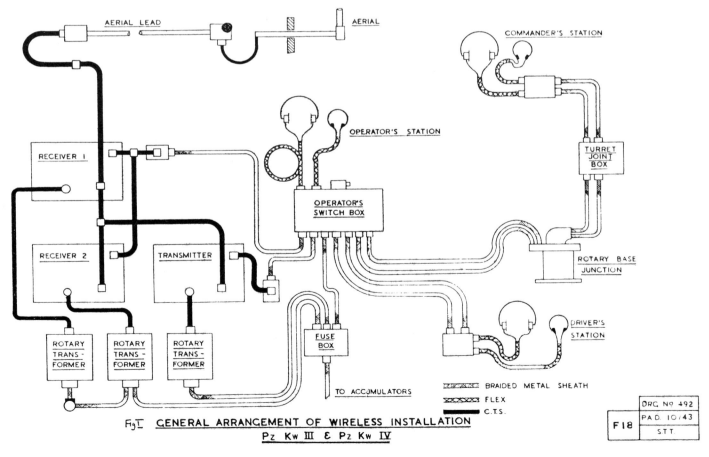

Fig I GENERAL ARRANGEMENT OF WIRELESS INSTALLATION
Pz Kw III & Pz Kw IV

These two PzKpfw III Ausf Fs are in Brest, on guard duty outside the HQ of 5th Panzer Division. Some Ausf Fs were still in service in 1944 (Rudolf Wulff).

in front of him under the glacis plate. There is a revolver port by his right shoulder inset into the right-side of the superstructure. Neither the driver nor the wireless operator have access hatches in the top of the superstructure.

'The fighting compartment surmounted by the turret is in the centre. On the PzKpfw III there is no floor in the turret, although seats for the commander and gunner are suspended from the turret wall. The loader, who stands on the right-hand side of the gun, has no seat and must therefore walk around with the turret as it traverses. He has a vision port protected by a glass block and an outer flap on the right-hand side of the turret. The gunner sits forward on the left-hand side of the gun. The 5 cm gun is fired

600 PzKpfw III Ausf Gs were produced and all but the first 50 were armed with a 5 cm gun with external mantlet, as seen here. This tank is ferrying wounded back to a dressing station during the siege of Tobruk.

The Ausf H had a newly-designed turret and a new transmission, sprocket and idler. This Ausf H is seen in Salonika in April 1941, driving past their Commanding General.

With 50 mm frontal armour (instead of 30 mm) and a new ball-shaped mounting for its bow machine-gun, the Ausf J was produced in larger quantity than any other model. This tank is crossing the Desna River in Russia during October 1941 (Rudolf Wulff).

electrically by means of a trigger on the turret traverse handwheel, and the co-axial MG mechanically by a foot-operated trigger. A vision port, similar to the loader's, is provided on the left-hand side of the turret. The commander sits in the middle at the rear of the turret, directly behind the main armament. His cupola is integral with the turret, and six ports fitted with bullet-proof glass blocks and sliding steel shutters provide all round vision. The cupola hatch consists of two hinged flaps. An auxiliary turret-traversing handle on the loader's side allows dual control for quick traversing, as no power traverse is provided on this tank.

'The engine compartment is at the rear and separated from the fighting compartment by a bulkhead. The engine is mounted in the centre with a petrol tank and a battery box on either side. To the rear of the engine are situated two radiators lying across the tank. A cardan shaft runs to the front of the tank under the "dummy" floor of the fighting compartment. There is an escape hatch on either side of the hull in line with the fighting compartment.

'The normal target and turret position indicating devices are provided for the commander and gunner, respectively, and a gyroscopic compass (Kurskeisel) is fitted for the driver.'

Battle history

Between 1935 and 1945, 15,350 ZW chassis were produced,[29] a reflection of its reliability and value to the German Army. The first PzKpfw IIIs to see action were 98 which were used in Poland, but they represented only a tiny fraction of the German tank force used in the operation. By the time of the campaigns in France and the Low Countries, the numbers of available PzKpfw IIIs had risen to 349, and they continued to rise

The Ausf L was built in 1942 and had thicker frontal armour, plus spaced armour on the gun mantlet (clearly seen here) and front of the superstructure. Also skirting plates (Schürzen) were fitted, together with extra stand-off armour around the turret to provide protection against HEAT projectiles. Armament is now the longer-barrelled L/60 gun.

The Ausf Ms were used mainly to replace losses suffered in combat, 250 being produced in the winter of 1942/43.

thereafter. PzKpfw III rapidly became the main weapon in tank v tank battles owing to the vulnerability of PzKpfw I and II and the use of PzKpfw IV in the infantry support role. It more than proved its worth during the early campaigns, but it soon became very apparent that it required both upgunning and uparmouring. Later the PzKpfw III saw action in North Africa, Russia and in North-West Europe. As we have seen, it was initially uparmoured and upgunned to maintain its superiority, but then lost its place as the main battle tank of the Panzer divisions to the PzKpfw IV, which was in turn replaced by the Panther and saw its main role become one of close support again rather than tank v tank. However, as Bryan Perret points out in his book on the PzKpfw III (published in the Osprey-Vanguard series): 'During the high years of *Blitzkrieg* it was the only weapon in the German tank arsenal that really counted and thus, like Napoleon's *vieux moustaches*, it did not merely witness history in the making — it made it, from the Channel to the Volga and from the Arctic to the North African desert,...it was the PzKpfw III that brought Hitler close to achieving his wildest dreams.'

Much has been written about the relative merits of the firepower of the PzKpfw III vis à vis its counterparts in, for example, the battles of the Western Desert. Initially the Allies considered that the penetrative power of the British high velocity 2-pdr and the American high velocity 37 mm were better than that of the short-barrelled, low velocity 5 cm on the PzKpfw III. Even Liddell-Hart, writing well after the war in 1959, concluded that the 2-pdr was better, basing his findings upon figures which had been published in the official British history of the desert war. However, these figures were revised in a later volume of the same official history, which showed conclusively that the 5 cm KwK was superior. In addition, these calculations had been made taking the performance of the three guns against homogenous armour plate, but from late 1941 many PzKpfw IIIs had extra face-hardened plates fitted, for example, on to the frontal areas, which defeated the 2-pdr and 37 mm except at very short ranges. British tank gunners, at that time, were complaining that their AP shot just bounced off the enemy tanks.

The redoubtable Major (later Colonel) George B. Jarrett, who is described in the US Army official Ordnance history as 'the one-man technical section of the MNAM Ordnance Section', arrived in the Middle

East in February 1942 and tested all German and Allied tank guns. He concluded that the British and American guns were ineffective against both the PzKpfw III and PzKpfw IV, while both the short 5 cm KwK and 7.5 cm KwK did much damage to all Allied tanks, with the possible exception of Matilda. Even at long ranges between 2,000–3,000 yd (1,829–2,743 m), the enemy shells were capable of damaging tracks and suspensions and thus putting tanks out of action.[30] Of course there were exceptions

Last of the line was the Ausf N, which was equipped with a short-barrelled 7.5 cm howitzer, having changed roles with the PzKpfw IV to become a close-support tank. These Ausf Ns were photographed while surrendering to the Allied forces in Norway.

and the Americans must have been very heartened when they first came up against German armour in northern Tunisia in late 1942. Several companies of 1st Armored Division, equipped with M3 Stuarts, ambushed a small force of six PzKpfw IV

Driver's seat in a PzKpfw III, showing steering levers and other controls.

Good view of the early PzKpfw III armament with internal mantlet showing 3.7 cm KwK L/46 and twin machine-guns.

'Specials' and three or more PzKpfw IIIs on 26 November 1942. 'Swarming around the German tanks the Stuarts with their 37 mm guns firing on flank and rear at close range, managed to knock out all the PzKpfw IVs and one of the IIIs.'[31] However, as the Ordnance history goes on to explain: 'this was a victory of superior numbers rather than superiority of matériel'.

The arrival of more powerful Allied tanks, such as the M3 medium Grant and the M4 medium Sherman, more than redressed the balance for a while, although by mid-1942, the Germans also started to receive new tanks like their PzKpfw III Specials (ie, the Ausf J onwards with thicker armour and the long-barrelled gun) and, by mid-June, a few PzKpfw IV Specials, mounting the new long-barrelled, high-velocity 7.5 cm KwK

40 — 'the ominous forerunner of the formidable gun on the Panther tank that was to be introduced in Italy'.[32]

There are many battle accounts written by Panzer crewmen who served in this reliable tank. I have chosen one sent to me by Justus-Wilhem v. Oechelhauser which comes from a book he wrote on his wartime experiences entitled *Wir Zogen in das Feld*. I am most grateful to him for allowing me to use it. It describes vividly a task undertaken by two PzKpfw IIIs in Russia. He writes: 'A new

Lieutenant has arrived in the Company, a teacher by profession and a Reserve Officer. For the inside measurement of our tank he was much too tall. His first assigment was to find and recover a car containing three Staff Officers, which had been trapped by the Russians during a recce, and was, according to radio messages, somewhere in the countryside. Two Panzers were to search for them, the tall Lieutenant, who had not had a vehicle allotted to him, took command of Tank No 921 — my tank.

'I ejected the loader and sat myself on the small seat between the ammo rack and the cannon. No sooner had we got cracking and were about a quarter of an hour away from our Company, than I saw through my small view slot Russian infantry just a few metres away in a little wood. The Lieutenant had not seen the shadowy figures and still had half of his body poking through the open top of the turret. I kicked him in the back of his knees and he slid into the tank. "What's the matter, you idiot? Damnation", he shouted and looked at me with rage. But already the burning oil was running inside the turret. The Lieutenant screamed with pain. The Russians had thrown a Molotov Cocktail into the open lid of the turret and the burning contents were running over the Lieutenant's neck and back into the tank.

'At first I wanted to get out, but then I thought of Ivan outside waiting for us. During that moment of indecision I saw a fire extinguisher handy and orderly in its bracket. Usually extinguishers in tanks are empty. This one by the grace of God was full

Turret access door on a PzKpfw III Ausf J.

and working. As quickly as the oil flamed, it was put out with the foam robbing it of oxygen.

'Ruhn, the gunner, was holding on to the legs of the Lieutenant who, suffering intense pain, tried to jump out of the turret. At last he became unconscious and slid down. I covered him with the rest of the foam, finally putting out any flames. I struggled over the top of him, into the commander's place and could hear heavy fire directed against us. Two grenades exploded on the rear of the tank and MG fire peppered like hailstones on the sides. Our tank was moving at moderate speed. I didn't know where to go as I could not see, something was lying in front of the view slot. The turret lid, which I would have liked closed, was still open. Looking upwards I saw a cloudless summer sky. Ruhn was pushing something to me. Looking closer I saw the half burned headphones he had pulled off the Lieutenant's head. The radio was still working and I heard the excited voice of Feldwebel Rietsh, the commander of the tank behind us. "Stop", he cried, "stop 921, stop! Where are you going. Can't you see you idiots. The area is full of Russians. Turn back, but carefully. On the front of your tank lie two Russians, and there is another one sitting on the turret. Shut your lid or he will throw hand grenades into the tank. I will try and shoot them down. Drive slowly, and turn round."

'Not only in front of my view slot but also in front of the driver a Russian was sitting. We drove blindly through the countryside. I didn't have a microphone for the radio. I squeezed past the gurgling Lieutenant and reached down to the driver's seat. In the meantime Ruhn fired one belt of ammo after another. As I reached Logo, our driver, I hit him on the left shoulder and, as drilled into to him, he pulled the left steering level. The tank started a large circle, the noise made communications by speech impossible. Suddenly the driver had free vision. The Russian was hiding behind the turret on the back for cover, because Titsch was spraying our tank with MG fire. The voice was back on the headphone; 'That's good, a bit further round, a bit more. Now straight on — slower, or you'll get stuck, one of the Ivans has had it, the other two you will have to finish off yourselves.'

'I thought of the egg hand-grenades, but their splinters would fly through the air vents in the engine compartment, that was out of the question. I made a decision to take out the glass blocks from the view slots and fired my pistol into the dark cloth. Two, three, four shots. I emptied the magazine. The dark mass outside shifted and I hoped...but now the open turret hatch

darkened. Above my face came a swinging arm with a dirty hand, an earthbrown shoulder and part of a head. My pistol was empty. I slid down and screamed "Ruhn". He didn't hear me, he was firing with his eyes on the optic. I dropped my '08 in despair and grabbed for the signalling pistol. Upwards I aimed and pulled the trigger. The rocket gas hissed upwards. I definitely didn't hit him I thought. Now, now he dropped the Molotov Cocktail, now he pulls the hand-grenade...now. I fled into the far corner of the loader's seat, my whole body was trembling. The turret hatch was still dark, but nothing happened. I had lost my earpiece during my jumping about. An MG hammered on the outside of our tank.

'Somebody pulled on my leg. I turned round and looked into the pale face of our

Good close-up of a PzKpfw III with its crew engaged in air co-operation with a Fieseler Storch air OP (Emil Thran).

radioman. He handed me a loaded pistol. Thank God. Again I pushed my arm into the turret and pressed the trigger. The damned devil has to get off the turret opening. Two more shots. Nothing! It is still dark. The tank comes to a sudden halt. Now what? I force myself back into the turret and look upwards. Warm blood drips into my face.

'I gave myself a shove and pushed with all my strength against the swinging arm and bleeding shoulder. It wasn't difficult to push him away. At last I saw the sky again.

'The firing outside was not too strong. Quickly I pushed my head through the turret and looked directly into both barrels of Ritsch's tank MGs, his turret only three metres away was covering us. A dead Russian was lying at the back, a second, lying on the turret, I had pushed aside. Two Molotov Cocktails and a bundle of hand grenades by the side of him. Of the other Russian, nothing was to be seen. Ritsch carefully manoeuvered his tank backwards, he held his earphone aloft, a signal that he wants to communicate. I crept back into the command seat, and in doing so trod on the Lieutenant's chest. Ruhn had his eyes still on the optic, and was turning the turret to and fro. He fired one more belt of MG into the wood. I called for the headphone but because of the noise I was not understood. Not until I chucked the empty pistol at the radio operator's back, he turned round and apologetically handed me the head-set and mic. At last I could talk to Ritsch.

'Ritsch said his tank was fully operational. I answered that we were no longer fighting fit and must return to the Company, also the Lieutenant needed medical attention. Ritsch agreed, let's turn round and make for home. As I wanted to bandage up the Lieutenant, I let Logo simply follow the other tank.

'A terrible stench was in our tank, gunpowder, foam and burned flesh. After a quarter of an hour we arrived back in the circle of our Company. I jumped from the tank before it came to a halt and ran into the bushes. I wanted to be sick. I cried and remained lying on the ground until our Medic, Ruebener, found me. Without a word he went away and came back with a tin bucket which was our cooking pot and also our washing-up bowl. He washed me like a child with cold water and bandaged my arm.

A group of radio vehicles belonging to 15th Panzer Division are seen here in the desert. They include both four- and eight-wheeled armoured cars and the PzKpfw III *Befehlswagen* (Karl Wilhelm).

I had burns from putting out the fire. When he had finished, I grinned, and he said "Go and see the chief and make your report."

'Charley sat between the two tracks of his Panzer. Close to him, lying on a stretcher in a thick white bandage, was the tall Lieutenant. I saluted and reported to him. "Why did you not carry on searching for the officers? It's damnable simply to turn back. If later you want to command, firstly you will have to learn to carry out orders without being held up by such interruptions. We shall always have interruptions. The war is no dancing lesson."

'"Jawohl, Herr Oberleutnant."

'"Is your wound serious?"

'"No, Herr Oberleutnant."

'"Well, you and Ritsch, drive off again, you know the area now and carry out your orders."

'"Jawohl, Herr Ober." I made an about turn. Already tears were close to my eyes. Oh God, once again back into this hell.

'The two tanks were ready to move and Ritsch was already in his turret. I pulled myself up on the gun barrel and climbed in. As the engine started, I wiped my nose and eyes with the end of my bandage. I must have gulped a few times, because Ritsch inquired through the radio "What is wrong with our communications, it made a klunking sound?".

'We reached our previous position. We used both machine-guns and sprayed the wood with MG fire and cautiously approached the clearing where the staff car stood. The Russians were nowhere to be seen. A grey body was lying in front of the car, in the grass lay the driver, a Sergeant. We drove closer, Ritsch got out, two leaps and he was beside the car. He dropped down next to the body and turned it on to its back to take off the identity disc. He then crawled back, looked questioningly at me and shrugged his shoulders. No sign of the officers. I searched

Excellent view of another PzKpfw III *Befehlswagen*, showing frame aerial on the rear decks. This command vehicle belonged to 24th Panzer Division in Russia (Ernst J. Dohany).

the dark green bushes around the clearing with my binoculars. I took a look into the countryside and thought where could I have taken cover had I been surprised by the enemy. I directed my tank there, and yes, there they were lying in a shallow ditch, a Colonel, a Major and a very young Lieutenant. Our crew put the dead on the the back of the tank and we returned.

'I reported to the chief, he was still in the same place. The others unloaded the dead. He listened quietly, did not once interrupt me and did not speak when I came to the end. The tall Lieutenant who could have justified my action had been taken to the main Field Clearing Station. His stretcher had gone. There was an unpleasant silence. At last I heard Charley's voice —

'"If you had kept on the first time and carried out your orders, the four of them might still be alive today."

'I could not answer this, I felt he was right.'

Variants

Tauchpanzer III Developed in 1940 for the intended invasion of England (Operation SEALION), the 'diving tank' was a converted PzKpfw III Ausf F, G, H or *Befehls*, with all external openings protected by a special sealant to make them watertight. The gap between hull and turret was sealed by a rubber ring (inflatable) while waterproof covers shrouded the cupola, gun mantlet and hull MG. When under water the engine drew its air by means of a flexible hose, 18 m (59 ft) long, which was attached to a float, while the exhaust gases escaped via two tall pipes fitted with non-return valves. The tank crew drew their air from another pipe which was also attached to a float and incorporated the radio aerial. The *Tauchpanzer* could operate at depths of up to 15 m (50 ft) and remain submerged for some 20 minutes.

A good shot of a platoon of PzKptw IIIs, belonging to Panzer Regiment 7 of 10 Panzer Division (note the divisional sign of front of superstructure), photographed just before the start of *Barbarossa*, the assault of Russia, summer 1941 (Maj Karl-Heinz Maass).

When Operation SEALION was cancelled it was decided to modify most of the 168 *Tauchpanzers* built for use in river crossings, with a fixed schnorkel pipe fitted through the commander's cupola. The *Tauchpanzers* had their 'moment of glory' when they were used for the crossing of the River Bug on 22 June 1941, at the start of Operation BARBAROSSA. This is well described in Paul Carell's book *Hitler's War on Russia*, in which he explains how the 18th Panzer Regiment worked on the 'U-boat tanks' until they were ready for action on the opening day of the operation. 'At 04:45 hours Sergeant Wierschin advanced into the Bug with diving tank No 1. The infantrymen watched him in amazement. The water closed over the tank. Playing at U-boats!... Tank after tank — the whole of 1st Battalion, 18th Panzer Regiment under the battalion commander, Manfred Graf Strachwitz — dived into the river...' The crossing was highly successful as Carell explains: 'And now the first ones were crawling up the far bank like mysterious amphibians. A soft plop and the rubber caps were blown off the gun muzzles. The gun-loaders let the air our of the bicycle inner tubes round the turret ... Eighty tanks had crossed the frontier river under water. Eighty tanks were moving into action.'

A most interesting report on underwater tanks was obtained from a prisoner captured near Saarbrüchen on 1 December 1944. It covers not only the PzKpfw III, but also mentions the Panther and a number of general points on underwater operations.

'Tanks for Underwater Travel

'**General** PW states that German experimentation with submersible tanks was started shortly after the conclusion of the French campaign. An experimental station and a school were set up at Putlos (GSGS 408/9). Tank crews for training were specially selected for intelligence, ability to withstand high pressures, eardrums, etc. PW was at the school for 10–12 days at the time that the entire project was being disbanded, in the autumn of 1941.

'**PW's diving experience** PW did not receive any official instruction at Putlos. He participated in two submersions, one lasting

The kind of problem which tank crews do not relish. A pair of PzKptw IIIs endeavouring to rescue a third from a flooded area in Russia, during the advance in the summer of 1941 (Maj Karl-Heinz Maass).

15 mins and the other 5 mins. A special concrete runway was constructed on the Putlos beach for these submersions. He personally submerged to a depth of 25 m [82 ft] in both cases, but he knows of submersions at Putlos of up to 40 m [131 ft].

'**Units and combat employment** PW states that in the autumn of 1941 Versuchs Pz Tauch Abt were formed in Germany. They made the normal third Abt of Pz Regts 3, 18 and 6, with the designations A, B, and C. These Pz Abt had each approx 60 tanks, PzKw III, equipped for submersion. The 3rd Abt of Pz Regt 6, the Versuchs Pz Tauch Abt C, commanded by the Ritterkreuzträger Hptn v Schneiderkostellki, crossed the river Dnieper in '41 in PzKw III. PW states

that the river at the point of the crossing was about 3,000 m [3,282 yd] wide and 10–15 m [33–49 ft] deep. During this crossing, two tanks became embedded in the mud and had to be abandoned. PW believes that a crossing of the river BUG was also made in 41. PW has had no combat experience with submersible tanks, and was never a member of a Versuchs Pz Tauch Abt. The Versuchs Pz Abt C lost its tanks in the Russian campaign, and was converted into the normal 3rd bn of Pz Regt 6.

Oblt Wisnewsky, who has since been killed in action, was the great expert on underwater tanks.

'**Types** PW states that the following types were specially constructed for "U-Fahrt",

An evocative shot of a column of PzKptw IIIs, belonging Panzer Regiment 7, in the deep snows of Russia, winter 1941/42 (Maj Karl-Heinz Maass).

underwater travel: PzKw II, III, IV, V, VI. PzKw II and IV were mainly built for experimental purposes, whilst several series of PzKw III were built exclusively as U-tanks.

'**Air intake in Panther** PW states that a rubber tube with floats is used when *Panther* tanks submerge. He has seen a connection for the tube on the rearmost air intake vent on the engine hatch, but he has never seen it used.

'**Wireless aerial on PzKw III** PW states that the wireless aerial for the PzKw III is supported by the air-pipe float. The float has a special hook for the aerial. PW does not know whether this arrangement was used in the crossing of the Dnieper. It was always used at Putlos, where the tks travelling under water were controlled by WT. The direction of travel could clearly be followed by the rubber float and the aerial mast.

'**Oxygen cartridges** PW states that at depths below 30 m [100 ft], the use of oxygen cartridges was intended. He has never seen these used.

'**Stalling of engine under water** PW states that experiments were made to restart the engine under water, if it had cut out, but that no solution was found and the results were that the crew had to bale out and abandon the tank. During the experiments carried out at PUTLOS, the abandoned tks were hauled to the surface by recovery ships, but during operations the tanks had to be blown up.

'**Methods of making the Panther Tk submersible** PW states that gun mantlet, hatches, etc, are sealed off by means of rubber sheeting specially prepared with a rubber solution. The KWK is sealed by means of a rubber cartidge, whilst the gun barrel itself is not sealed in any way and the water which penetrates has to be emptied out by pointing the barrel downwards before the gun can be fired.

'**Underwater direction** The underwater travelling is done by means of the ordinary *Kurs Kreisel* (gyroscopic course indicator) which is to be found in all tanks. There are no other means of direction.

'**Action of waterpump** When the water in the hull of the tank reaches 5 cm the Lenzpumpe is clutched in by the driver.

'**Underwater fire fighting** There are no special precautions or measures to fight a fire whilst the tank is submerged. The normal fire extinguishing apparatus would be used.

'**Danger of carbon monoxide poisoning** During the whole time that the tank is submerged, it is the gun layer's duty to make CO (carbon monoxide) tests with a chemical liquid. If carbon monoxide is established, the crew must bale out by means of the escape apparatus. Before they can do this and open the hatches, the fighting compartment must be flooded to create equalisation of pressure.

'**Track Adhesion under water** PW states that before the underwater crossing of a river is attempted, the condition of the surface of the riverbed, which should be fairly firm, should be reconnoitred. The buoyancy of the tank reduces its pressure on the surface and track adhesion is considerably diminished. PW had the peculiar experience during his first submersion experiment that the gyroscopic course indicator was spinning round. He discovered that he had pulled too hard on the left steering lever, and had spun the tank around.

'**Preparation for submersion** PW participated in preparing a PzKw III for underwater travel. The whole procedure, in which the five members of the crew take part, takes 45 mins. The *Lüftergetriebe* (driving gear for radiator fans) must be switched off; the UK *Tauchklappen* (UK diving shutters underneath the hull and beneath the engine) must be closed and all other vulnerable points where rubber scaling fixtures are fitted must be closed.

PW states that the air in the fighting compartment does not get too hot, as might be expected. The cold water provided a perfect cooling system for both the fighting compartment and the motor.'[33]

PzKpfw III (Flam) (SdKfz 141/3) 100 of these medium flamethrower tanks were produced in early 1943, based largely upon the Ausf M. A large 1.5 m (5 ft) long flame thrower replaced the 5 cm gun in the turret, with elevation −10° to +20°. Fuel was a black, sticky oil, smelling of creosote and was sufficient for 70 to 80 shots of two to three seconds' duration. Range of the weapon was 50–60 m (55–65 yd). The fuel 1,023 l (225 gallons) was carried in the tanks mounted inside the right- and left-hand sides. Extra protection was obtained by welding 30 mm plates on to the hull front.

An example of the way in which the flamethrowing tanks were employed is contained in a wartime US Military Intelligence Bulletin: 'Two German flamethrowing tanks, together with three other tanks, supported a German platoon in an attack on a forward position occupied by a platoon of US infantry. The attack was preceded by an artillery and mortar barrage which continued for one hour. The tanks moved forward, and shelled and machine-gunned the position at a range of 50 yards When US troops attempted to withdraw from the sector, the flamethrowing tanks joined the action, using their primary weapon against the personnel. In this action the German infantrymen, equipped with machine pistols, moved forward with the armoured vehicles. The flamethrowers were used intermittently over a 30 minute period and were reported to have a range of 30 yards [27 m].'[34]

Panzerbefehlswagen Small numbers of Ausf D, E and H (220 total) were built as command tanks, all with a fixed turret, a dummy gun, and a large fixed frame aerial over the back decks. These were followed by two properly armed command tanks with fully revolving turrets — there had been a continuous demand for such vehicles from the operational command tank crews, who had only their personal weapons and a single machine-gun with which to defend themselves in battle. Although this made the tanks less vulnerable it did make the turret rather cramped. The Panzerbefehlswagen mit 5 cm KwK L/42 was the first, 81 being built from scratch while later, a further 104 were converted from gun tanks. These were followed by a build of 50 Panzerbefehlswa-gen mit 5 cm KwK 39 L/60 (also known as the Ausf K) which had basically the same hull as the Ausf M. The frame aerial was replaced by a much smaller star antenna which made the tank considerably less conspicuous on the battlefield.

Karl Wilhelm of Dieburg served as a radio operator in a Signal section of 15th Panzer Division, then part of Rommel's Afrika Korps. He writes: 'Most of the armoured radio vehicles of our company were loaded on to four German transport ships which then attempted to cross the Mediterranean from Naples to Tripoli. The convoy was attacked and all four ships sent to the bottom by a British naval formation of cruisers and destroyers in the latitude of Sfax, Tunisia, on 16 April 1941. So the Signal Company had to make do with unarmoured vehicles during the first months of the campaign in North Africa, even light Opel Blitz lorries were used as radio cars. In these vehicles we did not feel at all safe, we often had to leave our car at the last moment to take cover in a trench or behind a small rise when we were attacked by British fighter aircraft, or when we came under shellfire. When we were passing messages during such a surprise attack there just wasn't time to signal "Wait" to receiver, although they would have guessed that the interruption was caused by enemy action. This often caused considerable delays, especially during longer messages.

'Some months later the Funkpanzer III, together with four- and eight-wheeled scout cars were available again, and we felt much safer in them than in our improvised radio cars. Now machine-gun bullets and shell splinters could not hurt us, but when the British fighter aircraft attacked with cannons, the thin armour of our scout cars did not provide sufficient protection, however, we were still safe in the radio tanks. The

radio operators of the group allocated to Panzer Regiment 8 of 15 Panzer Division had only four-wheeled scout cars and often had to shelter behind the Regimental Commander's tank when under fire. Dealing with the radio messages in such circumstances was a great strain and members of this radio crew were awarded the Iron Cross for outstanding devotion to duty in many tank battles.

'During the German-Italian offensive at El Alamein towards the end of August 1942 (known as the "Six-Day Race"), we were attacked constantly during the day by RAF bombers, with little chance of proper protection. We were in an eight-wheeled scout car and were allotted to Field Marshal Rommel as part of his direct escort, consisting of two ex-British lorries which mounted 2 cm AA guns plus our radio car. We had the advantage of being able to get out of the terrible carpet bombing from time to time, so the strain on us was far less than on the combat units. This non-stop bombing had decisive results and led to the British 8th Army's victory at El Alamein and then the great

withdrawal as far as Tunisia began for us which ended in the march into captivity,'

Oberst (Colonel) aD Hermann Rothe of Panzer Regiment 5 also served in a Panzer III Befehlswagen and writes: 'It was not until the spring of 1941 that the Regimental staff were issued with properly equipped PzKpfw III command vehicles. These Panzers had wooden cannons, all the necessary antennae and five crew — commander, signals-officer, two wireless operators and driver — complete with a battery charging system. The tin boxes on the outside were for storing our personal belongings, ration packs, etc. Unfortunately our command tank was put out of action on the first day of the assault on Russia, by a direct hit on the engine compartment. It brewed up. Fortunately we were all able to bale out safely, but despite this a rumour spread like wildfire that we were all dead. In fact we had boarded our reserve tank. There is a superstition that once a soldier has been mistakenly declared dead, that he will in fact survive whatever may happen later. This certainly came true for us as we all survived the war!'

Other variants A number of other variants were produced including, in 1943, an artillery OP tank (*Artillerie-Panzerbeobachtungswagen*) with a four-man crew, to enable artillery Forward Observation Officers to accompany Panzer formations in action. It replaced a light tracked carrier which had been used by FOOs earlier in the war. The only armament was a ball-mounted MG 34, while an artillery plotting board and extra radios occupied the space in the turret. A *Bergepanzer III* (armoured recovery vehicle) was the only other variant produced in any quantity, being converted from existing tank chassis, as was the case with the *Schlepper III* (supply carrier) and *Pionierpanzer III* (engineer vehicle). These three types were normally fitted with wider tracks (*Ostketten*)[35] for use in Russia. Other variants which only reached prototype stage

An early StuG III driving through a snowbound Russian village with a German column. The short-barrelled 7.5 cm Stuk 37 L/24 had a low muzzle velocity (450 m/s/1,476 fps) and poor penetration, but was designed to provide armoured support for infantry.

included a mine-clearing tank (*Minenraum-panzer III*) and a railway track vehicle for use against partisans (*Schienen-Ketten Fahrzeug*).

Assault guns

If the PzKpfw III proved its reliability and adaptability over its long in-service life, then the *SturmGeschütz* (assault gun), which used the same basic chassis, proved its outstanding battlefield ability, accounting for far more enemy tanks than did the conventional PzKpfw III. The decision to develop a special armoured assault gun for the close support of infantry, and also for anti-tank purposes, was made in June 1936 and the 7.5 cm L/24 gun chosen. In order to keep the silhouette as low as possible it was decided not to mount the gun in a revolving turret but directly on to the hull. The chassis chosen for production was that of the PzKpfw III Ausf F resulting in a StuG which was only 1.95 m (6 ft 5 in) high as compared with 2.44 m (8 ft) for the PzKpfw III Ausf F. Despite not having a turret the weight was 19.6 tons as the StuG had considerably thicker frontal armour (up to 50 mm) than the Ausf F tank. StuG Ausf A was built in 1940, with a four-man crew, a top speed of 40 km/h (25 mph) and a range of 160 km (100 miles). Forty-four rounds were carried for the main armament, but there was no secondary machine-gun fitted until StuG III Ausf E. The early AFVs saw service in France in 1940 and were followed by the StuG III Ausf B which had only minor differences and was produced in quantity in 1940–41. In September 1941, it was decided on the Führer's personal orders to up-armour and up-gun the StuG III. The weapon chosen was the 7.5 cm StuK 40 L/43, but mass-production of the StuG III Ausf F, with the new gun and armour thickness increased on the front to 80 mm, did not begin until February 1942. These alterations put the StuG's weight up to 22.8 tons. After some 120 had been produced it was decided to fit the longer 7.5 cm StuK 40 L/48, which continued to be used up to 1945. Extra protection was also gained by the fitting of stand-off side plates. The final model, StuG III Ausf G, had a partially cast superstructure and mantlet (known to the crews as *Saukopf* as it resembled a pig's head). Variants included an assault howitzer, mounting a 10.5 cm StuH 42 L/28, a flamethrower and an ammunition carrier. Total build of StuG IIIs was in excess of 9,000, the vast majority being the Ausf G (over 7,700), while over 1,200 StuH were also produced.

What was it like to serve on a StuG? Max

A StuG III Ausf C/D negotiating a steep, muddy slope during training.

Flemming, who now lives in England, was a member of the *Fallschirmpanzerkorps HG* ('Hermann Göring'). He joined the then Brigade HG in April 1942 and after basic training in Utrecht, Holland, was sent to an Army training camp for tank crews at Luckenwalde, near Berlin, where he was taught to drive a StuG. From there he was posted to France where the Brigade HG was enlarged to form a Panzer Division, and from there they went on to Italy. He writes: 'The *Sturmgeschütz* without a turret but otherwise a Panzer in its own right, should not be confused with the various types of self-propelled guns or other open-topped tracked

vehicles. It used the Panzer III chassis and had the same power unit. The gun, 7.5 cm short, was later changed to the 7.5 cm long, after lessons learned on the Eastern Front against Russian T-34s. The limited elevation and swing from left to right (only 20°) put extra responsibility on the driver as he had to position the wagon towards the target for the gunner to aim and fire. An MG 34, later MG 42, was mounted behind a folding armoured shield, and was used by the loader, exposing him to enemy fire. The biggest advantage over a conventional tank was its low, squat shape. A good driver could take advantage of the low silhouette against the sky-line and use the countryside — like shallow depressions, ridges or anything offered by nature or man-made, to minimise the risk of becoming a target.

Bombing up a StuG III (probably an Ausf G). The long-barrelled 7.5 cm StuK 40 L/48 had a much improved performance.

Bound for the Russian front. This trainload of StuG III Ausf Gs belonged to the 24th Panzer Division (Ernst J. Dohany).

Internal view of the StuG III, showing breech of main armament.

A heavier weapon was needed to complement the 7.5 cm, so the StuH 42 was introduced from early 1943 onwards, over 1,200 being produced of this hard-hitting assault howitzer, which was armed with a 10.5 cm StuH 42 L/28. This particular late model has lost its muzzle brake and is fitted with a remotely-controlled machine-gun.

'A well-trained crew is like a family and should be kept together at all costs. A good commander will foster a feeling of belonging and comradeship, often bypassing the normal strict military code of relationship between officer, NCO and men. I belonged to an elite Luftwaffe Division and the Army, with its experience and training facilities, seconded instructors to us, while we also went to Army tank ranges for intensive training on the AFV. Getting in and out of the vehicle at lightning speed was one thing we practised, knocking us black and blue in the process. We cursed under our breath, but how we came to appreciate it in action, when life depended upon such speed. Driving practice day and night had the aim of welding the crews together.

'Strength was also required: disaster once struck three of our StuGs, they got stuck right in front of the enemy, up to their bellies in a ditch along a narrow dirt path. Volunteers, one driver and one NCO per AFV, plus a platoon of infantry as protection, went forward to recover the vehicles. We got there without any trouble and with another of our StuGs acting as tractor, we managed to pull out the first casualty. Then we came under heavy fire from the wooded hills close by. The American infantry must have been asleep until then. I was unlucky enough to have the last StuG which had also damaged its steering gear. As the other two disappeared towards our lines I had great difficulty in holding mine in a straight line, and what made matters worse, my guide disappeared. Suddenly all the firing stopped and I didn't feel too happy sitting on my own in a damaged StuG, close to the Yanks, as I struggled on along a path in the direction of our lines. I had to cross a narrow bridge over a small gorge about 20 m deep and the moment I had crossed my vehicle sheered off the path to the right and in seconds I was hanging over the side, rocking backwards and forwards. I got out, not a soul about, darkness. I started walking towards our lines when a figure came towards me. I took the safety catch off my pistol and waited. Before I could fire a German voice asked me what the hell I was doing. It was an infantry Lieutenant, and, after explaining the situation, he got about ten men to sit on the back of the StuG as a counter-weight, while I reversed and managed to get back on to the path. I drove then to the repairs shop behind our lines. While there, getting something to eat, we came under heavy artillery fire and I was wounded in the head, so I finished up in a hospital in Germany.'

Max Flemming also gave a new relevance to the nickname *Saukopf* on the StuG, in this more light-hearted reminiscence: 'An army marches on its stomach. That saying was true for us in Italy in 1943, behind the Volturno defence line. Our StuG unit was in support of some Panzergrenadiers, it was September, still very warm and our field kitchen, further back, used to send us up warm rations by a motor cycle equipped with a sidecar. The food was well mixed by the time it reached us and often sour. Self-help was the answer and it just so happened that some pigs got loose close to our position. A pig hunt was agreed to supplement our rations and several of us set out . . .

'I had a piece of rope which I found handy when we eventually managed to wrestle one of the pigs on to its back. The rope was fastened to one of its hind legs, but then the animal took over. It went hell for leather across the fields which attracted the English artillery observers. They did not want us to have pork for dinner and such a barrage of shells added to our difficulties. However, the thought of a good meal gave me the strength to hold on and with the help of my comrades I managed to drag the pig to a safe place, and the butcher's knife. Nice tasty pork chops cooked over a fire, the pan supported by three track connecting bolts, gave us strength for the next day!'

7
Pz Kpfw IV and variants

Background development

As already explained, following a meeting of the *Heereswaffenamt* on 11 January 1934, at which basic agreement was reached on what would be the major items of equipment for the Panzer divisions, the PzKpfw IV made its first appearance under the innocuous name of the medium tractor (*Mittleren Traktor*), later changed to yet another 'camouflage' name, *Bataillonführerswagen* (BW), which remained until all such names were discarded. At that meeting, the basic roles and characteristics of the various classes of AFVs were agreed, the role chosen for the medium tank being that of close support. The armament would be a short-barreled 7.5 cm gun, it would have an all-up weight not more than the standard bridge loading of 24 tons, while its crew, general layout and armour thickness, etc, would be as already outlined in the last chapter for the other medium tank, the PzKpfw III.

Development work began that same year, Rheinmetall Borsig AG being the first firm to produce a wooden mock-up, which was followed in 1935 by the first prototype, known as the VK 2001/Rh. It weighed about 18 tons, was constructed of mild steel and was immediately sent to the Kummersdorf[36] testing grounds. Two other firms also submitted proposals to the *Heereswaffenamt* during 1935, namely Krupp AG and MAN. The former produced a proposal (VK 2001/K) which made use of some of the features of the unsuccessful design which they had submitted for the *Zugführerswagen*, while the latter's design (VK 2002/MAN) had an interleaved suspension. After trials of all three prototypes, the Krupp design was

chosen and they were appointed as the main developer and manufacturer for the tank, their first production model, with the designation 1/BW, appearing in 1936. PzKpfw IV thus beat PzKpfw III into service. The initial order was for 35 and all were produced between October 1937 and the following March. Thus began the production of what was to prove Germany's most important tank, which was to remain in quantity production throughout the war and become the backbone of the Panzer divisions. The soundness of its design and its general reliability and fightability, were a tribute to its designers, particularly as they had ensured that it was capable of being up-gunned and up-armoured without any radical alterations being necessary to its basic design.

In many respects the Ausf A set the pattern for the first few models of the tank, being armed with a 7.5 cm KwK L/24 gun plus a co-axial machine-gun, together with a second MG in the hull. The vehicle was powered by a 12-cylinder Maybach HL 108 TR petrol engine, producing 250 bhp, while there was a 500 cc DKW auxiliary two-stroke petrol engine, to power the motor for the electric turret traverse. Combat weight

PZKPFW IV AUSF A (SDKFZ 161)	
Date of origin	1935 (first production 1937)
Weight (tonnes)	18.4
Overall dimensions (m)	**Length** 5.6 **Height** 2.65 **Width** 2.9
Armament/Ammunition carried	
Main	1 × 7.5 cm KwK 37 L/24 122 rounds
Secondary	2 × 7.92 mm MG 13
Armour thickness (mm)	Max. 15 Min. 5
Engine Type	Maybach HL 108 TR **bhp/rpm** 250/3,000
Crew	5
Max. speed (km/h)	32
Range (km)	150
Remarks	First model

was 17.3 tons and armour thickness was up to 20 mm. The suspension consisted of four bogies on each side, each carrying a pair of rubber-tyred roadwheels with quarter elliptic leaf springs, front drive sprocket, rear idler and four top rollers. This suspension

First of the highly reliable PzKpfw IVs — 'backbone of the Panzer divisions' — was the Ausf A of which only some 35 were built in 1937–38. Based upon the original *Bataillonführerswagen*, the main armament was a short 7.5 cm KwK 37 L/24 gun which meant it was a medium support tank, designed to overwatch the PzKpfw II and later the PzKpfw III. The Ausf A saw service in Poland, France and Norway.

PzKpfw IV Ausf B seen here outside a newly-built Panzer barracks. The Ausf B had thicker armour, a new type of cupola and a larger engine. They were in service from 1938 until late 1943 (Oberst aD Hermann Rothe).

This Ausf E has suffered damage to its rear, bending up the catwalks. The Ausf E had a new cupola and extra armour. Note the spare track plates carried above the roadwheels. Some 220 were produced in 1940/41.

became the hallmark of the PzKpfw IV, remaining virtually unaltered throughout its long career. Another feature was the drum-shaped cupola with eight vision slits, located at the back of the turret.

The Ausf B incorporated a number of improvements including a more powerful engine, the 320 bhp Maybach HL 120 TRM, and a new six-speed SSG 76 gearbox replacing the five-speed SSG 75. Frontal armour was increased up to 30 mm which raised the combat weight to 17.7 tonnes (17.4 UK/19.5 US tons). Forty-five Ausf Bs were ordered — known then as the 2/BW — but only 42 were completed, due to lack of certain components at the Krupp factory. The Ausf C also appeared in 1938 and was practically identical to the previous model, except that the hull machine-gun had been removed and replaced by a vision slit. There was also an armoured sleeve over the co-axial MG and a redesigned gun-mantlet housing together with a different pattern of aerial deflector. The Ausf C was heavier at some 19 tons and approximately 140 were produced. These first three models had all been fitted with an internal mantlet which, on operations, had proved vulnerable, allowing bullet splash to enter the turret, so the Ausf D was fitted with a completely new type of

gun mantlet, the edges of which overlapped, and thus protected, the mantlet joints. The bow machine-gun was also re-introduced and the side and rear armour increased from 15 to 20 mm. After the Ausf D had been given a thorough testing an Army Regulation was published (No 685 dated 27 September 1939) which stated that: 'the PzKpfw IV (7.5 cm) (SdKfz 161) is hereby declared fit for service following successful troop trials.'[37] Although over 220 Ausf Ds were produced, only a handful were built before the outbreak of war, some of these being returned after the Polish campaign for refit. Battle experience showed that the armour was too thin and had to be reinforced by attaching plates to the front and sides. British intelligence reports of the period suggest that this was often done without proper authority, as they captured an order which expressly forbade the welding on of additional plates under unit arrangements. After pointing out that this practice, if not done properly, could have the effect of reducing the level of protection rather than improving it, the order went on to refer to instructions issued by the German HQ regulating the fitting of additional plates. The next model, the Ausf E, reflected this need for extra basic protection with an increase to its front glacis plate thickness to 50 mm, while additional 30 mm plate was fixed to the front plate and 20 mm to the hull sides. The additional armour raised the weight to 21 tons. This model also had a new type of cupola which was positioned further forward on the turret, while a simpler designed sprocket was fitted, which enabled the use of wider tracks.

The major improvement made when the Ausf F$_1$ appeared was again to the armour, the basic thickness being increased to 50 mm over all the frontal arc (hull, superstructure and turret), while the sides were 30 mm thick with no bolted-on armour. This model still had the low velocity 7.5 cm gun as its main armament, but it was the last PzKpfw IV to be so equipped, Hitler personally ordering that they be upgunned by the fitting of the long barreled 7.5 cm KwK 40 L/43. The Ausf F$_2$ had to have its ammunition stowage modified so that it could take the larger rounds. The fitting of the new gun changed once and for all the role of the PzKpfw IV from support to that of main tank killer, while the PzKpfw III was relegated to the supporting role. The muzzle velocity of the new gun was 740 m/s

(2,428 fps) as compared with 385 m/s (1,263 fps) of the former, increasing the penetrative power from 41 mm to 89 mm (steel plate at 460 m (500 yds) and 30°). Without doubt its appearance on the battlefield caused the Allies considerable problems.

To date some 1,300 PzKpfw IVs had been built from Ausf A to Ausf F_2. The next model, the Ausf G, was to more than double that figure — over 1,600 being produced between May 1942 and June 1943. Early Ausf Gs were almost identical to the F_2, but various modifications were introduced during the long production run. These included an improved KwK L/48 gun which had a muzzle velocity of 750 m/s (2,461 fps), additional bolted-on armour, including for the first time thin steel side plates known as *Schürzen* (skirts) which were fitted to the sides of the hull and around the back and sides of the turret. These were designed to defeat hollow-charge weapons, such as the bazooka, and were also fitted to the Ausf H which again was produced in larger numbers than any other model to date, nearly 4,000

PZKPFW IV AUSF H (SDKFZ 161/2)		
Date of origin 1943		
Weight (tonnes) 25		
Overall dimensions (m)	**Length**	7.02
	Height	2.68
	Width	2.88
Armament/Ammunition carried		
Main 1 × 7.5 cm KwK 40 L/48		
87 rounds		
Secondary 2 × 7.92 mm MG 34		
Armour thickness (mm)	**Max.**	80
	Min.	10
Engine Type Maybach HL 120 TRM		
bhp/rpm 300/3,000		
Crew 5		
Max. speed (km/h) 38		
Range (km) 210		
Remarks Main model, nearly		
4,000 produced		

The long-barrelled 7.5 cm was introduced to counteract the battlefield superiority of the Russian T-34 and KV 1. This PzKpfw IV is safely loaded on board its flatcar bound for the Russian front (Horst Riebenstahl).

chassis being built, although not all were used for the production of tanks (see later). Major changes included even thicker armour — now up to 80 mm on the front glacis — a new gearbox (SSG 77) and other modifications, all of which put up the combat weight to 25 tons, resulting in a slight drop in performance. The final model, Ausf J, was in production up to March 1945, over 1,700 being built, which brought total production for the PzKpfw IV to over 8,500, representing over one-third of Germany's total wartime tank production. This last model had increased fuel capacity which greatly improved the tank's range to 320 km (200 miles), but unfortunately was at the expense of losing the electric power traverse, a most retrograde step.

Basic description

General The hull, superstructure and turret were of orthodox welded construction. The main hull carried a detachable superstructure which, being wider than the hull, projected over the top of the tracks, providing useful stowage space and a wide base on which to mount the turret. This meant that a large turret ring could be used and turret ring protection fitted. The turret had escape doors on each side and a fixed cupola with

five windows in it, each fitted with *Ersatz-glaserblocks*, with sliding bulletproof shields which could be raised or lowered by a small lever situated immediately below each window. The turret floor was carried by brackets on the turret ring and thus rotated with the turret. The main armament, consisting of the 7.5 cm (long or short) gun, together with a co-axial MG, was mounted in a gun mantlet in the turret face, while a further MG for use by the wireless operator/hull gunner was mounted in a ball mounting in the offside of the superstructure front plate on all models except the Ausf C. Two bulkheads divided the hull into three compartments. The engine, mounted in the rearmost compartment, drove a propellor shaft which passed under the turret floor to a clutch and gearbox in the front compartment. From the gearbox the drive was taken through a bevel box and cross-shafts, thence through clutch-and-brake type steering units and spur reduction gears, to the front driving sprockets. An auxiliary petrol-driven generator set for the electric power traverse was located on the nearside of the engine, which was offset some 12–15 cm (5–6 in) to the offside of the centre line. Three petrol tanks, with a total capacity of 477 L (105 gal), were mounted on the floor of the central compartment of the hull, underneath the turret floor. The driver and wireless operator/hull gunner sat in the front compartment of the hull, one each side of the gearbox, with the driver on the nearside. The three other crew members (commander,

gunner and loader) were all housed in the turret.

Armour Basic armour was all welded and got thicker and thicker as new models were produced. Frontal armour was usually harder and thicker than side armour, but substantial facehardening of the armour was not in widespread use until the Ausf D, which had a face-hardened nose-plate. The turret base was protected by an inverted 'V' section ring. This did not, however, completely encompass the turret, so the back and nearside were partly unprotected (due to the fact that the turret was offset). Bullet splash protection was provided by splash channels fitted to the escape doors, and sheet metal splash guards fitted top and bottom of the mantlet aperture. A British investigation of an Ausf G, using the 'Poldi' Brinell[38] testing equipment, showed an increase in the use of face-hardened plates, which were apparently treated by a flame-hardening process to the following levels: front nose plate, outer surface — 460 to 490 Brinell; front vertical plate, outer surface — 500 to 520 Brinell; inner surface — 250 to 260 Brinell; turret front plate, outer surface — 490 to 510 Brinell; side superstructure, outer surface — 500 to 520 Brinell; inner surface — 270 to 280 Brinell; side hull plate, outer surface — 470 to 500 Brinell. Turret side plates were of homogeneous armour of 340 to 360 Brinell.

The final 'add-on' armour was the additional spaced armour mentioned earlier, known as *Schürzen*, which were of 5 mm (3/16 in) mild steel plate, in sections 114 cm

by 99 cm (3 ft 9 in by 3 ft 3 in), extending from the top of the superstructure to about the tops of the bogies, some 38 cm away from the hull. Turret spaced armour was of 6 mm ($\frac{1}{4}$ in) mild steel plate, positioned around the sides and rear, which had doors in them immediately opposite the doors of the turret.

Armament As already explained, the main armament was initially the 7.5 cm L/24 short gun (on Ausf A to Ausf F$_1$). This was a low velocity weapon, 24 calibres in length, with a vertically sliding breech block, a muzzle velocity of 385 m/s (1,263 fps) (APCBC) and was the same gun as fitted to the PzKpfw III Ausf N and the early StuG IIIs. Although a full range of ammunition was available, including HE, APCBC, HEAT, Smoke and Cased Shot, the weapon was essentially a howitzer and used in the fire support role. The elevating gears were of the pinion and rack type, controlled by a handwheel which enabled the mantlet cover to be moved through 32° (from −11° to +21°), requiring 15 full turns to cover the complete 32°. All-round traverse was by hand or power, current supply for the latter being controlled by a trigger switch on the hand traverse wheel, while a lever on the traverse gearbox provided

for the change to power from hand. The auxiliary engine was a water-cooled, two-cylinder, two-stroke Auto Union. There was a turret position indicator on the left of the gunner, which indicated where the turret was in relation to the hull and was graduated like a clock face from 1–12. Another gearing also drove an annular toothed ring in the cupola via a universally jointed shaft. This ring was also graduated from 1 to 12 and there was a fixed pointer on the outside of the cupola scale which corresponded with the gunner's dial. By this means the commander could indicate the approximate position of a target to the gunner. Co-axially mounted were an MG 34 and a TZF 5b sighting telescope. The belt-fed MG was fired by means of a footpedal by the gunner, while the telescope had three range scales for HE and AP (main armament) and MG 34. Eighty rounds of main armament ammunition were carried, plus 2,700 rounds for the machine-gun.

From the Ausf F_2 the short-barrelled gun was replaced by the more powerful KwK 40 L/43 and then from Ausf H with the improved L/48, which was 37.5 cm (14.75 in) longer. Early guns were fitted with a single baffle muzzle brake, but most had the double baffle type. The longer gun meant that the weapon system was muzzle heavy, so it was necessary to compensate for this by means of a heavy compression spring, carried in a cylinder anchored to the forepart of the turntable floor to the right of the centre line.

Mobility The first engine was the same unit as fitted in the PzKpfw III, namely the 250 hp 12-cylinder Maybach HL 108 TR (later replaced with the more powerful 320 hp HL 120 TR) which ran best on 74 octane fuel. It was generally very reliable in temperate climates, but suffered from overheating and other problems in the dusty hot conditions of North Africa and southern Russia. This meant that every effort had to be made to keep the engine temperature down by careful driving and the use of low gear where necessary. Engine layout was different from that of the PzKpfw III as the engine compartment was a different shape, which led to both exhausts being fitted on

the right-hand side of the tank. Transmission was similar to the Mk III's, the three-plate clutch being mounted on the rear end of the gearbox. Steering was by a Wilson-Krupp clutch and brake system. The tracks had 98 links on each side, were 400 mm (15.75 in) wide and were made of manganese steel, total weight of a set of

tracks being 1,270 kg (2,800 lbs). The tracks were of the 'skeleton' type which made them lighter and tension was maintained via adjustment to the rear-mounted idler. This was fitted on to an eccentric axle, which was rotated by means of a 1.5 m (5 ft) long ring spanner. A ratchet ring then prevented the eccentric axle from moving back to the slack

A first-class close-up of an Ausf H/J. Note the extra jerricans stowed on top of the turret. These 20-l (4.4 gal) cans were much superior to their Allied equivalent (Oberst aD Helmut Ritgen).

Battle history

First operational service for the PzKpfw IV was in Poland, where they performed extremely well although the numbers employed were very small. Just over twice as many PzKpfw IVs saw action in Poland as compared with PzKpfw IIIs, but that was still only 211 as compared with 98. They did so well as to be singled out by Guderian as being such an effective weapon system that he advocated they should be produced in quantity. Only 19 were lost in Poland out of a total of 217 tanks knocked out between 1 and 30 September 1939.

Here is an account of the part played by one brigade HQ command tank in the operations to capture Warsaw, as recorded in the regimental history of Panzer Regiment 35. The story was entitled 'Blown up in Warsaw' and was written by Hans Schaufler. 'It was five days ago that I joined the Panzer brigade HQ as their Signals Officer. The suburb Ochota, on the road leading from Rawa to Warsaw, was our final RV. The second attack on Warsaw was imminent. Waiting, closely lined up, were tank after tank and further behind were riflemen and engineers at the ready. It was unusually quiet. No rifle or machine-gun fired and the artillery was silent on both sides. Only now and then was the silence broken by the appearance of a reconnaissance 'plane up in the clear sky.

'I was sitting next to General von Hartlieb in the Panzer command tank. The Brigade Adjutant, Hauptmann (Captain) von Harling, spread out the position map. Space was tight. Both radio operators were poised by their sets. One was intently listening for the "Stand To" codeword from Division, whilst the other one had his hand on the switch ready to pass on the command to the Degiments. The engine was ticking over, the driver ready with his foot on the clutch. Then, a sudden whine through the air, burst upon burst close by, some to the right, then to the left, and then some behind us. Barrage after barrage swished and swirled through the air. Already the first wounded of the day groaned and moaned. The Polish artillery had sent us their usual "Greetings".

'Now we receive the command to advance. Immediately this is passed on. The heavy engines of our tanks roared into action. The big fight for Poland's capital, Warsaw, had

position. An interesting and effective track repair device was trialled with the PzKpfw IV, consisting of some industrial belting which was the same width as the track and had perforated edges to match up with the teeth on the driving sprocket. If a track was broken for any reason, then the belting could be clipped to the broken end, led forward over the top rollers and then linked with the sprocket teeth. By starting the engine and engaging the gears, the sprocket turned and pulled the belting and track forward until the latter engaged with the sprocket teeth. Anyone who has tried dragging a heavy length of track up over a sprocket in the rain and mud, using a piece of rope, will fully appreciate what a boon this simple system must have been to the crews.

just begun, this being the ninth day of the war. We reached the outskirts of the city. We can hear the rattle of heavy machine-gun fire, the thuds of exploding hand grenades, shell splinters strike against the armour plate. Inside the command tank one message chased another. "Ahead — street barricade," reported the 35th Regiment. "Anti-tank fire — five tanks destroyed — ahead mined barricade," came over the radio. "Command to Regiment. Turn due south," bellowed the General. You had to shout to be able to communicate because of the bedlam going on outside. "Send this" I ordered, "message to Division. Have reached outskirts of Warsaw. Streets barricaded and mined, turning south." Message from the Regiment: "Barricade taken".

'There was another sudden shower of shell splinters, followed by a burst to our right and then to the left. Someone kicked me in the back. "Enemy position 300 metres [330 yd] ahead" shouted the General, who was observing from the turret. "Turn right!" — the tracks ground on the cobbles as we drove across an empty square. "Faster! Faster!" bellowed the infuriated General, for the Poles were very good shots. "Meeting heavy enemy fire," reported the 36th Regiment. "Message to Regiment. Give Grid Reference for artillery support," answered the General. Stones and shell splinters thundered against the steel walls. The impacts were very close. Then — another explosion, my head was rammed against the instruments. The tank rose up before being thrown sideways.

'Yellow sparks were forced through the turret lid. Gasmasks, webbing, mess-tins, scattered all around us — artillery hit! A few seconds of terrifying hesitation passed. A quick check from face to face, a quick touch, all was well. The driver engaged third gear. We all looked at each other in anticipation. The tank moved. However, there came a suspicious knocking sound from the left-hand track and sprocket, but we seemed to get away OK. Suddenly all hell broke loose, there was a thump to our right and to our left, machine-gun fire came from all the windows. Bullets thudded against our armour. Hand grenades and petrol bombs were hurled at us from the cellars. We were outnumbered at least 100 to 1 — but we didn't stop.

'Overturned trams, barbed wire, tramrails ramped into the ground, as well as anti-tank fire, all slowed down our advance, as we continued on our route south. "Please don't

View through the left-hand door of an Ausf G, showing the gunner's controls.

break down now!" we all prayed, for this would have meant our certain death. Louder and more worrying came the knocking from the tracks. Then we noticed an orchard and managed to mingle with the trees. Some sections of our Regiments had already reached Warsaw's main station, but all too often

we received message: "Advance stopped, heavy enemy fire — tank destroyed by enemy anti-tank and mines — request artillery support".

'Our temporary peace was shattered by artillery fire landing around us. The Poles have spotted us. We couldn't move right or left. We have no alternative but to try to repair the damaged track, yet time does not allow us to do so as the Regiments need our support. The General dictates message after

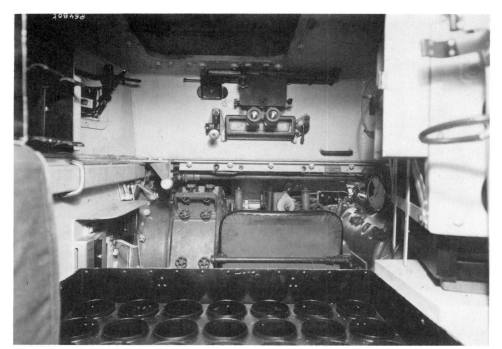

the command tank, so that we almost forgot our own desperate position. Once all the sections had been recalled our work was completed. We now faced the problem of our own withdrawal. Once more we had to run the gauntlet in that hell, from which we had been lucky to escape a first time. We decided to return via the same route by which we came.

'It was very quiet out there, suspiciously quiet in fact. This silence was nerve-wracking. We could feel the watchful eye of the enemy upon us. We were also aware that he was only waiting for an opportune moment. We passed the point where we had been hit. Only one more turn to take and then we would head back along the long, straight road. But there was also one more barricade to pass, and that meant caution. We reached the straight road and silently rejoiced.

'A heavy thud shook the rear deck, and again — in all, four times. Anti-tank fire! The engine kept going. Then, a shrill, deafening detonation, the tank swung to the right and stopped, destroyed in the last minute! Bale out! The next shot will destroy us for sure. But outside all hell has broken loose again. The best thing we could do was to throw our machine-guns out and then just tumble over the sides. But what is this? Thick smoke rose from the rear deck. Our first thought was that the engine was on fire. Yet there was an unusual hissing sound. It was almost unbelievable, but the anti-tank fire has ignited the smoke grenades. A light breeze spread the smoke to the barricade. Undoubtedly the enemy thought we were on fire. Their hesitation, together with the covering smoke, made our safe getaway possible.

'"Brigade to Division," dictated the General, but it was no use, the antenna was shot off. The track lay stretched out behind us, the rear deck was badly deformed. It wasn't an easy decision, but we had to leave our tank behind. It was impossible to repair it on the spot. We ripped out the machine-gun and radios and took the secret files with us. Now and then we had to duck to avoid incoming shells. We should have set fire to our command vehicle, but none of us could do so, instead we tried to camouflage it with branches. Perhaps, if the opportunity arose, we would be able to retrieve it. We gave each other covering fire whilst sprinting from house to house and garden to garden. We all made it.

Right-hand access doors on an Ausf G. The double doors were introduced on the Ausf F.

message, command after command. A sudden welcome break in the enemy fire followed. But as soon as we opened the hatch, intense gunfire hammered against the armour plate. Somewhere out there the Poles were watching us, yet we couldn't see them. We sat in the bramble bushes and tried to make our tank look as small as possible. The armour plate of our AFV was buckled in the front. The track guards were ripped to pieces, all the light metal parts were missing or hanging loose. The tracks and roadwheels were damaged. We pulled off all the loose parts and managed to free the tracks. We inserted two new track pins.

Luck might be on our side and let us carry on for another few kilometres. We vanished back inside our tank.

'Air support was impossible to get, the Division informed us. Our artillery was much too weak to keep supremacy over the enemy counterattack. Division ordered: "Fall back to last RV". Section after section was withdrawn under covering fire. In some places this proved more difficult to arrange than in others and it was a busy time for us in

Although this PzKpfw IV was knocked-out in the Western Desert, it still provides an excellent close-up shot for modellers. Note especially the five rear smoke emitters and linkage which was worked from the turret.

'With our limbs feeling as heavy as lead, we fell into an unsettled sleep. Every so often we would start up and then realise that we had left our B O1, blown up, with the turret wide open, near a Polish barricade. It must be in a sorry state. Once again I woke up and stared into the clear September night. Suddenly, the rough voice of our driver asked: "Are you coming?" I asked him where he was going. "I have organised a recovery vehicle," he replied and we all got up. That same night we managed to recover our B O1, which looked just like a Panzer IV[39], but with a fixed turret and aluminium gun. Once the Poles opened fire on us, but we were already on tow and got away. Our tank was damaged but none of us could have left it behind for the enemy to gloat over.'

Sustained operations over the bad Polish roads, and even worse terrain, had been extremely wearing on all German AFVs, so that extensive repair work was necessary before the opening of the campaign in the West. It was also necessary to improve the existing organisation for the repair and recovery of damaged tanks. The success of this can perhaps be judged from the following account which appeared initially in a contemporary German newspaper and was then circulated to British units by MI 1O in May 1941. It was entitled 'The secret of the fighting efficiency of the German AFVs' and gives an accurate account of the organisation of the repair and recovery elements of the Panzer division.

'The secret of the success of the German AFVs was the thorough organisation of the system for the replacement and repair of damaged tanks in the shortest possible time. The greater the distances covered in the advance and the farther the vehicles went from the technical services on which they normally depended, the more important it was to have a well organised maintenance and repair service in the field. The organisation of the service is described below.

'(1) Each tank squadron and the headquarters troop of each tank battalion has a light aid section. This is the smallest repair unit and the one which is employed nearest the front line. It consists of the necessary motor drivers, mechanics and wireless instrument mechanics. It is equipped with light lorries for spare parts and tools and a converted tank for transporting spare parts and mechanics across country to stranded tanks. The light aid section attached to the headquarters troop of each tank battalion is under the command of an officer who can, when necessary, arrange for all the light aid sections to proceed together to any part of the front where their services are urgently required.

'It is important to ensure that the light aid sections should have an ample supply of spare parts and all the necessary transport. The tank mechanic of the squadron light aid section always carries in his MC combination a sack containing spare parts most

Over the Don. A first-class shot of a PzKpfw IV belonging to the 24th Panzer Division being ferried across the River Don (Ernst J. Dohany).

commonly required, s that the minor running repairs can be carried out without loss of time. The light aid section of each squadron and battalion headquarters troop has a medium-sized semi-tracked lorry which carries a further stock of spare parts.

'If a tank is so badly damaged that special machinery would be required to repair it, or if the process would be a long one, the vehicle is returned to the manufacturer or to some maintenance depot in Germany.

'(2) Every tank regiment has a workshop company, which is equipped with power tools, produces its own power and light and can charge batteries, carry out welding operations, vulcanise tyres, etc. The equipment it carries includes a crane, a field smithy, milling, cutting, boring and tool-grinding machines and sets of tools for locksmiths, carpenters, tinsmiths, painters, etc. It is, therefore, completely independent.

'The regimental workshop company con-

sists of two identical platoons, one of which may be attached to each battalion of the regiment. In practice they leap-frog behind the regiment so as to ensure continuity in repair work. Each workshop platoon has several lorries used mainly for carrying spare parts or fetching them from the rear. The company also has a breakdown platoon which can bring stranded tanks to the work-

shop company or to some place where they can be fetched in order to be sent back by rail for more extensive repairs. In addition to these platoons the company has an armoury and a signals repair shop.

'(3) The light column of the tank battalion has two lorries also, specially detailed to carry spare parts, more particularly the heavy and bulky components.

'(4) If suitable workshops exist behind the lines or in occupied territory they are frequently used in order to save transport and reduce the volume of railway traffic. The necessary staff and equipment are brought from Germany.

'Without this careful organisation of the repair and maintenance service it would have been impossible for our AFVs to cover the

British troops. This issue, of February 1941, had much to say about the PzKpfw IV, describing how each Panzer battalion had one squadron of ten Mk IVs which were used mainly in two ways, firstly as highly mobile artillery, and secondly as an important component of fast-moving tank columns. Because field artillery could not be made immediately available to support armoured operations, the 7.5 cm gun of the PzKpfw IV was used in its place. The two most important aspects of this use were: that the range of the 7.5 cm gun (1,800 m (2,000 yd) effective and 8,000 m (9,000 yd) maximum) would dictate the time and placing of a battle; and that the speed of the PzKpfw IV was such that it could easily take part in a rapid advance.

The notes went on to explain that, on occasions, a troop of six Mk IVs had been used as artillery against forward columns, also as sniper guns, and in ambushes into which British tanks had been lured by armoured cars. Their use in defensive battles was cited with an example of how, on 16 June 1941, they had engaged British troops in Capuzzo, from outside the range of the defenders' anti-tank guns, while by their own mobility were then able to take avoiding action when engaged by artillery fire. The notes revealed that the British had discovered the Germans developing the following 'drill' for attacking prepared positions: 'The initial contact is made by armoured cars operating on a wide front. These cars operate in twos and threes, and, if seriously opposed, turn back. These are followed up by lorried infantry and a full-scale attack. The general standard of gunnery is high. Tank crews are instructed to gain the greatest opportunity of registering hits at 80°–90°. Their own tanks must be so positioned that front and sides present an acute angle to the opposing guns. They rarely fire on the move. Stationary gunnery from the PzKpfw II and PzKpfw III is preferred, the tanks moving rapidly from bound to bound, firing from "hull-down" positions. On occa-

tremendous distances and achieve the unparalleled successes they did in the recent campaign.'

When it came to the campaign in the West, PzKpfw IVs were again only available in small numbers — only 278 out of a total of 2,574 tanks (as compared with the Allied total of over 3,000 — mostly French — tanks opposing them). Many of these French tanks were more powerful, with better guns and thicker armour than even the handful of PzKpfw IVs available to Guderian. However, by concentration of force and the use of *Blitzkrieg* tactics — typified perhaps, by one of Guderian's favourite catch phrases, '*Klotzen nicht Kleckern*' (Don't feel with the fingers but hit with the fist!), the Germans fought a highly successful and lightning campaign, in which the PzKpfw IVs showed themselves to be highly effective. Despite the fact that they clearly needed thicker armour and more powerful guns, the German Panzers built a reputation which far exceeded their true capabilities.

Rommel's Afrika Korps contained its share of PzKpfw IVs, now available in greater numbers, but still being used in the supporting role. They received special mention in an issue of periodical notes on the German Army which were circulated to

The *Möbelwagen* (Furniture van) had a single 3.7 cm FlaK 43 L/60 and a crew of six. It was quite successful despite its cumbersome appearance, approximately 240 being built. The photograph shows it with its superstructure sides lowered.

sions, the PzKpfw IV tanks produce a creeping barrage by advancing firing their guns, not at specific targets, but between 3,000–4,000 yards [2,700–3,600 m] ahead of their course; the object, it is to be assumed, was to intimidate defence pockets and OPs.'

The first action between Americans and German tanks in Tunisia was on 26 November 1942, when a detachment of 190th Panzer Battalion DAK advanced towards the Chouigui Pass from Mateur and came up against the 2nd Battalion of 13th Armored Regiment, 1st Armored Division, which had spent the previous day near the Tine Valley at the entrance to the pass. The German detachment contained three or

more Mk IIIs and at least six Mk IV Specials, with the long-barrelled 7.5 cm gun. 'The Old Ironsides' battle history covers the engagement thus:

'The enemy detachment approached from the north after Waters' battalion had had time to place its tanks and guns in hull-down, camouflaged positions, to dig deep foxholes and in general to get itself into good shape for defense or possibly a day of rest. When the approaching column was first seen Siglin's company got ready to roll while its commander hurried back from the battalion CP. The assault-gun platoon under Lt Ray Wacker moved out ahead of Company A to intercept and delay the enemy. From the edge of a widely-spaced olive grove, at a range of perhaps 1,000 yd [900 m], the three 75 mm pack howitzers on their half-tracks ranged on the leading German tanks and fired rapidly with the best ammunition they had. The enemy tanks withdrew unhurt out of the resulting dust clouds and replied with

flat trajectory armor-piercing ammunition which came close but did no serious damage. Then, on battalion orders, Wacker switched to smoke shell and pulled his guns safely back.

'Siglin's unit then attacked the enemy's west flank with twelve M3 lights. The 1st Platoon was on the right nearest the enemy, but all were in range of his powerful guns drawing the full attention of the German-Italian force. Company A lost six tanks in a matter of minutes, but drew the enemy vehicles into positions which permitted Tuck's Company B to fire at their vulnerable rears. They knocked out six Mark IVs and at least one of the Mark IIIs before the rest withdrew.' In subsequent engagements the Americans were not so fortunate, being more often than not on the receiving end of the superior enemy firepower. However, in this first engagement, thanks to good defensive positioning, they had certainly scored a resounding success.

Ostwind 1, or *Flakpanzer* IV as it was also called, mounted a single 3.7 cm Flak 43 in a six-sided turret. It was due to be replaced by the *Kugelblitz* (Lightning ball) but the war ended before the new AA tank could go into production.

While there had been a distinct improvement in the numbers of PzKpfw IVs available by the time the invasion of Russia was imminent, they still formed only about one sixth of the total tank force (439 Mk IVs out of 3,332), but at least there were more PzKpfw IIIs and PzKpfw 38(t)s and many fewer little Mk Is and IIs. The vast majority of Russian tanks, although present in large numbers, were inferior to the Panzers who quickly made short work of them. However, the T-34 and KV 1 were a different matter altogether, being, for the most part, better than anything the Germans could produce until Tiger and Panther entered the lists. PzKpfw IV, especially the long-barrelled Specials, had the capacity to defeat the T-34s, so the situation did improve somewhat when they began to appear in reasonable numbers during 1942. Here is a description of one PzKpfw IV Special, in action against the Russian armour during an attack on Woronesh in summer 1942. This is how the history of Panzer Regiment 24[40] described it: 'On the second day of our attack on Woronesh, heavy house-to-house fighting was the order of the day, even by the late afternoon the resistance of the brave defenders had not been broken. Then the Soviet tanks which were the hub of their defence tried to break out through our encircling forces. It developed into a tank versus tank fight at close quarters which was decided through the better fighting spirit of our crews.

'Here is a report on the engagement by the then Panzer commander *Wachtmeister* [Sergeant Major] Freyer: "On 7 July 1942, I took up position with my PzKpfw IV long barrel at an important crossroads in Woronesh, well camouflaged, we stood next to a house in a garden. In front of the Panzer was a wooden fence, covering us from view from the street. Our orders were to support our Panzergrenadiers who were attempting to clear the town, and to protect them from enemy t anks. During the day our only problems came from scattered Russian troops, but the actions between friend and foe in the town kept us on our toes. It was a hot day, but we didn't realise that the evening was going to be even hotter. At about 8 pm a T-34 appeared from a side street to our left and attempted to get past us at high speed. He was followed by a column of some 30 more tanks and we had to prevent this breakout. In quick succession we engaged and knocked out the first three T-34s, then our gunner Unteroffizier [Lance Sergeant] Fischer reported 'The gun is jammed'. Our gun was new and had had teething troubles, because every second or third round, the empty shellcase got stuck in the breech. Our driver, Unteroffizier Schmidt and I jumped out of the Panzer, screwed the barrel cleaner together and with it pushed the empty shell out of the breech. The next Russian tank fired wildly round about and wounded our loader Gefreiter [Lance Corporal] Groll in the head. We pulled him out of the Panzer and our radioman took his place to help operate our weapon. We fired time and time again and kept on hitting our targets. A few more times we had to grab the barrel cleaner and push out jammed shells and then take cover quickly. The Russians cut the fence in front of us to pieces with their fire, but didn't hit our Panzer. We, however, hit 11 enemy tanks, the only time they got past us was when our gun jammed again. The fight took about 20 minutes, by then 11 enemy tanks

The StuG IV was really just the StuG III superstructure fitted onto a PzKpfw IV chassis. A large number were built once it was found that this could be done successfully.

Close-up of the front of a StuG IV showing the mounting of the 7.5 cm StuK 40 L/48 and driver's cab which was further protected by concrete slabs. Note also the antimagnetic mine paste on most other surfaces.

Jagdpanzer IV was developed as an improved version of the StuG IV, mounting the 7.5 cm PaK 39 L/48 gun. Combat weight was 24 tons, crew four men and 79 rounds of ammunition were carried. This *Jagdpanzer* was photographed in Warsaw, September 1944 (OTL aD Rolf Düe).

The Panzer IV/70 (V) was an improved version of the *Jagdpanzer*, produced by Vomag. The 7.5 cm PaK 42 L/70 was held in a travelling lock when moving. The photograph shows a late production model with only three return rollers, which was knocked out in Vilsen on the road to Bremen. Over 900 were built between August 1944 and March 1945.

were on fire in front of us, the flames and explosions giving the place an eerie appearance. That is how the rest of our company found us, despite the dark, and brought us back to the regimental leaguer on the southern edge of Wornonesh. We could not sleep, the day had been too hot. Oberst [Colonel] Riegel expressed his appreciation of this brave action in the following Regimental Order:

REGIMENTAL ORDER

The Führer and Higher Command is decorating Wachmeister Freyer 4 Company with the Knights Cross of the Iron Cross. Wachmeister Freyer destroyed nine heavy T-34s and two light T-60s with his PzKpfw IV at Woronesh. When the Panzer enemy which remained in the town tried to break out with over 30 Panzers, Wachmeister Freyer remained with exemplary bravery at his post. He let the far superior enemy approach him and then destroyed them. The hard fighting Russian Panzer brigade was scattered and to a large part destroyed. Our infantry managed to occupy the town after heavy fighting.

In the name of the Regiment, I wish to express my congratulations to Wachmeister Freyer for his high war decoration. The Regiment views with pride and pleasure our Knights Cross bearer and wishes him further success and best wishes for the future. At the same time I take the opportunity to thank the brave crew of the AFV:

The Gunner   Uffz Fischer
The Driver   Uffz Schmidt
The Loader   Gefr Groll
The Operator   Gefr Mueller

and to express my thanks and admiration for the action of this tank on 7.7.42. It will go down in the Roll of Honour of our glorious Regiment.

The Allied landings in North-West Europe opened up yet another battleground for the ubiquitous PzKpfw IV, especially in the early days when they were fighting defensively from carefully concealed well reconnoitred positions and still in fairly large numbers. There were few Allied tanks or tank destroyers that could take on and knock out the Mk IVs from long range, the Sherman Firefly and M10 Achilles, both armed with the British 17 pdr, being the most successful. When forced to move, then the Panzers had just the same problems as any AFV operating in the close bocage countryside. 'I never saw a German tank employed singly,' wrote one GI in an Intelligence Bulletin[41] of the period. 'In nearly all instances, a section or platoon was employed. One tank may try to draw your fire; then if you react as the Germans expect you to, you are immediately subjected to the remainder of their firepower. German tanks have a tendency to bunch up and it is quite common for them to expose their broadsides. We found them vulnerable to cross fire from firepower deployed on an extended front.

'I found that the enemy employs his tanks in groups of six or more, and that they are usually two or three types in a group. The most common we found were PzKpfw IV and VI, and, in most cases one or two SP guns. These guns, I believe, are intended to delay our advance in the event that the tanks

have to withdraw or maneuver to a more advantageous position. The Germans frequently use a single tank as a decoy to draw your fire, with the hope that you will present yourself as a more vulnerable target. The enemy's main fault, it seems to me, is bunching up his vehicles and trying to get too much through a single avenue of approach or withdrawal.

' If a German tank is not completely destroyed — set afire with HE shells, for example — the enemy is likely to sneak back into it and deliver unexpected fire from its weapons. Also a crew baling out may leave one man behind to cause us trouble. Once, we fired on a PzKpfw IV Special, and hit it on the track. The crew baled out immediately and we thought the tank was out of action. However, the gunner remained in the vehicle. After we had stopped watching this particular tank, the gunner fired two rounds at us. We weren't hit fortunately, and lost no time at all in demolishing the tank.'

PzKpfw IVs went on being used right up to the end of the war, despite losses and reductions in production caused by the Allied bombing of the factories. A fair number of Mk IVs were supplied to various allies of Germany, such as Bulgaria, Rumania and Hungary, and to sympathetic nations like Spain and Finland. The latter remained in service for some years after the war, while the last recorded battle action of the PzKpfw IV occurred on the Golan Heights, during the Arab-Israeli conflicts. The Syrians had some old PzKpfw IVs which they had obtained from the French and put them into strongpoints of the Golan Heights, where they could engage the Israeli settlements down on the plain below. They were used in 1965 and again in 1967, until finally captured by the Israelis during the Six Day War.

Before moving on to describe the variants, here is one more story about a PzKpfw IV in Russia, which gives an excellent impression of the traumas for average crew of a Mk IV in action; it concerns the tank RO-1 of the 7th Company of Panzer Regiment 35, returning from workshops to rejoin the Company near Preklun in October 1944 and was written by the tank driver.

'We set off in a southerly direction towards Preklun, it is noon and the sun shines weakly from the sky. On the way my Panzer engine starts to misfire, performance deteriorates badly and I have to pull out of the column to examine the carburettor. As far as is necessary, I dismantle the double down-draught carb, to clean the jets, float and valve. It isn't difficult for me as I have had training in tank maintenance. While I work a lot of fighter planes perform in the air, the weather is ideal for flying. They don't bother us, we are prepared and have manned our turret MG in the air defence position. After a good hour the engine sounds OK again and we continue our drive to catch up with our comrades. Our route goes through Preklun, then in an easterly direction. Instinctively we follow the track marks to find the right way and our "nose" is right again. Approximately three to four kilometres after leaving the settlement the land begins to rise to a ridge and there we see our 7th Company, attacking with some 13 to 14 Panzer IVs. After approaching very close we have another look from the so called "Fieldmarshal's Hill". Already we can see that several Panzers have run on to mines. Some of these are out of action, others are moving backwards.

'My main concern is to find a good position and having found a suitable hole we move on and join up with the attacking 7th Company. Today the Regiment is commanded by Oberstleutnant [Lieutenant] Petreli. The attack moves slowly forwards. Ivan defends the heights with a mass of tanks and other material. For us the heights are of strategic importance, as one can command from the ridge the whole of the main supply road as far as Libau. More and more Panzers fall out through strong enemy fire, reducing our numbers, but slowly we move up the hill against the stubborn defenders, until night comes. My commander, Unterfeldwebel [Sergeant] Ernst, orders me to the left towards a burning farm house. It is burning well! By the light of this fire we approach an opening in a hedge of fir trees surrounding the farm. As we approach, about 20 m from the entrance, I recognise with a big shock, that at the end of the hedge there is an enemy heavy anti-tank gun, with its barrel pointing straight at me! The shock goes right into my bones and I can't get a word out. It appears that neither the commander nor the gunner has seen it, because I don't hear any fire orders and our gun is pointing in a different direction. Our only salvation is to give the Panzer full throttle, and the needle of the rev counter moves quickly into the red field. A tenth of a second is decisive, as the muzzle of the anti-tank gun appears directly in front of my view slot, only to be crushed before they can fire, by the tracks of our Panzer. I assume that the gun crew are killed. At the same instant, the

commander recognises the danger — we both breathe a sigh of relief.

'Downwards we move into a depression, the glow of the burning house does not penetrate through the hedge into the hollow. Soon we stand again on a firm path surrounded by darkness. As we roll quietly along we see to the left and right of the path the silhouettes of two more Panzers. We stop between them and poke out our heads, discovering to our horror that they are T-43! We disappear immediately into our Panzer and train our cannon on them, but it would certainly have been too late if they had been "live". Instead, we find that they have both slipped off the path and are stuck in the mud. Their crews had abandoned them. To make sure we shoot a grenade from close range into their engine compartments. Now the flickering light of the fires comes in useful and we discover that we have only four friendly Panzers left.

'The top of the hill is within reach, perhaps no more than 50 metres. Suddenly from close range the crack of gunfire and the other three Panzers are all hit and set on fire. Fortunately, we have time to take cover back in the hollow before the fourth shot. In the firelight we must have presented a good target to a dug-in Russian Sturmgeschütz. Because of this the retaking of the hill has to be abandoned and we spend the night until first light, on our own, unsure of our surroundings. Early in the morning the first Panzers with Oberleutnant Petreli reach us and from then on our main function is to secure against enemy counterattacks. Towards noon, Unteroffizier Goos comes from Regimental HQ with his Panzer RO 3. As he is trying to move into a suitable position he crosses the firing arc of the Russian Sturmgeschütz which we have been unable to eliminate and is shot up. His gunner is killed. The same afternoon we make a counter-attack with our infantry to plug the enemy break-in. At the foot of the hill we go forward to the right. Countless dead German soldiers lie on the ground. We miss them with difficulty, we don't like to drive over the dead. We succeed in cleaning up the incursion, inflicting very heavy losses on Ivan and reposition our infantry in their old foxholes. We are being raked by heavy small arms fire when orders come to return to Oberleutnant Petreli. Turning round in very heavy going I stall the engine. I try to restart but the electrical starter doesn't work. The radio operator and loader have to get out amidst heavy enemy fire and use the starting handle on the flywheel starter — not a very easy job, but they succeed.

'After rounding the hill in order to get back to our previous position we come into

view of a Russian forward artillery observer. He chases us around with heavy artillery fire from several batteries for over an hour, until we can get out of his sight and join Oberleutnant Petreli. Days later we get relieved and I can get my starter repaired.'

Variants

General conversions A small number (approximately 40) of PzKpfw IV Ausf Ds and Es were converted into *Tauchpanzer* for underwater operations against England in 1940. After Operation SEALION was aborted the vehicles were issued to 18 Panzer Regiment and used for the crossing of the River Bug in Russia in 1941. This model was very similar to the diving tank described in the last chapter. Twenty Ausf C and D chassis were used, again in 1940, to produce bridgelayers (*Brückenleger IV*), which then served with the armoured bridging platoons of Panzer divisions. Weight with bridge was approximately 28 tons. Another bridge carrier was the infantry assault bridge (*Infanterie Sturmsteg*) of which two only were produced. It resembled the ladder of a fire engine, having a telescopic catwalk. Fitters (*Bergepanzer*) were converted from turretless chassis with the addition of a box-like wooden superstructure and a crane, while other chassis were converted for use as ammunition or stores carriers (also minus turrets). Two prototypes of a tracked amphibious ferry, known as *Panzerfahre*, were produced. These had a large pontoon-type upper hull, mounted on the drive train, engine and running gear of the Ausf F, but did not go into production.

Panzerbefehlswagen IV and Panzerbeobachtungswagen IV Less PzKpfw IVs were converted to the command and OP roles than were PzKpfw IIIs. It was not until 1944, when shortages of armoured command vehicles with adequate levels of protection became acute, that action was taken to produce the Pz Bef Wg IV and Pz Beob Wg IV. The former conversions — some 100 during the summer and autumn of 1944 — were mainly from Ausf Hs. They had the normal dummy gun, extra radio and antenna base (with star aerial) as for other Bef Wg. The Ausf J was the model chosen for the artillery OP tank, again about 100 being converted between mid-1944 and March 1945. They were fitted up as per artillery requirements, in order to provide the OP officer with all round communications, including a link back to the guns.

Anti-aircraft weapons After the early war years Germany had lost air superiority and never regained it except in certain isolated instances, so the need for air defence weapons became more and more pronounced, especially by fast-moving armoured columns. The use of the 8.8 cm anti-aircraft gun in the anti-tank role did not help the situation either although its prowess as a tank killer was legendary. There were four FlaK weapons mounted on the PzKpfw IV chassis:

the Bulge,[42] in which he recounts the experiences of an aiming gunner, Karl Wortmann, who was part of the crew of the third of four flak tanks which were closely following the leading Panther tanks of *Kampfgruppe Peiper*, as they entered Honsfeld, early one foggy morning. As the first flak tank edged around an S-bend and past some buildings a US anti-tank gun opened fire on

advance. Although the anti-tank gun fired a third time, it missed Wortmann's vehicle. Wortmann could see that the gun was firing from a barn concealed by a hedge. Taking aim with his 37 mm piece, he knocked it out with one round.'

Tank destroyers The Pz Kpfw IV chassis was used for a number of excellent tank destroyers (*Panzerjäger*), over 3,500 being produced and used to great effect in battle. The best were (*see* table below):

Name	Armament	Superstructure	Nos produced/converted and dates
Wirbelwind	Quad 2 cm AA guns (FlaKvierling 38)	Open-topped, many-sided turret	90 approx, 1944
Möbelwagen	Single 3.7 cm FlaK 43 L/60	Four-sided, open-topped superstructure which could be let down horizontally	240 approx, 1944–45
Ostwind	Single 3.7 cm FlaK 43/1 L/60	Six-sided, open-topped turret	45 approx, 1944–45
Kugelblitz	Twin 3 cm MK 103/38	Modern-looking low, rounded, open-topped turret	2 only, early 1945

The *Wirbelwind* (Whirlwind) had 16 mm armour, was quite effective and better suited to rapid engagements than *Möbelwagen* (Furniture Van) which also lacked protection once the sides had been lowered. *Ostwind* (East Wind) had thicker armour (25 mm) but a lower rate of fire with its single 3.7 cm than the quad 2 cm which it replaced. All save *Kugelblitz* (Fireball) entered service with the AA platoons (*Flugabwehrzeug*) of the Panzer regiments. There was also another 2 cm Flakvierling which was mounted in a similar way to the Möbelwagen but this model never got beyond the prototype stage.

The effectiveness of the *Ostwind* in the ground role was well described by Charles B. MacDonald in his account of the Battle of

them. The first round hit the leading flak tank but it kept on moving, then the second Ostwind was hit and knocked out: '...Bypassing the immobilized tank, the driver of Wortmann's flak tank continued to

StuG IV had a combat weight of 23 tons, thick frontal armour (80 mm) and a four-man crew; 63 rounds were carried for the main armament of this most effective TD, which was used, together with StuG III, to equip assault artillery brigades from late 1943. It was replaced in 1944 by the Jagdpanzer IV, after a pilot model had been demonstrated to Hitler in October 1943. Combat weight was 24 tons and 79 rounds were carried. Vomag were then tasked to fit the more powerful, long-barrelled 7.5 cm PaK 42 L/70 gun to the chassis and produced a prototype in May 1944. The gun had a performance similar to that on the Panther. It entered service in August 1944, was a match for all contemporary AFVs and

Name	Armament	Superstructure	Numbers produced/converted and dates
Sturmgeschütz IV	7.5 cm StuK 40 L/48	StuG III superstructure on top of PzKpfw IV chassis	Over 1,100, Dec 1943–Mar 1945
Jagdpanzer IV	7.5 cm Pak 39 L/48	Improved version of StuG IV	Nearly 800, 1944
Panzer IV/70(V)	7.5 cm Pak 42 L/70	Improved version of JagdPz IV produced by Vomag	Over 900, Aug 1944–Mar 1945
Panzer IV/70(A)	7.5 cm Pak 42 L/70	Alkett version of Panzer IV/70 (V)	Nearly 300, Aug 1944–Mar 1945
Nashorn (also called Hornisse)	8.8 cm Pak 43/1 L/71	Gun mounted on lengthened hull with centrally positioned engine	500, 1943–45

Side view of a knocked-out *Nashorn*. Built between February 1943 and March 1945, they were issued to heavy Panzerjäger detachments.

earned the nickname 'Guderian's Chicken'. It was, however, reputedly not very easy to steer on rough terrain and inclined to be top heavy. *Hornisse* (Hornet) had its name changed to *Nashorn* (Rhino). It was issued to heavy Panzerjäger troops in early summer 1943 and proved highly effective. From the summer of 1944 StuGs had their externally-mounted (self-protection) MGs replaced by a remotely-controlled MG mount, which enabled the MG to be sighted and fired without exposing any member of the crew.

Self-propelled guns Various other weapons were mounted on the PzKpfw IV chassis including: (*see* Table at top *page 97*)

The Sturmpanzer IV or *Brummbär* (Grizzly Bear) first saw action in the summer offensive at Kursk in 1943, and was designed

Name	Armament	Detail	Numbers and dates
Brummbär	15 cm StuH 43 L/12	Box-like superstructure housing a heavy infantry assault gun	Approx 300, 1943–45
Hummel	15 cm sFH 18/1 L/30	Heavy howitzer fitted on to tank classis in a similar way as for the Nashorn	Over 600, from 1944

Hummel (Bumble Bee) seen here moving into action, was a 15 cm heavy howitzer mounted upon the PzKpfw IV chassis.

JAGDPANZER IV AUSF F (SDKFZ 162)
Date of origin 1943
Weight (tonnes) 24
Overall dimensions (m) **Length** 6.85
 Height 1.85
 Width 3.2
Armament/Ammunition carried
  Main 1 × 7.5 cm PaK 39 L/48
   79 rounds
  Secondary 1 × 7.92 mm MG 42
Armour thickness (mm) Max. 80
 Min. 10
Engine Type Maybach HL 120 TRM
 bhp/rpm 300/3,000
Crew 4
Max. speed (km/h) 40
Range (km) 210
Remarks Excellent tank destroyer

These *Hummels* belonged to PzAR 89 of the 24th Panzer Division (Ernst J. Dohany).

primarily for street fighting. *Hummel* (Bumblebee) was the final development of a heavy tank howitzer. It had a combat weight of 23.5 tons, a crew of six and stowage for 18 rounds only. Like the *Nashorn*, the engine had been repositioned in a central position to leave the rear of the hull clear for the gun. Early models had a muzzle brake but this was dropped during the production run. There was also a *Munitionsträger Hummel* issued to units, some 150 being built. The forward access plate could be unscrewed and the howitzer replaced if necessary. The main problem with *Hummel* was that it had too

high a silhouette and poor crew protection.
Miscellaneous A number of other AFVs used the PzKpfw IV chassis, and were either produced in too small numbers to be significant, or never got into full production. The former group included an SP gun, the 10.5 cm K 18 *auf* Panzer *Selbstfahrlafette* IVa of which only two were produced in 1941. It was intended to deal with Allied superheavy tanks which never materialised so, although the two performed excellently, no more were ever built. Among those which never entered full production were three SP light field howitzers, all mounting the 10.5 cm leFH 18. They were intended to provide an answer to the poor protection and high silhouette of the *Hummel* and *Wespe* but, although eight of the first of the trio were built and saw service in Russia, the other two

did not get past the prototype stage and the idea was dropped. The three models were: the 10.5 cm leFH 18/1 (Sf) *auf Geschützwagen* IVb, the 10.5 cm leFH 18/1 L/28 *auf Waffenträger* GW IVb (also known as *Heuschrecke* 10), and the *leichte* PzH 18/40/2 *auf Fahrgestell* PanzerKampfwagen III/IV (Sf).

Pz Kpfw V and variants

Background development

Without a shadow of doubt, one of the biggest shocks the Panzertruppen ever received during the war was their first meeting with the Russian T-34 tank. Guderian, in his book *Panzer Leader*, tells how, in October 1941, in the Mzensk area 'numerous Russian T-34s went into action and inflicted heavy losses on the German tanks'. He goes on to explain how, until that time, the Panzertruppen had always considered their tanks to be far superior to anything the enemy could produce, but that now the situation was clearly reversed. Had the German authorities not been quite so smug about their apparent superiority, then perhaps the reversal might never have occurred. This was evidently Guderian's personal view, as he tells about a visit made in the spring of 1941 by a Russian delegation, which Hitler had invited to Germany to look at Panzer training schools and tank-building factories. He recalled how insistent the Russians had been that they were not being shown the latest developments, despite the Führer's promises. They could not believe that the PzKpfw IV was the best and heaviest type of tank in service and their sceptical attitude led some

people, including himself, to conclude that perhaps the Russians had already built bigger and better tanks themselves.

This conclusion was, of course, not borne out by the ease in which the initial German assault swept through Russian armour when Operation BARBAROSSA began, so meeting the T-34 came as a nasty surprise and clearly something had to be done about it very quickly indeed. In his report to Army Group, describing the marked superiority of the T-34 over the PzKpfw IV, Guderian requested that a team of experts be sent out at once to make an on-the-spot examination of the problem. The team, composed of experts from the Army Ordnance Office and Armaments Ministry, tank designers and tank producing firms, arrived in the 2nd Panzer Army front on 20 November 1941. They examined captured and knocked-out enemy tanks, and talked with soldiers at 'the sharp end' in order to get their views. Many were clearly of the opinion that the simplest and best answer would be to take an example of the T-34 home and then mass-produce it, but the designers did not agree. Guderian is at pains to explain that he does not think that this was due to the designers' 'natural pride in their own inventions', but rather because

of the more practical problems the proposal raised. For example, it would be impossible to mass-produce such essential T-34 components as its aluminium diesel engine, while shortages of raw materials from which to manufacture steel alloys was an insurmountable problem for Germany. It was therefore decided to adopt a compromise solution, in that, while work would continue on the design and construction of the 60 ton Tiger tank (see next chapter), a new vehicle would be designed, a heavy medium tank weighing about 35 tons, which would be called Panther.

On 25 November 1941 the *Heereswaffenamt* put out contracts to Daimler-Benz and MAN, to produce designs for this new heavy medium tank, in the 30- to 35-ton class, as quickly as possible. It was given the designation VK 3002[43] and was to have the following specifications: armour thickness (minimum) — frontal arc 60 mm, sides and rear 40 mm; front glacis and sides to be sloped as for T-34; and speed — 55 km/h (35 mph) max, 40 km/h (25 mph) cruising. The two firms produced very different design proposals, the Daimler-Benz VK 3002(DB) closely resembling the T-34, while MAN's offering, VK 3002(MAN), was far closer to other contemporary German designs. Basic differences were that the Daimler-Benz model weighed 34 tons, had a hull shape very similar to the T-34's, an MB 507 diesel engine with drive to rear-mounted sprockets, paired steel bogies suspended by leaf springs, the driver located within the turret cage, and armament of a 7.5 cm L/48 gun. The MAN model weighed 35 tons, had a hull shape higher and wider than that of the T-34, with a large, set-back turret to offset for the overhang of a long gun, a Maybach HL 210 petrol engine with

This is one of the first 20 Panthers ever produced. These were originally called the Ausf A but this changed to Ausf D₁. Note the way the cupola protrudes into the side of the turret, also the ball-shaped muzzle brake and smoke dischargers on the sides of the turret which were other features of the early model.

An early Panther Ausf D, now with the double muzzle brake, leaving the factory in company with a pair of Tigers.

drive to front sprockets, torsion bar suspension with interleaved roadwheels, the driver and hull gunner in a front compartment, layout as per normal German tanks, and proposed armament of the 7.5 cm long-barrelled L/70.

Initially Hitler favoured the Daimler-Benz design, although he felt it should have a more powerful gun. This led to an order being placed for 200 of the VK 3002(DB) model. However, the 'Panther Committee' preferred the MAN design, particularly because the MB 507 diesel had never been tested, while the new gun which Hitler wanted would never fit into the small turret. They asked the firm to produce a mild steel prototype as quickly as possible. This was ready by September 1942 and was trialled at the works test ground at Nuremberg. A second, completed soon afterwards, went for testing at the *Heereswaffenamt* test ground at Kummersdorf. Ing Kniepkampf[44], chief engineer and designer of Waffenprüfamt 6, had taken personal charge of the detailed design work on the MAN model and the project was given top priority.

As a result of these trials, the MAN design

Excellent shot of an Ausf D with its crew. The commander is Oberfeldwebel Herbert Elsner, who features in one of the battle accounts at the end of this chapter and was awarded a Knights Cross for bravery (Herbert Elsner).

was chosen for production. Whether the 'Panther Committee' had the temerity to overrule the Führer's wishes, or whether he did in fact authorise the change is not clear, but the Daimler-Benz order was conveniently ignored and later rescinded. The new vehicle was ordered into immediate production and given the designation PzKpfw V Panther (SdKfz 171). It was planned to produce 250 a month initially then, at the end of 1942, this target was raised to 600 a month. Clearly MAN could not handle such a large order alone and Daimler-Benz was quickly switched to Panther production. Other companies joined the production group later, either as main producers (eg, Maschinenfabrik Niedersachsen of Hanover — MNH, Henschel and later DEMAG) or as sub-contractors for engines and other components.

In mid-July 1941, Rheinmetall-Borsig had been given a contract to develop a tank gun which could penetrate 140 mm of armour at 1,000 m (1,090 yd). At the same time they were authorised to design a turret for the VK 3002 project, which would take the new gun. By early 1942 they had pro-

duced a test barrel L/60 but the performance did not reach the required specification, so an L/70 barrel length was chosen and delivery fixed at June 1942. This target date was met and the gun went into full production, initially with a single muzzle brake, which was later changed to a double baffle. It was a gun of superlative performance and feared by every Allied tank crew.

So began the development of what many experts consider was the best tank built by any nation during World War 2. Some 6,000-plus would be built in all and it was to become the most important tank on the production lines, because two Panthers could be built in the same number of man hours required to build one Tiger. The first 20 Panthers to come off the production line at MAN from November 1942 onwards were designated Ausf A in the normal manner, although as we shall see, this designation was later changed. The Ausf B was to have been a version to be fitted with the Maybach-Olvar gearbox instead of the specially-designed ZFAK 7-200, but this proved abortive and the designation was never used. It could be said that the original 20 Ausf As

were really pre-production models as they did not have any of the design improvements which had been proposed following the pilot model trials. They were built to the basic specifications which the VK 3002 project had demanded, namely the Maybach HL 210 petrol engine, armour up to 60 mm thick in front, the earliest type of L/70 gun and a ZF 7 gearbox, with clutch and brake steering. From early 1943 Panthers were produced with various improvements: for example, the engine capacity was raised from 21 to 23 litres by enlarging the cylinder bore, the engine then being known as the HL 230 P 30, a V-12 petrol engine that produced 700 bhp; the front glacis was thickened to 80 mm; and the turret cupola was moved slightly to the right (purely to make turret production easier). What happened to the designation Ausf C remains a mystery, but it was presumably allocated to another model

that never left the drawing board, so the first full production model was designated Ausf D. To try to keep the records straight the Ausf A batch was later given the designation Ausf D$_1$, while the Ausf D was sometimes called Ausf D$_2$.

PZKPFW V AUSF D (SDKFZ 171)
Date of origin 1942 (pre-production models); 1943
Weight (tonnes) 43
Overall dimensions (m) **Length** 8.86
Height 2.97
Width 3.43
Armament/Ammunition carried
Main 1 × 7.5 cm KwK 42 L/70
79 rounds
Secondary 2 × 7.92 mm MG 34
Armour thickness (mm) Max. 100
Min. 16
Engine **Type** Maybach HL 230 P30
bhp/rpm 700/3,000
Crew 5
Max. speed (km/h) 46
Range (km) 200

Four companies — MAN, Daimler-Benz, MNH and Henschel — were now producing the Ausf D, some 600 being built between January and September 1943. Unfortunately, as the development had been so rushed, the early Panthers suffered from numerous mechanical faults, especially as regards their transmission and steering which, having been designed for lighter tanks, was not really up to the stresses caused by the increased weight and power of a larger engine. The same also applied to the engine itself which was prone to overheating, often causing fires.

In March 1943, Guderian requested a breathing space, explaining to Hitler that he did not believe the Panther would be operational before July 1943.[45] Even that date proved too optimistic. Writing after the first major battle test of the Panther on the Russian front,[46] Oberstleutnant (Lieutenant-Colonel) von Grundherr wrote: '...In closing, I can't get around adding a few words on a very sad story, despite the fact that it was exactly the way I had thought it would be: Panther. There were a great many who expected the decision to come from the new, untried weapon. The initially complete failure therefore had a somewhat depressing effect, particularly since, on the basis of the Führer Order, special expecta-

tions had been aroused... So long as one builds such a valuable weapon, one must not build in an unusable gasoline pump or deficient gaskets. There is no shadow of doubt that the majority of technical deficiencies resulted from substitute materials which simply did not measure up to standard.'

Depressing reading for those at home, but at least he goes on to say:

'...the effectiveness of the Panther weapon is noteworthy. At a range of 7,224 m a T-34 was knocked out with the first round.'[47] Of the 200 Panther tanks that took part in this debut 160 were out of action by the end of the first day and nine days later only 43 were left. Many had broken down between the rail-heads and the Front, towing proving extremely difficult due to their weight. Of course these teething problems were sorted out and the Panther rapidly gained a reputation for its all-round excellence although, as we shall read later, there still could be problems.

The next production model was for some reason designated as Ausf A instead of the expected Ausf E. It first appeared in August 1943 and some 1,788 were built by the four firms, MAN, Daimler-Benz, MNH and DEMAG. The 'second' Ausf A had an improved cupola for the commander, replacing the 'dustbin'-shaped earlier model, with better vision via armoured episcopes rather than vision slits. The hull machine-gun had a new ball-mounting, while there was improved sighting gear for the gunner — TZF 12A monocular telescope, replacing the older TZF 12 binocular telescope. There were a number of minor changes made to the turret as well, such as the elimination of the ammu-

nition loading hatch on the left-hand side, removal of the pistol ports, and the addition of a roof-mounted close-in defence weapon[48] plus a roof-mounted periscope for the loader. To ease production and to help with the weight problems, the number of tyre bolts in the wheels was increased from 16 to 24.

The final production model of the Panther was the Ausf G and this was built in larger quantities than any of the others, 3,740 being constructed between March 1944 and April 1945 by MAN, Daimler-Benz and MNH. It had a redesigned hull, with more sloping, thicker sides (50 mm instead of 40 mm), and the side plates were now all in one piece. The front glacis was strengthened by the removal of the driver's vision port, which was replaced by a rotating periscope in the roof of his compartment. Hatches for the driver and hull gunner were improved by making them hinged, rather than swinging pivot, and they were fitted with springs to make them easier to open.

Ammunition stowage was increased from 79 to 82 rounds, while in later models there was a new mantlet, and resilient steel roadwheels were fitted. On the final production versions of the Ausf G the ZF AK 7-200 gearbox was replaced by the ZF AK 7-400. The designation of this last model was changed to Panther Ausf G, the PzKpfw V designation being dropped following a directive from the Führer dated 27 February 1944. Both infrared night sights and a stabiliser system for the main armament were planned for the Ausf G, but never produced in time for operational use before the end of the war.

Basic description

As we have seen, thanks to Ing Kniepkampf and the 'Panther Committee', Panther was designed on standard German lines, with a driving compartment in the front, turret and fighting compartment in the centre and an engine compartment at the rear, the drive being taken through the centre of the tank to a front-mounted gearbox and thence to the driving sprockets. It was larger and heavier than the tank it had been built to defeat, viz:

	Panther Ausf D	T-34/76A
Combat weight	43 tonnes (42.3 UK/47.4 US tons); Ausf A and G were both heavier at 44.75 tonnes (44 UK/49.4 US tons)	26.3 tonnes (25.9 UK/29 US tons), later models went up to 30.9 tonnes (30.4 UK/34.1 US tons)
Length (gun forward)	8.86 m (29 ft 1 in)	6.1 m (20 ft 0 in)
Overall width	3.43 m (11 ft 3 in) (with side skirts)	3.0 m (9 ft 10 in)
Overall height	2.97 m (9 ft 9 in)	2.5 m (8 ft 2 in)

The driver sat on the left with a vision port (removed on the Ausf G) directly in front of him in the glacis plate, fitted with an armoured cover which measured 24.8 cm by 10 cm ($9\frac{3}{4}$ in by 4 in) and was operated by a single spring-loaded lever. When driving closed down the driver used two fixed episcopes in the roof of his compartment, one facing directly forward, the other half facing left. Visibility was not good, so the advent of the fully rotating periscope on the Ausf G was a welcome modification. He had

normal driving controls with the gear lever on the right and handbrake on the left, plus an instrument panel (with speedometer, rev counter, oil pressure gauge and ammeter). There was also a button on the panel for the electrical starter, but during very cold weather or if the vehicle batteries were low an inertia starter could be used, the crank handle being inserted through the rear plate. It needed two men to swing the handle; later models had an improved version (*Durch-drehenanlasser*) which was easier to operate.

The radio operator/hull gunner sat on the right of the driving compartment on the other side of the gearbox and transmission. He manned an MG 34 which he fired through the glacis plate via a vertical 'letter-box' type flap. On later models this was replaced by a proper ball mounting (*Kugel-blende*), which incorporated a sighting aperture. To his right, fitted into the sponson, was all the radio equipment, while above him were similar fixed episcopes to the driver. Both had large oblong escape hatches

which opened by first raising slightly, then swivelling outwards (hinged and spring-assisted in the Ausf G).

Between the two men was the ZF AK 7-200 gearbox, which had seven forward and one reverse gears. It was not an easy box to operate and needed skill to get the best results. It provided syncromesh for all gears at 2,000 to 2,200 rpm, but double-declutching was necessary over 2,500 rpm or when changing down at under 1,500 rpm. The drive passed from the gearbox through a transfer box and a single reduction gear to the forward-mounted driving sprockets. While normal hydraulic disc brakes were used for steering by braking the tracks, the epicyclic gears could be used to help steer by driving one or other of the sprockets against the main drive, thus slowing down the track on that side and allowing tighter turns to be made. This type of controlled differential steering was also used on the Tiger. Turning circles were wider the higher the gear used, varying from a radius of 5 m (16 ft 5 in) in 1st gear to 80 m (87 ft 6 in) in 7th. A neutral turn was also provided. The driving sprockets had detachable rims with 17 teeth.

Suspension and tracks The suspension was of the twin torsion bar type with eight double interleaved bogie wheels on each side. The wheels were dished with solid rubber tyres, although a few late production models were fitted with all-steel wheels

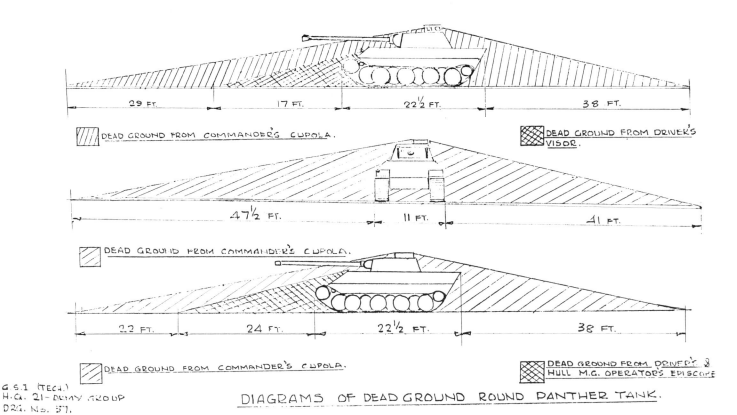

29 FT. 17 FT. 22½ FT. 38 FT.

DEAD GROUND FROM COMMANDER'S CUPOLA.   DEAD GROUND FROM DRIVER'S VISOR.

47½ FT. 11 FT. 41 FT.

DEAD GROUND FROM COMMANDER'S CUPOLA.

22 FT. 24 FT. 22½ FT. 38 FT.

DEAD GROUND FROM COMMANDER'S CUPOLA.   DEAD GROUND FROM DRIVER'S & HULL M.G. OPERATOR'S EPISCOPE

G.S.1 (TECH.)
H.Q. 21 ARMY GROUP
DRG. No. 57.

DIAGRAMS OF DEAD GROUND ROUND PANTHER TANK.

(Ausf G). It was a complicated suspension, difficult to maintain and heavy to work on, but did give an excellent, smooth ride. Tracks were 660 mm (2 ft 2 in) wide with 86 links per track, and tension was controlled by rear mounted idlers. The drive sprockets were quite high off the ground so the tank had an excellent vertical step performance (91 cm (3 ft) as compared with 60 cm (1 ft 11 in) for PzKpfw IV and 79 cm (2 ft 7 in) for Tiger). For really difficult going grousers were provided for fitting to every fifth link, but speed had to be severely reduced when they were fitted.

Turret The turret was centrally placed on the fighting compartment and was complete with sides and a rotating floor. The 7.5 cm KwK 42 L/70 gun was mounted on the gun cradle, with its breech block, buffer and recoil system. The gunner's telescope was on the left and the co-axial MG 34 on the right. The cast mantlet was secured to the front of the cradle which was elevated or depressed by a toothed elevating arc between −8° and +20°. The turret sides consisted of two large plates, bent inwards near the rear ends to meet the edges of a comparatively narrow rear plate, so that the sides and rear together were roughly in the shape of a horseshoe. The roof sloped down towards the mantlet at about 6°, while the sides and rear were set at 65° and the mantlet at 78°. Three members of the crew (commander, gunner and loader) occupied the turret, with the commander left rear under his cupola, gunner left front and loader on the right. The large breech of the main armament almost divided the turret into two. The commander's cupola was some 26 cm (10¼ in) high with six horizontal slots around it. These were closed by operating a handwheel which caused a 56 mm (2½ in) thick steel ring to rotate around the cupola. It also had a circular hatch which could be raised or lowered and then swung to one side. As has been explained, this cupola was replaced on Ausf A by a much improved version with armoured periscopes. Over the hatch was a ring mount for an MG 34 for air defence. A Panther crew always suffered from poor close-in visibility, due to the height and shape of the tank, although the better cupola, and later the loader's periscope, did help. As the drawing shows, watching out for tank hunting parties must have been a continual nightmare in close country or built-up areas.

The gunner's main controls comprised an elevating handwheel, which incorporated

the trigger to fire the main armament (electrically); a traversing handwheel, used for both hand and power and a foot pedal for the co-axial MG. He had a TZF 12 binocular telescope (later TZF 12a monocular). It had range scales for APC BC, HE and AP40, the HE scale also being used for the machine-gun. It gave dual magnification and included a range plate and a sighting plate. The range plate had the scale for main armament and co-axial MG ranges marked around its edge. It rotated about its own axis, while the sighting plate, which contained sighting and aim-off markings, moved up and down. Both plates turned together. Thus, to obtain a selected range, the gunner turned the range wheel until the correct marking was opposite a pointer on top of the sight, then laid the sighting mark on the target by using his traverse and elevating handwheels. Power for the hydraulic traverse was obtained from the main drive shaft via a fluid coupling, so the rate of turn depended upon engine speed and the driver and gunner had to work as a team to produce fast traversing. For example, in high ratio, at 2,500 rpm, the turret could be traversed in 17–18 seconds, while in low ratio at 1,000 rpm it took 92–93 secs. Final lay was always made by hand, so the power traverse lever on the gunner's right then had to be in the vertical (neutral) position. It was pulled back to go left and pushed forward to go right. Hand traverse was not easy, one full turn of the handwheel only moved the 7.5-tonnes (7.4 UK/8.3 US tons) turret a mere 0.36°.

Gun position in relation to the tank was shown via a two-dial azimuth indicator for the gunner (the left dial having an inner scale marked 0–12 and an outer scale 0–64, for

coarse adjustment, while the right-hand dial was graduated in mils for finer adjustment). There was also a 1–12 clock scale marked on a toothed ring around the inside of the commander's cupola. The cupola scale worked on the contra-rotation principle, so that when the turret was traversed a pinion, which engaged with the teeth of the turret rack, drove the scale in the opposite direction but at the same speed. This meant that the figure 12 on the scale always remained looking directly forward along the vehicle centre line. The commander used this to work out the approximate bearing of the next target. The indicator was less used when the later cupola was fitted because the commander then had to be in a 'head down' position in order to use his episcopes, so could see the azimuth indicator himself.

The 7.5 cm Kwk 42 L/70 gun was a formidable weapon, 5.85 m (19 ft 2¼ in) long with muzzle brake. It could penetrate 90 mm of armour plate at 457 m (500 yd) or 80 mm at 915 m (1,000 yd) (both at 60°). It could knock out a T-34 headon at 800 m (875 yd), or a Sherman at 1,000 m (1,090 yd), while for side and rear engagements the official range was 2,800 m (3,060 yd). As we have already seen, however, it could knock out enemy tanks at much greater ranges if the strike was in the right place. Types of ammunition fired were:

Type	Muzzle velocity
AP 40 (Pzgr Patr 40)	1,120 m/s (3,675 fps)
APCBC (Pzgr Patr 39)	935 m/s (3,068 fps)
HE (Sprgr Patr 42)	700 m/s (2,297 fps)
Hollow charge (Pzgr Patr 38)	N/A

A ball mounting for the bow MG replaced the 'letter box' flap of the earlier models on the Ausf A, which was the next model after the Ausf D (Horst Riebenstahl).

Good action shot of the rear of an Ausf A with crew, one of whom is busy fixing an MG 34 on to the AA (*Fliegerbeschussgerät*) mounting, which was fitted on to many PzKpfw IIIs, IVs, Panthers and Tigers from late 1943 onwards (Horst Riebenstahl).

Seventy-nine main armament rounds were carried on Ausf A and D (increased to 82 for Ausf G), stowed in racks and lockers within the lower half of the fighting compartment; 4,200 rounds of MG ammunition were carried in bags.

On the Ausf D there was a bank of three smoke grenade dischargers on either side of the turret, but later the close defence grenade launcher (*Nahverteidigungswaffe*) was fitted into the turret roof, with its 92 mm calibre short barrel angled at about 60°. It had all-round traverse, was hand-operated and fired by a simple cocking ring. It could be used for local smoke or to fire an HE grenade against tank hunters.

The loader had no outside view until Ausf A and in the event of a 'bale-out' had to use the large circular replenishment port in the rear face of the turret as an escape hatch. The pistol ports in the rear and sides were done away with on the Ausf G, and there was an electric ventilation fan on the right of the turret roof. There were three locks for the turret and main armament — a turret lock on the right of the turret race, an elevation lock on the gun and a barrel clamp, the latter being hinged and located on the front superstructure roof of the tank, the barrel being locked at 0° by means of a chain and clamping nut.

Engine compartment The V 12 Maybach HL 230 P30 engine occupied the rear compartment. It produced 700 bhp at 3,000 rpm. Access was via a large inspection hatch located in the centre of the rear decking. It was a water-cooled engine, with two radiators (one on each side of the engine compartment), linked by a compensating tank. Twin fans drew air through them, the hot air being expelled via grilles in the engine decking. Some heat could be directed into the turret via an air duct in order to assist the crew with the thankless task of keeping warm in the bitter Russian winter. It was also a difficult engine to keep cool, especially in the summer, because of its size and its tight confinement in the engine compartment. There was a fire extinguisher system fitted which came into action when the engine temperature rose over 120°C (normal running temperature was 80°C). Special extinguisher liquid was then sprayed automatically from six nozzles on to the fuel pump and carburettors, while a warning light appeared on the driver's instrument panel, so that he could let the engine cool off. Fuel (727L/160 gals of petrol) was

carried in a total of five fuel tanks, two each side of the engine compartment and one at the rear. Fuel consumption varied from 0.25 kpl (0.7 mpg) on roads to under 0.14 kpl (0.4 mpg) on cross country. The Panther had a top speed of about 46 km/h (25.5 mph) and a range of 200 km (125 miles).

Initially there had been a requirement for Panther to be able to ford in water up to 1.9 m (6.24 ft) deep and to be able to travel fully submerged in depths up to 4 m (13 ft). However, although the fording depth for all models was only 1.7 m (5.6 ft), the full 1.9 m was achieved for both the recovery and command versions (see later). Full waterproofing was never properly developed.

Protection The Ausf D was of all-welded construction, and apart from the cast mantlet and cupola, all the armour was homogeneous rolled plate of good machineable quality. An early report from Russia gave a Brinell hardness figure of 262 for the front glacis.

Thickness of the armour was: turret front — 100 mm (110 mm on Ausf A and G); sides and rear — 45 mm; top — 16 mm; Hull upper — 80 mm; lower — 60 mm; sides and rear — 40 mm; top — 16–30 mm; and mantlet — 100 mm. Thin skirting plates, 5 mm thick, extended down to about 76 cm (30 in) above the ground on either side of the suspension.

The British carried out comprehensive firing trials against an Ausf G in late 1944 and came to the following conclusions:

It was immune to small-arms fire from

ground level, but SAA fire directed downwards at 30° into the inlet louvres of the engine compartment caused severe damage to the radiators. Even greater damage might result from 20 mm attack from the air or airburst HE.

Projectiles (both AP and HE) of 6 pdrs and larger guns which struck below the horizontal centre line of the gun mantlet were likely to penetrate, blow the roof off the driving compartment or jam the turret.

Side penetrations were likely to cause ammunition or petrol fires.

The rolled armour proved brittle and flakey, while the brittle nature of the roof plates made them vulnerable to HE grenades or close airbursts.

The use of interlocked joints provided major stability even when the main welds were fractured.

Frontal attack with a PIAT[49] was useless, but side attacks were effective.

Mines with 4–15 lb (1.8–6.8 kg) of explosive charge were only likely to break the track if detonated at the centre of its width, while detonations under the tracks were unlikely to affect the floor plates or their side joints.

The report ended by saying: 'The design of the vehicle is such that its structural stability is considerable, the effective use of interlocking joints being chiefly responsible. The Panther tank, judged on the results of these trials done, remains a most formidable weapon with few weaknesses, and its value if used with adequate flank protection should not be underrated.'[50]

User comments

Both the Panther and the Tiger earned a formidable reputation, so it was not unnatural for the 'powers that be' to try to play down their superiority over Allied tanks. The following comments on Panther, which were purported to have been extracted from German official documents, were circulated in June 1944 by MI 10 under the heading 'Panthers and Tigers (a German view)'.

'A lot has been written in recent months in praise of these two heavyweight German beasts. The following extracts from German official documents throw another light on the subject, and may excite interest, if not encouragement: —

'PANTHER

'a. It is particularly important to ensure flank protection for the "sensitive" sides of the Panther tanks. The Pz Regt commander must always keep a reserve of tanks up his sleeve, which he can use at a moment's notice to block any threat from the flank... This reserve should normally be about 1,100 yards [1,000 m] in the rear. It has been found advisable to let the available Mark IV tanks in the Pz Regt take over the task of protection from the flanks, while the Panthers quickly press on and drive a wedge into the enemy position...

'b. In spite of the improved engine performance the Bn of Panthers averaged 450 miles [720 km] per tank with only 11 engines having to be changed. Panthers should not be driven over stretches greater than 62

miles [100 km], as this causes much harm to the suspension, particularly in winter.

'c. Tracks and track adjustment: the Panther track is correctly adjusted when the track just touches the second bogie wheel from the front, ie, when further tensioning would lift it off this bogie wheel. Consequently, when the final stage of the track tensioning process becomes a heavy job, negligent drivers often allow the track to remain too loose. Adjusting collars and retaining pins easily fall off, so it is essential that the driver should inspect the tracks frequently.

'd. The third gear of the Panther gearbox is the one most often in use. When changing gear it should therefore be nurtured carefully. In five out of seven cases the gear-box had to be changed because third gear could no longer be engaged. As the cog-wheels of the third gear are always in constant mesh, it is impossible to engage a higher gear.

'When travelling in second gear, and it is desired to change up to third gear, the vehicle should be accelerated so that during the process of changing gear, (particularly over bad ground or steep incline) it does not come to a halt. If insufficient time for changing gear has been allowed, ie, if the tank does slow up, the driver should not make the mistake of trying to make up this time shortage by changing gear quickly. Changing gear too quickly overstrains both the teeth on the cogs and the synchromesh apparatus and incidentally overloads the main drive. When the going is heavy or when a steep hill has to be negotiated, it is therefore preferable to remain in third gear.

Good views of the last Panther model, the Ausf G, which had the driver's vision port removed from the front glacis plate in order to strengthen it.

'e. The track of a Panther or Tiger sometimes slips or becomes disengaged from the teeth of the driving sprocket and jams, owing to the assemblage of undesirable matter. The consequent tensioning of the track is so great that it is generally not possible to free the track by knocking out a track pin. The German report adds that a certain Tiger Bn solved this problem when the overtensioned track was cut by exploding hand grenades under it, but adds that the practice should not be resorted to unless the tank would otherwise have to be written off.'[51]

Further development

Panther II German tank designers were never allowed to rest on their laurels for very long and it was early in April 1943, soon after Panther production started, that the *Heereswaffenamt* commissioned MAN and Henschel to work jointly on a new project to produce improved designs of both the Panther and the Tiger. They were told to try to achieve as much standardisation as possible between the two tanks, so as to make production, training, maintenance and repair that much simpler. The two designs were desig-

nated Panther II and Tiger II. The latter, as we shall see later, successfully entered service, but Panther II never got further than the building of a few prototypes. The new tank was to weigh about 50 tons, have considerably thicker armour, but still be capable of the same performance as Panther I. The running gear chosen was as for the Tiger II, but with only seven wheel stations and single torsion bars on each side. Two prototype hulls were produced and one was equipped, for trail purposes, with an Ausf G turret. This model was captured by the US Army and shipped to the USA. It is still in existence and still in running order at the Patton Museum of Armor, Fort Knox, Kentucky, and gets an airing on most public Open Days. The Panther II design study was overtaken by a new project, the E 50, which was intended to replace both Panther I and II. However, this did not even get off the drawing board before the war ended.

Panther Ausf F In 1945, Daimler-Benz produced about eight prototype hulls of the series successor to the Ausf G, which was designated Ausf F.[52] It had the same steel-rimmed running gear as fitted to Tiger II, but with eight sets of interleaved roadwheels, set as for previous Panthers. Other hull differences included a modification to the ball mount to enable the hull gunner/radio operator to fire the new MP/StG 44 assault rifle,[53] in place of an MG. The major change, however, was in the turret. Known as *Schmalturm* (small turret), the new turret was developed to be used for the Panther II/Tiger II programme and was to be capable of mounting either the new 7.5 cm KwK 44/1 gun or the 8.8 cm gun of the Tiger. It had many new features including thicker and better sloped armour, but because the new front plate and mantlet were lighter, there was no increase in the overall weight (still 7.5 long tons). The new thicknesses were: front of turret — 120 mm; sides and rear — 60 mm; and roof — 30 mm.

The small turret had a much lighter, conical gun mantlet, similar in shape to the *Saukopf* (pig's head) mantlet of the Tiger II, and improved elevating and traversing gear, to allow full all-round rotation in under 30 seconds, plus gun stabilisation. It had a new commander's cupola with seven episcopes (of Tiger), an IR telescope and searchlight

assembly, a new rear gun port for an MP/StG 44, and a close support weapon port on the rear right side of the roof. There was a transversely-mounted coincidence rangefinder and a permanent extra aerial base and fittings, so that the tank could be rapidly changed into a command model in the field. Finally, a co-axial MG 42 was substituted for the MG 34.

Three of these new turrets were produced[54] and one each was shipped to the USA and UK after the war, complete with its new KwK 44/1 gun. After investigation, the UK *Schmalturm* was sadly discarded and for many years has lain on the RA ranges at Larkhill, where it has been used as a target.

IR equipment On 31 July 1945, 21 Army Group, Tech Int, produced a report on German infrared equipment as fitted to the Panther. It was based on the examination of four Ausf Gs which had been equipped with IR, plus one captured crew member. The report explains how the four tanks had been at Fallingbostel with the **Panzer Jäger**

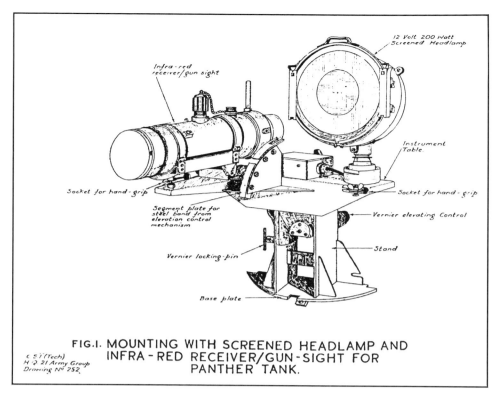

FIG.I. MOUNTING WITH SCREENED HEADLAMP AND INFRA-RED RECEIVER/GUN-SIGHT FOR PANTHER TANK.

Mounting with screened headlamp and infra-red receiver/gun-sight for the Panther tank. GSI (Tech), HQ 21 Army Group, Drawing No 252.

Lehr und Versuchs Kompanie. However, they had not been withdrawn northwards with the soft-skinned vehicles on the formation of *Kampfgruppe Uhu*, but were committed in a daylight role to the battle east of Minden. Three were subsequently burnt out and the fourth badly damaged. Their IR equipment comprised a screened car-type headlamp with 12 v 200 w transmitter lamp; an IR receiver gunsight for use with the main armament; a gun elevation control device; a power source (12 v batteries), vibrator unit and a transformer. The codename for the equipment was 'Puma', according to the crew member interrogated; however, another PW called it 'Sperba' (sparrowhawk). The equipment (see drawing) had to be lined up and checked against a source of light at 600 m (650 yd) before going into action. The tank commander alone could traverse, elevate or depress both the screened headlight and the receiver, by means of special hand grips. The tank commander only could see where he was going or spot a target, for the rest of the crew worked 'blind' on his orders over the intercom.

Variants

Panzerbefehlswagen Panther and Panzerbeobachtungswagen Panther As with the PzKpfw III and IV, there were both command and artillery observation post versions of the Panther. The former retained its main armament, so its correct title was: Panzerbefehlswagen mit 7.5 cm KwK 42 L/70 Panther. Although this reduced working space, it did make it more difficult to pick out from other Panthers in action, the only external difference being the extra antennae on the turret roof and rear of the engine decking. Space for an extra radio was found by reducing the number of main armament rounds to 64. There were two radio fits, either an Fu 5 with an Fu 8 (the main divisional link set), or an Fu 5 with an Fu 7 (ground-to-air set). The loader acted as operator for the second set, which was fitted close to him on the turret wall. Over 300 Panthers were converted to the command role.

The OP conversion was more drastic, as the main armament had to be completely removed. A dummy gun was fitted outside, together with an MG 34 in a ball mounting. The MG could traverse 5° left and right and elevate from −10° to +15°. Optical instruments on the PzBeobWg Panther included a 1.25 m (4 ft) base rangefinder, a turret observation periscope TBF 2 (*Turmbeobach-tungsfernrohr*), a commander's periscope TBF 2 and a 'Scissors' periscope. The Zeiss rangefinder was located at the front of the turret with vision slots on either side of the turret front plate. These slots had hinged cover plates which could be closed from within the tank. The turret observation periscope was mounted in the centre of the turret in a ball mounting in the roof plate, and could be traversed through 360°. The commander's periscope or the scissors telescope was mounted in an adjustable bracket in front of the commander's cupola. An elaborate automatic plotting board (*Blockstelle*) was located just in front of the commander's cupola and was used to give initial range and line to the pivot gun, then to give corrections based on the observation of fall of shot. The PzBeobWg Panther was considered by many to be the best artillery OP tank produced during the war by either side, but only some 40 Panthers were actually converted to this role.

Bergepanther It was increasingly apparent that the normal 18 tonne (17.7 UK/19.85 US tons) half-track recovery tractor just could not cope with the Panther heavy medium tank, let alone the even heavier Tiger. Stories of having to use half-tracks in pairs or even threes to deal with these heavyweights abound, while on many other occasions damaged tanks had to be abandoned because nothing was powerful enough to recover them. Only a small number of Tigers were ever converted to the armoured recovery role, but nearly 350 *Bergepanthers* were produced. The first dozen were created by simply using turretless chassis from the MAN factory's normal Panther production line. Thereafter, however, first Henschel then DEMAG took on their manufacture. The original batch had used Ausf D chassis, the rest were a mixture of Ausf A and then Ausf G. A square box-like wooden structure took the place of the turret and armament, the vacant space in the hull being filled by a winch which had a 40 tonne (39.4 UK/44.1 US tons) direct pull capability (which could be doubled using the appropriate gear). There was also a large spade, hinged to the bottom of the hull which was used as a ground anchor, plus a simple folding derrick with a 1.5 tonne (3,300 lb) capacity for lifting heavy equipment on and off the top deck. *Bergepanther* weighed 42.7 tonnes (42 UK/47 US tons), had a crew of four or five, although it could be operated by two men, and a top speed of 34 km/h (21 mph).

A British report on the ARV remarked that it was a very useful and serviceable armoured recovery vehicle and that the simplicity of the equipment stowed on the vehicle was most noteworthy (ie, the absence of the usual collection of heavy jibs, booms, welding plant, etc, which festooned most ARVs). During the testing of the *Bergepanther* it was used to recover a Churchill ARV which 'had been placed in a deep ditch with its nose against a 1.8 m (6 ft) high bank. The report reads: 'The Panther ARV winch cable was shackled to the nose of the Churchill via two Churchill tow ropes, in one of which was the FVPE dynamometer. The winch rope was paid out and the Panther anchor dug itself into the ground. A direct pull without any snatch blocks gave a maximum corrected reading of 46 to 50 tons in the winch rope while pulling the Churchill ARV up and over the bank. This was accomplished satisfactorily, the Panther engine revolutions dropping at one point to 700.'[55]

Jagdpanther Probably the most important variant of the Panther was the *Jagdpanther*, one of the best tank destroyers built by any nation during the war. As we have already seen, there was a wide variety of self-propelled guns, both assault guns and TDs built by the Germans, most of which were adaptations designed to make use of obsolescent tank chassis. However, by late

PzBeobWg **Panther with dummy gun.**

JAGDPANTHER (SDKFZ 173)		
Date of origin 1944		
Weight (tonnes) 46		
Overall dimensions (m)	**Length**	9.9
	Height	2.72
	Width	3.42
Armament/Ammunition carried		
Main 1 × 8.8 cm PaK 43/3 L/71		
57 rounds		
Secondary 1 × 7.92 mm MG 34		
Armour thickness (mm)	**Max.**	100
	Min.	16
Engine **Type** Maybach HL 230 P30		
bhp/rpm 700/3,000		
Crew 5		
Max. speed (km/h) 46		
Range (km) 200		
Remarks One of the best tank destroyers built during World War 2		

1942, it was clear that a better solution had to be found to meet the growing need for a fast, well-armed TD that would be able to knock out the heaviest enemy tank. The obvious choice of weapon was the formidable 8.8 cm FlaK gun, already used in the ground role to devastating effect as an anti-tank gun. However, the chassis of all tanks up to and

The *Schmalturm* (small turret) that was to be fitted to the Panther Ausf F, seen here at Bovington Camp on investigation before being used as a target on the Larkhill ranges.

including the PzKpfw IV was just not strong enough. It was decided therefore to use the new Panther chassis and Maschinenfabrik Neidersachsen-Hannover (MNH) were ordered to develop the new TD. The first prototype was shown to Hitler on 20 October 1943, during a demonstration in Arys[56]

and, with his approval, the new vehicle was put into full production in January 1944, at the Brunswick factory of MIAG (Muhlenbau und Industrie AG), who were joined at the end of the year by MNH. Both factories continued to produce *Jagdpanthers* until March 1945, by which time a total of 382 had been built.

The chassis used for the *Jagdpanther* was the standard Ausf A, with the ball mounted MG in the glacis. The top of the glacis and sides of the superstructure were extended all round to form a roomy, flat-topped fighting

Work in progress on a Panther at the workshops company of Panzer Regiment 31, 5th Panzer Division, in Russia (Rudolf Wulff).

compartment in which was mounted the 8.8 cm PaK 43/3 L/71 gun. The main armour plate was well sloped and varied in thickness from 80 mm on the front, 50 mm on the sides and 40 mm at the rear to 25 mm on the top. The *Saukopf* gun mantlet was 100 mm thick. The gun was mounted well back in the fighting compartment, giving complete access to all the controls and recoil gear. Elevation limits were −8° to +14°, while the full extent of traverse was only 11°, so the TD had to track in order to engage most targets. Overall length including the gun was 9.85 m (32 ft 4 in), while the combat weight, complete with five-man crew and 60 rounds of ammunition, was 46 tons. Top speed was just under 46 km/h (30 mph) and it had a range of 160 km (100 miles). Recommended engagement range was 2,469 m (2,700 yd).

Jagdpanther was well respected on the battlefield, British Technical Intelligence reports containing such comments as 'The 8.8 cm high velocity gun, comparatively thick, well sloped armour and more than average speed, make it a very formidable proposition as a tank destroyer, and it is believed that the Germans intend, as soon as Panther production is well enough advanced, to produce it and bring it into service on a considerable scale.'[57] Another report reads: 'The *Jagdpanther* was apparently designed as a mobile A tk gun for employment both in attack and defence. In the attack it is intended to follow closely upon the leading infantry, to destroy enemy armour counter-attacking or in hull-down positions. In the defence it is intended to be employed to strengthen the A tk defences, more especially those in forward positions. Its

thick armour permits its use in these forward areas, and its cross-country performance enables its manoeuverability to complement its firepower.'[58]

Jagdpanthers were organised as Army troops in heavy anti-tank battalions, which comprised three companies each of 14 vehicles, with three more in battalion HQ. Each company had three platoons of four, with the remaining two being at company HQ. According to the official German handbook, the *Jagdpanther* was designed as a *Schwerpunkt* weapon for the destruction of enemy tank attacks. Its employment as a complete battalion was considered to be the primary consideration towards achieving decisive success, while the employment of individual platoons was only permissible against fortified positions or in close country. It was not to be used either as a static anti-tank gun or as SP artillery except in dire emergency. Once they had completed their mission *Jagdpanthers* were to be withdrawn for 'repair and maintenance'.

Miscellaneous Various projects using the Panther chassis which never reached the production line included a *Minenraumpanzer* (mine exploding vehicle); two *Flakpanzers*, one mounting an 8.8 cm FlaK 41 gun in an open-topped fully-rotating turret, the other twin 3.7 cm FlaK 43 guns in a fully armoured turret, the latter version being known as *Coelian*; and a *Waffenträger*, (weapons carrier) with an open-topped hull. Also, various elderly Panthers were converted into munitions carriers by removing their turrets, while some old *Bergepanthers* had their winches and spades removed for use in the same role.

THE PANTHER IN DISGUISE

During the Ardennes breakthrough a small number of Panthers were camouflaged to represent the American M10 tank destroyer. The commander's cupola of the Panther was removed and in its place two semi-circular hinged hatch covers covered the opening. Sheet-metal was then used to mock up the distinctive shape of the open-topped M10 turret, the bow and along the sides as false skirting. In addition to their structural deception, US markings, even down to regimental and divisional signs, were painted on each tank, while all normal Panther external storage was removed. Crews were dressed in US Army uniforms.

The *Bergepanther* (armoured recovery vehicle) was created by using the chassis of a Panther from the normal production line and putting on the usual box-like wooden structure which the Germans favoured for their ARVs. Note also the spade anchor on the rear.

PANTHER TURRET PILLBOXES

Old Panther Ausf D turrets were put to another use in Italy at both the Hitler and Gothic lines, being used as static pillboxes. The following extract is taken from Mediterranean area AFV Technical Report: 'Panther turrets. These are not of course AFVs but their impact on the course of AFV affairs is thought to be sufficiently important to justify a few words. Panther turrets were first met in the Hitler line and were in fact the salient features round which the other defences were built up. They are actual tank turrets though perhaps of a slightly earlier vintage than those now on tanks. They are mounted on a turret ring fitted on an armoured box[59] built up of welded plate about 2½ inches [63 mm] in thickness. The whole of this box is sunk into the ground and earth is banked up close to the turret so that it is first cleared by the gun at depression and yet offers some additional protection to the

base of the turret skirt. Traverse is by hand only and no power is supplied. Access to the turret is either by the access doors in the turret itself or from underneath the armoured box by means of a steel ladder communicating with a deep dugout. It is obvious that the crews live in the turret and dugout permanently, as electric light is supplied and there are other signs of continuing operation.

'This system of static defence was backed up by SP equipment and ordering A/T guns. In front of each position there was a graveyard of Churchills and some Shermans; perhaps eight tanks to a gun and all within 200 yards [183 m] of it. This is, at present, the cost of reducing a Panther turret and it would seem to be an excellent investment for Hitler. Obviously these turrets are most formidable unless each one is dealt with by a carefully prepared and co-ordinated attack.

'The turrets are almost invisible till they fire and, when located, there is very little to shoot at and, unless the turret happens to be pointing elsewhere, it will not be penetrated either by the 75 mm or 6 pr guns. HE fire is obviously useless. In all cases where there was enough of the turret left to diagnose the method of destruction, penetration of the turret side had been effected. One Chruchill

crew who destroyed one with their 6 pr say that the turret blew up immediately it was hit. This was presumably due to the ammunition, since a large quantity is stored... If A/T defence is to consist of these turrets in the future it cannot but emphasise the need for a proportion of tanks to carry a really effective AP weapon, though it is not by any means accepted that attack by tanks is the best and correct method of dealing with them.'

Battle history

As we have seen Panthers were first used in action in Russia, in the battles around Kursk in July 1943. Thereafter they fought both in Italy and in North-West Europe as well as on the Eastern Front. Working as a team with the ever-reliable PzKpfw IV to guard their flanks, they formed a potent battle winning combination but there were, of course, never enough of them to go round. This is how Brigadier (later Major-General) Nigel Duncan, who was then commanding 30th Armoured Brigade in the famous British 79th Armoured Division, recorded his first view of Panther in his diary. 'I went to look at a Panther. A wonderful job, easily

teething troubles but once these had been overcome, it was much superior to the PzKpfw IV. The following are a few of the defects and their improvement: —

'1. The steering clutch had given trouble but this was due to the inexperience of the drivers.

'2. The inability on the part of the driver to engage third gear had been due to his lack of experience in synchronising engine speed with gearbox speed. This was no difficulty once the driver had got used to the tank.

'3. The final drive had given trouble but now had been improved.

'4. The faults in the pressure lubrication system had been due partly to the oil pump. This had been improved and an eighth main bearing fitted.

'5. There were no difficulties with the turret traverse.'[60]

Allied tank crews were of course delighted when they managed to knock out a Panther, as these two battle reports illustrate. The first is taken from a Mediterranean Area AFV Technical Report and reads: 'Our first Panther is claimed by the North Irish Horse of 25 Tank Bde who shot it through the side of the turret with a 6 pdr from a Churchill (other claimants have since appeared and someone is alleged to have found a 75 mm M61 round inside the turret, but so far NIH claim is the most likely). This particular machine was unlucky as it had got itself ditched while entering a sunken road. In this unfavourable position it seems to have had mechanical trouble, for the crew were seen with the engine hatches open performing some operation inside. When the turret was holed the crew made off, although one was killed. In consequence, the demolition charges were not laid and the tank is almost a perfect specimen, save for the binocular sighting telescope which disappeared in the prompt fashion of all optical instruments on the battlefield. When the battle had moved on somewhat, 25 Tank Bde Workshops were easily able to recover it with a Churchill ARV and took it to their leaguer, where AFV(T) were able to spend part of two days in examination. It was thereafter required for a demonstration to 8 Army Commander after which it was evacuated to 16 Base Workshops, Naples, who prepared it for shipment. This tank is now on the high seas, and will soon, we hope, be in England.

'The Panther struck us as a fine tank

accessible with a good gunner's position, room for the driver and an excellent look-out for the commander. All hatches are spring-loaded and the whole affair bears the imprint of a sound job. WT set forward with the hull gunner, hydraulic steering, easily adjustable valves and excellent optical instruments as one would expect.' These brief comments

are amplified by a POW report which was headed 'Panther — some teething troubles and their remedies', and went on to debunk some of the critisms which had been made about the tank in its early days. It read: 'PW denied the statement that the Panther, from the point of view of its engine, was a poor tank. He said that like all tanks it had had

which, in the desert, would have caused us a lot of trouble. Obviously, however, it depends for its success on being able to present its heavily armoured front to its opponents on all occasions. The sides of the hull and turret are so thin that they are very vulnerable to any of our existing A/T guns. Whether in the close fighting to be expected in Europe, it remains to be seen if it will always be possible for Panther to avoid being taken in the flank but GS opinion on this subject is that we have not really met him in a fair fight so far and must prepare for serious trouble. The Panthers were not committed until the general situation had deteriorated badly and, as is now known, many of those now in our hands were destroyed by their own crews through shortage of petrol. The actual cases of Panthers knocked out by our tanks are few.'

Alfred Johnson was a Corporal in B Squadron of the 4/7 Royal Dragoon Guards in Normandy in 1944, and writes: 'The Panther was undoubtedly the best tank of both sides engaged in the long Normandy struggle. It was more manoeuverable and faster than the Tiger. AP from its long 75 would penetrate a Sherman tank more easily than an infantryman could prod open a can of beans with a bayonet. Its frontal armour was too thick for us to have much hope with an AP shot from our 75 mm howitzers which lacked muzzle velocity. Even by August 1944, few tank troops had a Firefly [17 pdr Sherman]. The chances, therefore, of my troop knocking out a Panther were not very good, even after two months in Normandy. In the first place, we had to spot one before he got us, an unlikely occurrence when attacking in the bocage. Usually when we were supporting infantry the first sign of the opposition was seeing soldiers mown down by Spandau fire or one of our tanks going up in smoke. In the latter case, either the Sherman brewed up straight away or ground to a halt with some of the crew baling out.

'So it was on 1 August, when the Regiment was supporting 214 Infantry Brigade of 43 Wessex Division in an advance on Cahagnes, south of Caumont. During the night the objectives at Les Haies crossroads had been reached. This was part of the overall move to capture the Bois au Homme feature with Mont Pincon on its eastern end. German resistance therefore increased and the next ten days or so saw some of the most intensive action we had experienced. B Squadron took over the lead the next day, supporting 1st Worcesters. My troop was committed to crossing the crest of some rising ground in the middle of a fairly large field. L/Sgt Perry was the first over on the

left, followed by Lt Penrose, for whom I was loader/operator, in the centre. Sgt Collins with the third tank, on the right, was hit as he came on slightly to the rear, his driver being killed. Fortunately for the rest of us, L/Sgt Perry spotted the gun flash from a Panther 400 yards away to the left and concealed behind the usual huge hedgerow. He quickly brought his 75 mm to bear, knocking out the Panther with a lot of luck and a good shot into one side just under the gun turret. The crew baled out and escaped under cover... In the same area the next morning, while waiting for new orders, we had the rare sight of a war correspondent/photographer who was interested in the location of the knocked-out Panther. We pointed out the site and this "intrepid warrior" then drove off in his jeep, to pour a jerrycan of petrol over the wreck before taking graphic pictures for the mollification of the armchair critics back home who thought Monty was too slow.'

Normally the odds were far more in the Panther's favour, as this vivid account taken from the history of Panzer Regiment 35 explains. It tells how a certain Sergeant Christ and his crew shot up seven Russian tanks in one short action. The battle took place near Riga in September 1944 and reads: 'Hill 920 is now securely in our hands. Sgt Christ is commanding a Panther which is part of the attacking force and the rest of his crew are: Rehard — gunner, Mehling — loader, Gietle — driver and Faustman — radio operator.

'The tank has been playing up for some time, so Christ gets permission to drive into a layback position behind the hill and investigate the fault. Gietle discovers that there is an oil leak and that a steering brake is defective. The Panzer is no longer fit for operations, so must go back for repairs. Christ reports the problems then waits and waits. Russian fighters and bombers fly over and drop their bombs all around the tank, sensibly the crew stay inside their Panzer during the bombing. Suddenly they hear engine noises over on the right flank, beyond a belt of trees. Christ cannot see properly because the trees are blocking his view, but as the noise is far beyond the German positions, he reckons that they can only be Ivan. So he climbs out of his Panzer and goes on foot over to some supporting Panzergrenadiers. They tell him about some Russian T-43s[61] which they have seen in the forest opposite. Christ crawls through the undergrowth and can now see two T-43s, standing on the edge of the forest. He quickly fetches his gunner, Rehard, to show him the targets. Their faulty Panzer follows, carefully, manoeuvering into a good fire position.

Close-up of the front glacis of the *Jagdpanther*, showing the *Zimmerit* (anti-magnetic mine paste) coating on all surfaces and ball mounting for the MG 34.

They engage the first Russian and after the second shot see the crew baling out, but the tank does not catch fire. Next they engage the second T-43 which catches fire after the first round. During this action Christ observes the gunfire of two other Soviet tanks. They are firing, but fortunately not in his direction. Rehard traverses on to them and after a few shots another enemy tank is set on fire. The destruction of the fourth was later confirmed by a recce patrol. The Panther then return to its layback position, leaving Christ to continue observing through his field-glasses.

'Shortly afterwards he sees two new T-43s, close to where the two knocked-out tanks are lying, with their guns pointing in his direction. Now it is getting dicey as the Russians know where their enemy is located. Again he calls forward the "overdue for repair" Panzer. Very carefully Gietle drives into a firing position. Rehard aims and fires at one of the Russian tanks and that "smashing chap our gunner" hits him straight away with the first AP shell. The tank explodes with a tremendous bang, pieces flying through the air. That is number five.

'Now the very first T-43 which they engaged is trying to escape, its engine seems to be working still, but after another shot it also burns like a torch. With that our ammo comes to an end. Quickly two of the crew run off to scrounge more AP shells from other tanks. Christ cannot believe his eyes as yet another enemy tank starts to fire from a position next to his burning comrade over on

the right. Hopefully the rest of the crew will return soon with more ammo. Christ crosses his fingers and it helps! It does not take very long before the sixth enemy tank is burning. A further T-43 slips away because of our lack of ammo, but both men are soon on their way again and bring back two more shells. Another Russian tank is poking out its "inquiring nose". Number seven is burning after the very first shot. From now on the Russians shun this draughty corner and withdraw and our Panzergrenadiers can breathe a sigh of relief.

'As evening comes, Christ and his crew take their half-lame Panzer back to the workshop.'[62]

The Russian climate did nothing to help tank operations, the need for spare parts increasing considerably at low temperatures. The Germans had to cannibalise broken down or abandoned vehicles in order to get spare parts. The overall *Heereswaffenamt* policy of furnishing as many complete tanks as possible to the front was actually detrimental to the production of spare parts. It was by no means unusual for Panzer regiments to send their technical personnel on unauthorised trips back home to visit the factories in Germany in order to try to obtain spares through personal contact![63] Winter temperatures in Russia rendered self-starters useless. The Germans resorted to prewarming engines by building fires under them. In this way a few vehicles were started and then used for tow starting the rest. During alerts engines had to be kept running hour after hour despite severe fuel shortages.

It was no easier in the muddy season when the ice and snow melted. German losses of tanks and motorised equipment of all types were still extremely high, particularly in 1941, the first time they encountered the Russian mud. It remained a constant problem. For example, in February 1944 when two German Corps were surrounded at Cherkassy, an attempt by strong armoured forces to crack the Russian ring from the outside bogged down within sight of the encircled Corps, although the relief force did

View of Parther turret as used in both the Hitler and Gothic lines in Italy'.

manage to get close enough to its objective to make contact with some troops who had fought their way out on foot.

In another action, in March 1944, 6,000 German troops, cut off in the city of Tarnopol, were lost because a tank force of 35 Tigers and 100 Panthers attempting a relief thrust were prevented from reaching the beleaguered city by mud. The tank force had been able to cross the River Strypa and to knock out strong anti-tank defences, but had only covered half of the 12 miles to Tarnopol when mud forced them to give up. Thousands of hours of labour were subsequently needed in order to restore roads and small bridges sufficiently, so as to be able to recover the stranded tanks.

Many Panzertruppe were awarded medals for gallantry, a considerable number gaining the coveted Knights Cross,[64] so to complete this section on the Panther in battle, here is the account of an action which involved two such men, Oberleutnant (later Oberstleutnant) Gerhard Fischer and Oberfeldwebel Herbert Elsner, both of 23rd Panzer Division. I am extremely grateful to both of them for allowing me to publish their reminiscences. The action took place in the area of Kriwoi Rog (see map) in the late autumn of 1943. The Russians had made a series of determined attacks to reach the important industrial area around the town, but had been pushed back some 15 km (9–10 miles) to the north. After many attacks had been beaten off, the Russians launched yet another on 14 November 1943, with a motor rifle division supported by 80 tanks and heavy artillery. The attack was directed against 23rd Panzer Division with the aim of breaking through to Kriwoi Rog. The main attack was against the Sturm (assault) battalion of the 6th Army, who had only 300 men to guard a 6 km (4 mile) section of front each side of Nowo Iwanowka. Two regiments of infantry with 40 tanks in support finally overran the German positions and captured Nowo Iwanowka, the high ground at Point 138 and the area to the south and south-west. Panzer Battalion 506 was at Glijewatka under command of Major Fechner. He ordered Oberleutnant Fischer to position himself with his 11 Panthers on the high ground at Point 140.7. Having reached this high ground Fischer saw that the enemy were attacking on a wide front. He could also see the danger which these attacks presented to 128 Panzergrenadier Regiment who were positioned on the west flank, beside the stream (Ingulez) and south of Nedaiwoda, as the enemy tried to get around the western flank. He immediately gave the order to attack, even though some of his Panthers had broken down and were temporarily out of

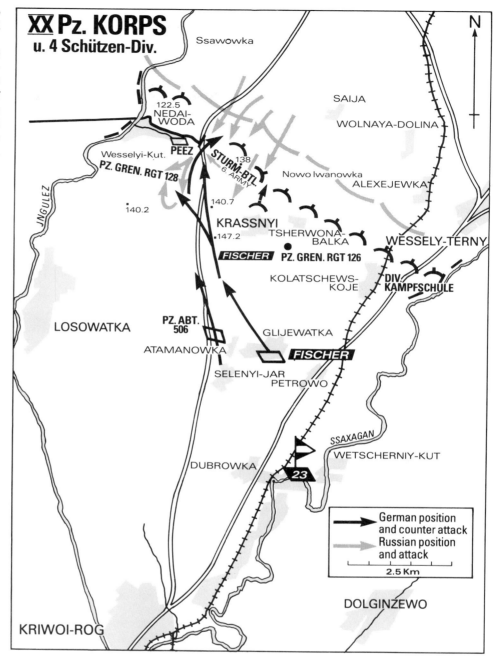

action. Fischer and his small force pushed the enemy back, knocking out at least two T-34s and causing heavy casualties to their infantry. He also picked up survivors of the *Sturm* battalion and with them he continued to attack.

In the meantime, some Tiger tanks from Panzer Battalion 506 arrived on the scene. Fischer briefed them on the battle and then guided them into an excellent position from where they knocked out 20 T-34s. By then the enemy attack was weakening and the combined force of Panthers and Tigers, with artillery support, was able to push the Russians further back and regain all the lost ground.

Oberleutnant (Lieutenant) Fischer now takes up the story: 'I had just arrived back at our rear area in Tross for some rest after the last battle and finished putting my bedding in my bunk, when a radio message came over: "Oblt Fischer come straight to Btn HQ and take over the Panther group". The journey there was very difficult and I had to drive my battered *Schwimmwagen*[65] against columns of the withdrawing troops. In Kriwoi Rog it was so bad that I had to use every bit of my authority to get past the Military Police. When I finally reached our headquarters it was very late, but my old tank crew were very pleased to see me. They told me straight away that there was a lot of

again I gave orders to my commanders to prepare to move out. I realised that the Russians had broken through our thinly held positions and were now behind our Panzergrenadier Regiment 128. We had to act quickly to re-establish contact with them before they were wiped out.

'With four tanks left and the rest right of the track, we moved off in the direction of Nedaiwoda. I ordered the tanks on the far right to make for Point 122.5 and Point 138. Soon after we had reached the high ground around Point 140.7 we were attacked by heavy anti-tank fire. Elsner was with the group on the left of the track and I ordered him to start attacking the Russian infantry, while I moved on in a northerly direction with the rest of the tanks. We moved from the high ground into a ravine in order to get to a good position from which to attack the anti-tank guns, but as we entered the ravine, we suddenly noticed enemy tanks not more than 800 to 1,000 metres in front of us. They were firing at Elsner's section as he moved forward. So the situation was clear, there were Russian T-34 tanks which during the night had positioned themselves in the ravine together with a battalion of infantry, and had cut off Pz Gren Regt 128.

'I radioed our situation back to HQ and then spoke to the rest of my tanks: "Fischer to all stations, attack the enemy tanks now!" The situation was at that moment very critical. We were under fire from all the enemy anti-tank and tank guns and could not stay in one position for very long. However, we rapidly knocked out some of the enemy and that gave my men a terrific morale boost. Then, while we were heavily engaged in the battle, five Tiger tanks came rolling towards us from Point 140.7. I put them straight into action.

'Suddenly my driver shouted "Eleven o'clock anti-tank gun" and without waiting for an order, turned our tank in the direction of the enemy gun. I was just going to tell him off when we were hit, but luckily it was only an HE shell. In the meantime, Elsner's tanks had been heavily engaged. On his own tank the turret had been hit and one of his tracks broken, but he kept on firing. After half an hour of fierce combat all the enemy tanks had been destroyed. We had forced the Russians back with heavy losses and regained out original positions. However, between Nedaiwoda and Point 138, there was still a 2 km gap and I was ordered

enemy activity all along the front. At 02:00 hours I was called to an "O" Group and Major Fechner gave me his orders. He told me in a few short sentences what the situation was on the divisional front. The tank crews who had just come in had bombed up, refuelled and eaten. He would have liked to have allowed them a few hours sleep, but the latest messages from the Panzergrenadiers made it necessary for all the tanks to move up to help them. In pitch darkness my 11 tanks and myself started moving in a northerly direction. We used the track which went northwards to Nedaiwoda to get to our forming up point. The weather was lousy,

raining and cold. All the tank crews were shivering and had no possibility of keeping dry.

'It was still dark when we arrived in the area of Point 140.7 and I was hoping that my commanders and I would have a chance to recce the area in daylight, so that we could select good fire positions in case of an attack. But it was not to be. I put three tanks into a layback position as mobile reserve and then sent Oberfeldwebel [Sergeant-Major] Elsner forward to observe. A few minutes later he radioed back to me: "The area in front of me is crawling with Russians and they are bringing up their artillery". Looking at my map

to secure it with my tanks. It was difficult and thankless task. The crews were all-but exhausted after the battle and had to be positioned far apart in order to cover the whole area. We could not replenish in the daylight, as the Russians were still firing at us, so our tank crews had to wait until the night for fresh supplies. Having been in over 100 battles, I well knew what hardship meant, but to secure over 2 km of front line with only a handful of tanks, by night, is an extremely difficult job. But we still had to do it.

'About midnight some soldiers from the assault pioneer battalion were sent to help me, so I was able to fill in some of the gaps. The tanks were occupied just by the commander, driver and gunner, while the other two crewmen were outside acting as infantry. We had to stay in these positions for a number of nights, and every night without fail the Russians would attack, try to get to our vehicles, and throw Molotov cocktails at them from short range. However, we stopped them with hand grenades, machine-guns and our pistols. By day the snipers gave us problems as we did not know where they were firing from for quite some time. Then we realised they were hiding in knocked-out enemy tanks, so we had to keep firing at these wrecks again and again. For many days they kept attacking, but each time we pushed them back with heavy losses. The only person we saw from the outside world was Lt Mengel who brought up our supplies and ammunition. I am sorry there isn't room to mention all the names of the men in the tank crews who fought in this battle north of

Kriwoi Rog, but they all gave of their best and I would like to thank each and every one of them.'

Herbert Elsner now takes up the story, to tell what happened when his tank was hit: 'We had been hit on our right side and the track had come off. In this critical situation the Russians naturally tried to finish us off with Molotov cocktails from close range. It was as though I could smell the danger in the air. At that moment I looked out of the turret directly into the eyes of a Russian. Quickly I got my gun from the turret and shot him down. We were hit a few more times, but fortunately there was no great damage. We destroyed two anti-tank guns — they were 12.2 cm guns[66] which we hadn't seen before.

'It was impossible to get out to repair the track, so our driver Hilmar Lang had a bright idea. He would try to manoeuvre out with only one track. He managed to get rid of the pieces of broken track first, by going backwards and forwards, accelerating and braking. Then he tried to reverse out of this dangerous situation. We managed somehow to get back as far as the ravine, then had to wait for hours until darkness so we could be towed away. During that night and the following day while the track was being repaired, the situation got really dangerous, and enemy tanks broke through and started firing at us. As soon as the repairs were complete we jumped back into the tank and made ready to leave. Just as I put the microphone around my neck and was about to give the order "Driver start up" an HE shell exploded on the tail plate and blew off all the camouflage, some of the stowage items

Oberfeldwebel Herbert Elsner, also a Knights Cross winner, enjoys a cigar on top of his Panther Ausf D. He wears a silver tank battle badge below his Iron Cross 1st Class (Herbert Elsner).

and two of the crew who had been sitting on the back decks — they were thrown high into the air. Both men picked themselves up off the ground and found that they had not been injured, just scared stiff! They climbed back into the tank and we started off. At the next road intersection we met up with two T-34s and set them on fire at close range, then rejoined our unit. Later the tank had to go back for more repairs to its rear.'

9
Pz Kpfw VI and variants

Background development

Although, as has already been explained, the 'new construction vehicle' (*Neubaufahrzeuge* or *NbFz*) which first made its appearance in 1933–34, was sometimes referred to as the PanzerKampfwagen VI, this was probably only done for propaganda purposes, and work did not really begin on the development of the true PzKpfw VI until 1937. Henschel und Sohn of Kassel were ordered to design and build a tank in the 30- to 33-ton range, to be known as DW1, the 'breakthrough tank' (*Durchbruchswagen*).[67] It was to have the role of close infantry support as its main task and would be armed with the same 7.5 cm howitzer as mounted on the PzKpfw IV. One chassis was built and trials commenced, only to be halted in 1938, when Henschel were told to switch their design team on to a much heavier 65-ton tank instead. Two prototypes of the VK 6501 were built, but once again, while they were

on trial, the project was halted and the firm told to go back to the development of the DW1. By 1940, Henschel had produced an improved design which was known as the DW2. It weighed 32 tons, had a crew of five, a five-wheel torsion bar suspension and was armed with the 7.5 cm L/24 howitzer, plus two MGs. Trials took place the following year, then the Army Weapons Branch altered the basic requirements by saying that the new tank was to be armed with the long-barrelled L/48 gun. At the same time they brought three other firms into the project, inviting Porsche, MAN and Daimler-Benz to tender as well as Henschel. The new tank was known as the VK 3001, and it would have a similar superstructure to the PzKpfw IV, but with a new suspension comprising seven interleaved bogie wheels and three return rollers. Henschel built four prototypes VK 3001(H), two in March 1941 and two in October 1941. By then, however, the T-34 had made its dramatic first appearance

on the battlefield and the VK 3001(H) project was scrapped, although two of the chassis were later converted to SP guns, by fitting them with a 12.8 cm gun. They saw service in Russia the following year. The Porsche version, the VK 3001(P), which was also known as the Leopard, incorporated a number of new features, including petrol-electric drive and longitudinal torsion bar suspension. MAN and Daimler-Benz also produced prototypes, but they like all the others became obsolete.

At the same time as ordering the work to start on the VK 3001 design, the *Heereswaffenamt* had placed an order for the design of a 36-ton tank, the VK 3601, the specifications coming from the Führer himself, which included a high velocity gun, thick armour and a top speed of 40 km/h (25 mph). Henschel built a prototype in March 1942, but before it had appeared, work on both the VK 3001 and VK 3601 projects had virtually ceased, in order to concentrate upon another new tank, the VK 4501, which was designed to mount a tank version of the 8.8 cm FlaK 36 gun. Hitler certainly favoured the use of this gun, which had already proved itself as formidable in ground combat, as an anti-tank gun, as it had in its normal Ack-Ack role. The *Heereswaffenamt* preferred a lighter gun, so as to keep the tank's overall weight down. Krupp designed the turret for the 8.8 cm, while Rheinmetall developed a lighter one (7.5 cm KwK L/70), but the latter never reached production. The order for the new tank had been first placed in May 1941 and had included the pronouncement that work was to be completed in time for a trial demonstration of prototypes on Hitler's birthday on 20 April 1942. In view of the limited time available, Henschel decided to incorporate all the best features of the VK 3001(H)

The VK 3001(H) was the original Henschel design for the improved *Durchbruchswagen* (Breakthrough tank) project, DW2. Note the seven interleaved road wheels. This trials vehicle has weights on it to simulate the missing turret.

Although the VK 3001 project was scrapped when the T-34 appeared, two of the four prototype chassis built were converted into self-propelled guns, by fitting a 12.8 cm gun. They later saw service in Russia.

and the VK 3601(H) designs into the new project, which was known as the VK 4501(H). Henschel planned two models, H1 to mount the 8.8 cm gun and H2 the 7.5 cm, so that they had covered both eventualities. Porsche had also been ordered to compete and took much the same short cuts, incorporating the best features of the VK 3001(P) design into their VK 4501(P), which was also known as Tiger (P).

After burning a great amount of midnight oil both companies were able to meet the required deadline and the demonstration trial took place as directed, at Rastenburg on Hitler's birthday. Dr Ferdinand Porsche was a personal friend of the Führer, so it must have been annoying for both of them to discover that the Henschel design, H1, was clearly the better of the two contestants, despite the fact that a production order for 90 Tiger (P) was already in full swing at Nibelungwerke of Linz, Austria, with first delivery scheduled for July 1942. As a result of this demonstration and further trials, the Henschel H1 design was chosen for production, to commence in July/August 1942, with some 285 to be built by May 1943. Thus began the production of the PzKpfw VI Tiger Ausf H, which over the next three years would also be called PzKpfw VI Tiger

Ausf E (from about August 1944 onwards), Tiger E or Tiger I. Whatever its official nomenclature, the mere mention of the word 'Tiger' was enough to cause a shiver down the backs of most Allied soldiers.

The Tiger (P) was destined never to be put in production as a tank, but some 85 of the chassis were later shipped to Alkett in Berlin-Spandau, where they were fitted with new superstructures, more armour and the long barrelled 8.8cm PaK 43/2 L/71 anti-tank gun, in a large fixed turret set back at the rear of the chassis. The original Porsche engines were replaced by two standard Maybach HL 120 TRM tank engines and a new heavy tank destroyer was born, the *Sturmgeschütz mit 8.8 cm PaK 43/2 (SdKfz 184)*. It initially was also called *Ferdinand*, presumably after its designer Dr Porsche, but later its name was changed to *Elefant*. At 65 tonnes (64 UK/71.7 US tons), with 200 mm of armour on its hull front, *Elefant* was a formidable TD, first to see action in Russia, at Kursk in May 1943, where its range and lethality soon earned it a considerable reputation.

First official British mention of the fact that the Germans might be designing a new heavy tank was contained in an AFV Technical Intelligence report, issued by MI 10, in February 1941. It described PzKpfw VI as being a 45 ton tank, with 75 mm thick armour, a 75 mm gun as main armament, with two further 2 cm guns and no less than four machine-guns. It was said to be 36 ft long, under 10 ft wide and over 6 ft high,

with a top speed of 25 mph and a crew of no less than 18 men — although it was commented that perhaps 13 was a more realistic number: clearly this was the product of a fertile imagination, some good German propaganda, and a mixture of facts gleaned from a study of such World War 1 monsters as the German A7V and of the abortive *Neubaufahrzeug* project. More accurate information was to follow, the first photographic proof of Tiger being a picture in the German press on 11 December 1942, which showed a Tiger of 501st (Heavy Tank Battalion) driving through the streets of Tunis.

Other firms were also asked to produce prototypes as well as Henschel, this being the Porsche offering, the VK 3001(P). It was also known as Leopard or Typ 100, and featured petrol-electric drive.

Following immediately on from the VK 3001 and VK 3601 projects came the heavier VK 4501. These two photographs show the Henschel version on trial. It was finally chosen in preference to the Porsche design for production, and some of the salient features of Tiger Ausf E can be clearly seen on this prototype VK 4501(H).

Production

Tiger I was in production for just two years (August 1942 until August 1944), during which time 1,354 were built. Henschel was the only producer, although several other firms did naturally produce many of the component parts. In view of Tiger's importance I deliberately chose Henschel and Sohn, Kassel, as the subject of one of the appendices to this book (Appendix A), which describes the factory in some detail. As will be seen from that report, there were just two months when production reached three figures, the maximum being 104 in April 1944. Tiger was an extremely robust and powerful heavy tank, more than was intended originally, as the production model actually weighed some 11 tons more than the prototype! Its sheer size, the thickness of its armour plate and its large, deadly gun made it a battle winner, but also made it costly in man-hours and very expensive to manufacture. Tiger took 300,000 man-hours to build and cost 800,000 Reichmarks per tank (£6,600/$26,600), so critics were not slow to point out that two Panthers could be built in the same number of man-hours as one Tiger, while three Messerschmitt Bf 109 fighters cost the equivalent of one Tiger.

In order to stand up to the enormous stresses which were set up when the large calibre gun was fired, plates of the largest possible size were used wherever possible. For example, the belly was a single plate, 4.88 m by 1.83 m (16 ft by 6 ft), while the sides and rear of the turret were also one plate, which was bent around in a horseshoe shape. Armour plates also had to be made to interlock, with special steps cut at the joints, so as to act as seats for the welds. The superstructure was welded on to the hull rather than being bolted on, while the hull was strengthened by means of a massive arched cross member which extended

through the driving compartment as well as by a robust engine bulkhead.

Tiger I was the first German tank to be fitted successfully with overlapping, interleaved roadwheels. These were initially constructed of dished steel discs with solid rubber tyres, but were later replaced in the last half of the production run by rubber-cushioned discs with steel tyres. This type both saved rubber and improved wheel life, but was very noisy. Each suspension axle carried three wheels and their movement was controlled by torsion bar springing. The overlapping wheels spread the heavy weight to advantage, giving a good, reasonably comfortable ride, but did bring new problems. For example, they could quickly get packed with ice and snow, which then froze solid if not cleared away, rendering the tank immobile. There are reports that on the Eastern Front this became such a hazard as to encourage the Russians to postpone their attacks until dawn, so as to catch the Tigers with frozen suspensions, unable to move. Very wide tracks (725 mm or 28.5 in) were used in battle, but these were too wide for travelling on the railways in Germany, so for such movement the outer roadwheels had to be removed and narrower tracks (520 mm or 20.5 in) fitted. These raised the average ground pressure from 14.7 psi to 20.6 psi (1.03 to 1.45 kg/cm²).

PZKPFW VI AUSF E (SDKFZ 181)

Date of origin 1942
Weight (tonnes) 57
Overall dimensions (m)   **Length** 8.45
  Height 2.93
  Width 3.7
Armament/Ammunition carried
  Main   1 × 8.8 cm KwK 36 L/56
    92 rounds
  Secondary   2 × 7.92 mm MG 34
Armour thickness (mm)   Max. 100
    Min. 25
Engine   Type Maybach HL 210 P45
    bhp/rpm 650/3,000
Crew 5
Max. speed (km/h) 38
Range (km) 140
Remarks   From May 1943 fitted with
    HL 230 P45 23-litre engine

Tiger I was initially powered by an HL 210 P45 Maybach V-12 petrol engine, but in

May 1943 the underpowered 21-litre capacity engine was replaced by a more powerful 23-litre HL 230 P45. Special air pre-cleaners (Feifel system) were needed to overcome the very dusty conditions experienced in North Africa. They were fixed to the rear of the hull and joined to the engine via the cover plate. The Tropical Tiger (*Tiger Tp*), as it was called, proved quite successful, but the Feifel system was discontinued after the surrender in Tunisia and not used again. One additional feature found in early Tigers was a built-in capacity to deep wade, using a schnorkel system, at a depth of 3.9 m (13 ft). This equipment was, however, both expensive to install and difficult to maintain at an operational level, so after 495 Tigers had been built with it fitted, the facility was discarded in order to simplify production. Normal wading depth for Tiger I was 120 cm (4 ft). Tiger's considerable weight made steering potentially difficult, so Henschel developed power steering to replace the normal clutch and brake system of the earlier Panzers. They designed a fully regenerative and continuous system, similar to the Merritt-Brown type found on the British Churchill tank. It was controlled by the driver using a steering wheel and had the added feature of a twin radius of turn in each gear. The Maybach Olvar gearbox gave eight forward and four reverse gears and was fitted with a preselector. The power steering and wide range of gears made the Tiger a surprisingly easy tank to drive, despite its size and weight.

MODIFICATIONS DURING PRODUCTION

Although there were, strictly speaking, no actual official different models of Tiger I, the change from Ausf H to Ausf E being just one of nomenclature, there are notable differences between Tigers, depending upon the production period in which they were produced. These differences can roughly be broken down into four periods: pre-production, early, middle and late production. Pre-production tanks had no side track guards on their superstructures, had rectangular bevelled exhaust pipe shields, pistol

ports on both sides of the turret instead of a single loading/escape hatch and no smoke grenade dischargers. The early production run all had squared-off turret rear bins and three smoke grenade dischargers on each side of the turret, while there were removable track guards, which had rounded front mudguards, and two headlamps were also fitted. Those for desert use had Feifel air pre-cleaners on the rear hull plate. Mid-production vehicles had the right-hand rear escape/loading hatch in the turret instead of the pistol ports, a 'dustbin' type cupola with vision slits and turret-mounted smoke dischargers, while the track guards had hinged flaps over the wide cross-country tracks.

Tigers of this period destined for the Eastern Front had 'S' mine dischargers fitted on five mounting points around the hull roof. All vehicles up to and including mid-production, had rubber-tyred roadwheels, while the first 495 were fitted for deep wading. Late production Tigers had resilient, steel-rimmed wheels, no air precleaners, turrets with Panther-type episcopes and a horizontally rotating hatch cover, and lacked any smoke grenade dischargers on the turret or 'S' mine discharger points on the hull roof. There was also just one centrally-placed headlamp instead of the usual pair.

All-round views of the PzKpfw VI Ausf E, Tiger I, taken in various locations and at various times during its highly successful career as the most feared tank of World War 2. There were a few changes made during the two years of production (August 1942–August 1944), a total of 1,354 Tigers being produced. A more powerful engine was introduced in May 1943, a better cupola was also fitted, while late production Tigers had resilient, steel-rimmed wheels. Tigers were adapted to suit all theatres of operation — for example, the fitting of *Feifel* pre-air cleaners for desert use, or wide cross-country tracks (*Ostketten*) for Russia.

General description

In October 1943 an example of the Tiger I was brought back to the UK from North Africa, after being knocked out in action (see later). This tank was minutely inspected and a full and comprehensive report was published. The following description of Tiger 1 is taken from that report, but of course, in the space available I have had to leave a great deal out.[68]

'**Introduction** The PzKpfw VI was introduced into service by the enemy in the autumn or winter of 1942 and appeared in North Africa in January 1943 and later in Sicily and on the Russian front. The vehicle which has been examined is a PzKpfw VI (H) or SdKfz 182[69] and is also known as the "TIGER". This model is known to have been developed by Henschel u Sohne GmbH. The "TIGER" is of course outstanding by reason of it being the heaviest AFV in general service, scaling approximately 56 tons in battle order. Its main armament is an 8.8 cm gun, whilst its heaviest armour (on the front vertical plate) is 102 mm. Another feature of outstanding tactical interest is its deep wading facilities, and limited underwater performance, to a depth of approximately 15 ft [actually 3.9 m, see above]. Its size and weight, however, impose certain tactical disadvantages, the most outstanding being the restriction on transportation due to its width and its limited radius of action, due to heavy fuel consumption (stated by the enemy as being 2.75 gallons per mile [7.77 L per km] on normal cross-country running). The workmanship appears to be of a high order, and the design has been executed freely from the drawing board, in general unhampered by the utilisation of existing components. There are exceptions, however, and certain points

of detailed design appear unnecessarily elaborate and costly to manufacture. An interesting development in German AFV construction is the introduction of plate interlocking in addition to the normal stepped jointing. This method has no doubt been made necessary by the use of thicker armour.

'The steering unit is in principle similar to the "Merritt-Brown" with the further refinement of a twin radius of turn in each gear. This adoption of a fully regenerative steering system is a distinct departure from the simple clutch/brake system hitherto employed on German tanks. The weight of "TIGER" no doubt enforced a radical change in the gearbox design and the adoption of this system is therefore of interest. The gearbox has much in common with other Maybach pre-selective units, and probably the outstanding merit of this design is the provision of a large number of forward ratios (in this case eight) in a relatively compact main casing. This use of a fully automatic change speed operation is in distinct contrast with current Allied practice. The transmission and steering units are extremely complicated and undoubtedly costly in man/hours to produce. The resultant light control of such a heavy vehicle may be some justification since those who have driven the tank comment favourably on this feature. As yet there is no indication that the Germans favour a compression ignition engine and the PzKpfw VI is powered by a V-12 Maybach petrol engine. This engine which has undoubtedly been expressly designed for a heavy tank, is a logical development of the Maybach V-12 type 120 TRM used in PzKw III and PzKw IV and is similar in general design. As this engine represents the very latest German practice it merits close study, and it must be conceded that the design has achieved its purpose in a great measure. It is compact, light and very accessible.

'**General description** As compared with other AFVs in service, the "TIGER" is outstandingly well armed and protected. Designed to carry an 8.8 cm gun and constructed of very heavy armoured plate, this vehicle is naturally of exceptional size and weight and it is therefore somewhat surprising to note how it is, to a certain degree, dwarfed by the main armament. Viewed from the side with the turret at 12 o'clock, the 8.8 cm gun extends beyond the nose of the tank by about a quarter of its length, and the length from the muzzle brake to the mantlet is rather over half the total length of the vehicle. From the front aspect the great width and extremely wide tracks present a clean, formidable appearance, whilst from

the rear, the abnormal height of the flat tail plate carrying the large cylindrical silencers and air pre-cleaners, presents by contrast an ungainly and untidy appearance. The use of heavy armour plate has imposed the necessity of employing flat plates wherever possible and the number of plates has been kept to a minimum to facilitate manufacture. This results in a simple boxlike contour. Both the super-structure and engine compartments are high and the former overhangs the tracks at each side. This arrangement permits of adequate turret ring diameter to accommodate the 8.8 cm gun. Apart from the tail plate already referred to, the exterior is of generally clean and simple lines.

'A notable departure from past German practice is the welding of the superstructure to the main hull; in previous German designs a bolted joint has been used. The turret is also of simple outline, the vertical sides and rear being formed of a single rolled plate, while the mantlet is a steel casting of rectangular section. A conventional German type of cupola is mounted on the nearside of the turret roof. Circular hatches are provided in the superstructure top for the driver and hull gunner. There are three hatches in the turret — a rectangular hatch for the loader in the roof and two circular hatches, one in the cupola top and one in the turret side. Massive cast manganese steel tracks of comparatively small pitch are driven by the front sprockets — consistent with normal German practice. Adjustment of the track tension by a rear idler is accessible through the tail plate, and the mechanism is all housed within the hull. The vehicle is sprung on torsion bars. The bogie wheels are arranged to overlap each other thus increasing the number of spring units and resulting in a soft suspension. This arrangement is not altogether unexpected since it has previously been encountered on German tracked vehicles and its merits are obvious, particularly when dealing with the suspension of an unusually heavy vehicle. Even distribution of the weight of the tracks is achieved by the use of triple rubber tyred bogie wheels. In order to accommodate the 16 torsion bars on the hull floor, trailing suspension arms are used on one side and leading arms on the other. The mechanical layout follows orthodox German practice although the elaboration and refinement in design has been carried to an exceptional degree. The engine is accommodated centrally at the rear and drives forward through the propeller shaft below the turret floor to the gearbox which incorporates the clutch. Bolted to it is the steering unit and each track is driven through a final reduction gear in each sprocket. A radiator and twin fan assembly is

installed in a separate compartment each side of the engine. Below each compartment two petrol tanks are carried.

'Arrangements for wading and total submersion are necessarily somewhat elaborate, but have evidently not been incorporated as an afterthought. All hatches and doors are rubber sealed, whilst the turret ring is sealed by an inflatable tube. The main air supply for the engine and crew is taken through a demountable telescopic standpipe mounted over the engine compartment. During submersion, the fan drives are disconnected and the radiator compartments flooded. The excessive width of the vehicle in battle order necessitates special preparation for rail travel. Narrow tracks are substituted and the outer bogie wheels removed as are the track guards and air pre-cleaners.

'The general layout of the fighting and driving compartments is shown [in the perspective drawing]. The seating arrangements for the crew follow normal German practice. In the three-man turret the gunner sits on the nearside of the gun with the Commander immediately behind him and the loader sits on the other side of the gun and faces to the rear. The commander is provided with a cupola in which there are five vision slits. In the hull the driver sits on the nearside and the hull gunner, who also operates the wireless, sits opposite on the offside. Although the turret is unusually spacious, the breech mechanism of the 8.8 cm gun reaches nearly to the rear wall dividing the compartment in two. The mechanism is of the semi-automatic falling wedge type and is, broadly speaking a scaled-up version of the smaller tank guns. It is electrically fired by a control on the elevating handwheel. A 7.92 mm machine-gun is mounted co-axially on the offside and is fired mechanically by a foot pedal. The gunner is provided with a binocular telescope and a turret position dial indicator to his left. The gun is balanced by a large coil spring housed in a cylinder in the offside front of the turret. Elevation and hand traverse are controlled by handwheels to the right and left of the gunner, and an additional handwheel may be used by the commander to give assistance. The hydraulic power traverse is controlled by the gunner with a rocking foot plate. Around the vertical sides and rear of the turret are various small boxes, brackets and straps for stowing such items as gasmasks, glass blocks, microphones, etc, as well as junction and fuse boxes for the turret electrical gear. The turret floor rotates with the turret and is suspended on three steel tubes. In the centre is a domed cover for the drive to the hydraulic unit which is bolted to the revolving floor. The drive is also taken to the

controls are normal. The driver's visor can be closed by a sliding shutter operated by a large handwheel, and a fixed episcope is provided in the escape hatch. A standard German gyrocompass and instrument panel are situated to the left and right respectively. The 7.92 mm machine-gun for the hull gunner is held by a ball mounting in the offside of the front vertical plate. It is fired by a hand trigger and sighted by an orthodox telescope. The wireless sets are carried on a shelf to the right of the hull gunner.'[70]

Armament After covering the detailed specification of Tiger, the British report goes on to look in detail at the main components. The remarks made about the main armament includes the following summary: 'The 8.8 cm (3.46 in) gun is mounted on a $70\frac{1}{2}$ in [179 cm] internal diameter ring and has 360° traverse. It is provided with 92 rounds of ammunition. This gun, known as the KwK 36, should not be regarded as a development of the FlaK 18 and 36 AA/ATk guns, but a parallel development with the 7.5 cm KwK 40 (long) and follows the well known principles of German tank gun design. The only similarity to the FlaK 36 lies in the ammunition and ballistics. The standard FlaK 18 and 36 ammunition is fired, except that it is fitted with the C/22 electric primer instead of the C/12 percussion primer. The combination of a muzzle brake, long recoil (22.8 in [58 cm]) and a heavy vehicle (approximately 56 tons) results in a stable gun platform, thus avoiding one of the difficulties of observation of fire present being encountered in British tanks. In addition to the KwK 36, the armament of the tank comprises two MG 34 7.92 mm machine-guns, one co-axially mounted with the 8.8 cm gun, and one in a ball mounting on the offside of the front vertical plate. A curious feature is the provision of a clinometer in conjunction with a simple type azimuth indicator, graduated in clock hours only, as on the PzKw IV with 7.5 cm KwK (short). On the PzKw IV with 7.5 cm KwK 40 (long), however, there is a more elaborate azimuth indicator, graduated in clock hours and mils, with a split pinion drive but no clinometer. Thus, neither of these vehicles has complete equipment for turret down shooting, although this is known to be practised by the Germans. It is surprising that no attempt has been made to protect the ammunition from splinters though there is good protection against dust.

The Germans appear to have discarded

turret rack through shafting and universal joints. Also mounted on the revolving floor is a rack for spare petrol cans and a fire extinguisher. The gunner's seat is carried on a welded tubular extension on the elevating gear and is situated forward over the hydraulic unit. To the rear on the engine bulkhead are mounted the petrol taps, certain other engine controls and the automatic fire extinguisher unit. Ammunition for the 8.8 cm gun is stowed in bins at each side of the fighting compartment. The remainder is stowed under the turret floor and alongside the driver.

Breech of the 8.8 cm KwK L/36 gun, the Tiger's main armament. The '88' earned a formidable reputation in the anti-tank role, also as a tank gun, and of course in its original role as an anti-aircraft gun.

'The driver is provided with a steering wheel which controls hydraulically the controlled differential steering unit. When the engine is not running this unit is inoperative and orthodox steering levers controlling skid disc brakes may be used. These brakes are also the vehicle brakes and are coupled to a foot pedal and parking brake lever. Other

tail smoke apparatus in favour of turret-mounted generator dischargers, obviously as a result of examination of British AFVs. As no extra generators are stowed, beyond those in the dischargers, and the fitting of the primer is not a quick operation, they obviously cannot be loaded after firing, until coming out of action. By comparison with those of present British tanks, the turret is fairly roomy and comfortable. It is observed that the standard of workmanship and design in the armament is of a very high order and shows no deterioration when compared with early German designs.'

The main types of ammunition fired by the 8.8 cm gun of the Tiger were as follows. The normal number of rounds carried, usually a mixture of types, was 92.

Type	Muzzle velocity
APCBC (AP 38)	810 m/s (2,657 fps)
AP 40	914 m/s (3,000 fps)
HE/ATk (Patr 39)	600 m/s (1,968 fps)
HE	820 m/s (2,690 fps)

A later, British report gave the following figures for penetration performance of the APCBC round against homogeneous armour plate:

Range	At normal	At 30°
500	130 mm	110 mm
1,000	119 mm	102 mm
1,500	109 mm	94 mm
2,000	99 mm	87 mm
2,500	90 mm	80 mm

All rounds were stowed horizontally, lying fore and aft, alternately nose and base forward, in unarmoured bins with folding doors. The rounds stowed in the fighting compartment floor were held at their bases by rests, sliding vertically in grooves in the bin sides. As the majority of rounds were stowed high up in the vehicle they were more vulnerable than those in British tanks which were lower down and stowed in armoured bins.

Battle history

Accounts of the first two occasions when the Tiger was used in battle tell of almost complete disaster, and it is very clear that, thanks to Adolf Hitler's impatience, the new tanks were used prematurely, in small numbers and on unsuitable terrain — almost an exact parallel of the hasty manner in which the British High Command had used the very first tanks ever built, on the Somme in 1916.

Guderian puts the blame squarely on Hitler, who, he says, was so consumed with desire to try out his new wonder weapon, that he ordered the premature use of the first handful of Tigers in minor operations, on bad going. The first unit with Tigers was the 1st Platoon of 502nd *schwere Panzerabteilung*, which had four. They were entrained at Fallingbostel, together with a small supporting echelon, containing some technicians from the manufacturer, Henschel, and were moved to the Russian front, arriving at Mga (to the south-east of Leningrad) on 29 August 1942. After detraining, they left Mga and were immediately moved up to the front line, arriving at their assembly point in a thick forest about 10:00 hr.

Just before 11:00 hr the platoon was told to mount up and start engines. Major Richard Maerker, who was commanding the party, got into the leading Tiger and they moved off, accompanied by a Kübelwagen (the German 'Jeep' made by Volkswagen), which contained Herr Franke, a Henschel technician, and an observer. They married up with their infantry support, crossed the Start Line and soon began engaging the enemy targets. Unfortunately, the ground was far too soft and the terrain totally unsuitable for heavy tracked vehicles. Although the enemy withdrew in front of the advancing force, they did call down retaliatory fire. On reaching a low ridge the platoon divided, two tanks moving right and two left. The Kübelwagen was held up by enemy fire, but eventually managed to get forward, only to find one Tiger stationary behind the next crest, where it had broken down with gearbox trouble. Later there was more bad news, another Tiger had broken down with engine trouble. Franke and the observer decided to leave their Kübelwagen and to go forward on foot to locate the second breakdown. They did so, and after a rapid inspection, decided to return to the nearest workshops and arrange recovery. As they reached their Kübelwagen, Major Maerker arrived in his Tiger, to say that the fourth tank had also broken down, this time with steering problems.

During the night, recovery of all three breakdowns was completed successfully, using three 18-ton recovery tractors (probably SdKfz 9s) to move each of the Tigers, through the thick, heavy going. Fortunately the enemy did not appreciate the importance

of the situation and, although they were shelled heavily during the operation, all went well. At the workshops the defective parts were stripped out and immediately sent back to the manufacturers by air, who in turn sent out replacement parts. The fitters worked night and day on the Tigers, so that by 15 September all four tanks were once again ready for action.

Sadly the second action was an even worse disaster. High Command decided to use the Tigers, together with some PzKpfw IIIs, to spearhead an attack by 170 Infantry Division on the Russian Second Army on 22 September. The area chosen was very similar to that of the abortive attack on 29 August. Vainly Major Maerker protested, as he had personally reconnoitred the ground and knew that it was totally unsuitable for heavy tanks.

However, the Führer himself had ordered the Tigers to be used so nobody dared to countermand his directive. The advance began after a series of airstrikes. A short distance over the Start Line the first Tiger was hit on the front plate. Although the tank was not penetrated, the explosion stopped the engine and it would not restart. The crew decided to abandon their vehicle and later someone who thought it was not going to be recovered, threw a hand grenade into the turret which started a fire.

Although the other three Tigers all reached their first objective, they were later either knocked out or got stuck in the mud when they tried to advance. Nevertheless, after a great deal of effort, two, plus the first Tiger hit were recovered. The fourth, which had advanced the furthest, had sunk so deep

into the cloying mud that it proved quite impossible to recover. Everyone was worried about leaving a Tiger so near the enemy but they were equally worried about destroying it. This indecision lasted for some time, while every possible method of recovery was tried. Eventually, on the night of 24 November, a workshop party went forward, removed all the useful parts they could, crammed the tank with ammunition to ensure its total destruction, and then blew it up. Alas, this was not the end of the saga as Hitler, who was entirely responsible for the debacle, would not accept his error and called for the unfortunate Major Maerker to explain what had gone wrong. Maerker continued to insist that the tanks should never have been used on such appalling terrain, but was made a scapegoat by the Führer, being transferred to 5th Panzer Division and later killed in action. As Guderian rightly commented, the outcome of these operations was 'not only heavy, unnecessary casualties, but also the loss of secrecy and the element of surprise for the future'.

Fortunately, the next time the Tiger was used in battle it was a very different story. Bryan Perrett, in his book *The Tiger Tanks*, tells how on 12 January 1943 the 502nd — now complete in Russia — received a call for help from the 96th Infantry Division, to the effect that they were being overrun by two dozen Russian T-34 tanks. 'The situation was critical and the four Tigers under Oberleutnant [Lieutenant] Bodo von Gerdstell were sent to the Infantry's relief. During the sharp exchange of fire twelve T-34s were blown apart and the remainder turned tail and drove for their own lines as they had never driven before.'

The US Department of the Army pamphlet No 20–233 entitled *German Defense Tactics against Russian Breakthroughs*, published in October 1951, talks about a slightly later action in March 1943 as being the first action in which Tigers took on T-34s. This particular action took place in the Kharkov area and concerned the *Grossdeutschland* Division and reads as follows: 'It was in this action that Tiger tanks engaged the Russian T-34s for the first time; the results were more than gratifying for the Germans. For instance, two Tigers acting as an armored point, destroyed a pack of T-34s. Normally the Russian tanks would stand in ambush at the hitherto safe distance of 1,350

Repairing a roadwheel station. Such work was extremely difficult and tiring in bad conditions.

Interesting shot of a Tiger in snowy conditions, with what appears to be a snowplough on its front.

yards [1,235 m] and wait for the German tanks to expose themselves upon their exit from a village. They would then take on the German tanks under fire while the Panthers[71] were still outranged. Until now, these tactics had been foolproof. This time, however, the Russians had miscalculated. Instead of leaving the village, the Tigers took up well camouflaged positions and made use of their longer range. Within a short time they had knocked out 16 T-34s which were sitting in open terrain and, when the others turned about, the Tigers pursued the fleeing Russians and destroyed 18 more tanks. It was observed that the 88 mm armor-piercing shells had such a terrific impact that they ripped the turrets off many T-34s and hurled them several yards. The German soldiers' immediate reaction was to coin the phrase: "The T-34 raises its hat whenever it meets a Tiger". The performance of the new German tanks was a great morale booster.'

General Guderian was certainly well pleased with the performance of the new tank, now that it was being properly employed in suitable strength, as is evidenced in this extract from a leaflet published under his signature in August 1943: 'With two fingers you can shift 700 hp, move 60 tons, drive at 45 km/h on the road or 20 km/h across country, and cross a water obstacle four metres deep... On the southern sector of the Russian front in one six-hour engagement a Tiger was hit 227 times by anti-tank rifle shots, beside receiving 14 hits by 52 mm shells and 11 by 76.2 mm projectiles — none of which penetrated the armour.

The roadwheels were shot to pieces, two torsion bars were knocked out, several anti-tank missiles were jammed in the transmission and the tank had run over three mines. Yet it managed to run another 60 km across country... You can destroy a T-34 at 800 metres, but the T-34 needs to get within 500 metres of you if you are in a Tiger!'[72]

Undoubtedly the Tiger had a highly successful battle record in Russia, until the new 44 tonne (43.3 UK/48.5 US tons). Joseph Stalin tank began to appear on the scene. With its thick armour (up to 120 mm) and increasingly large gun (initially an 85 mm, then 100 mm and then, by 1944, the definitive version was armed with a 125 mm gun), the Stalin was the most powerfully armed tank in combat at that time. In September 1944 the following article entitled 'Tiger versus Stalin' appeared in the German official Notes for Panzer Troops, which was later circulated by MI 10 to British Troops in early 1945, who commented rather caustically that it was 'presumably done as an encouragement to the German tank arm'. The article read: 'A Tiger squadron reports one of a number of engagements in which it knocked out Stalin tanks. The squadron had been given the task of counter-attacking an enemy penetration into a wood and exploiting success. At 12:15 hr the squadron moved off together with a rifle battalion. The squadron was forced to move in file by reason of the thick forest, bad visibility (50 yd) and narrow path. The Soviet infantry withdrew as soon as the Tigers appeared. The anti-tank guns which the enemy had brought up only $\frac{3}{4}$ hr after initial penetration were quickly knocked out, partly by fire partly by crushing.

'The point troop having penetrated a further 2,000 yd into the forest, the troop commander suddenly heard the sound of falling trees and observed right ahead the large muzzle brake of the Stalin. He immediately ordered "AP fixed sights — fire!" but was hit at the same time by two rounds from a 4.7 cm anti-tank gun which obscured his vision completely. Meanwhile a second tank in the troop had come up level with the troop commander's tank. The latter, firing blind, was continuing the fire-fight at a range of 35 yd and the Stalin withdrew behind a hillock. The second Tiger had in the meantime taken over the lead and fired three rounds at the enemy tank. It was hit by a round from the enemy's 12.2 cm tank gun on the hull below the wireless operator's seat but no penetration was effected, probably because the Tiger was oblique to the enemy. The Stalin, however, had been hit in the gun by the Tiger's last round and put out of action. A second Stalin attempted to cover the first tank's withdrawal but was also hit by one of the leading Tigers just below the gun, and brewed up. The rate of fire of the Stalin was comparatively slow.

'The squadron commander drew the following conclusions from all the engagements his squadron had had with Stalin tanks:

'1. Most Stalin tanks will withdraw on encountering Tigers without attempting to engage in a fire-fight.

'2. Stalin tanks generally only open fire at ranges over 2,200 yd and then only if standing oblique to the target.

'3. Enemy crews tend to abandon tanks as soon as hit.

'4. The Russians make great efforts to prevent Stalin tanks falling into our hands and particularly strive to recover or blow up such of them as have been immobilised.

'5. Stalin tanks can be brewed up although penetration is by no means easy against the frontal armour at long ranges (another Tiger battalion reports that Stalin tanks can only be penetrated by Tigers frontally under 550 yds).

'6. Stalin tanks should, wherever possible, be engaged in flanks or rear, and destroyed by concentrated fire.

'7. Stalin tanks should not be engaged under any circumstances by Tigers in less than troop strength. To use single Tingers is to invite their destruction.

'8. It is useful practice to follow up the first hit with AP on the Stalin with HE to continue blinding the occupants.

'The Inspector-General of Panzer Troops (who is responsible for this official publication) commented as follows on the above remarks:

'1. These experiences agree with those of other Tiger units and are correct.

'2. Reference para 4, it would be desirable for the enemy to observe the same keenness in all our Tiger crews. No Tiger should ever be allowed to fall into enemy hands intact.

'3. Reference para 5 & 6, faced as we are now with the 12.2 cm tank gun and the 5.7 cm ATk gun in Russia and the 9.2 cm AA/A Tk gun in Western Europe and Italy, Tigers can no longer afford to ignore the principles practised by normal tank formations. This means, *inter alia*, that Tigers can no longer show themselves on crests "to have a look round" but must behave like other tanks — behaviour of this kind caused the destruction by Stalin tanks of three Tigers recently, all crews being killed with the exception of two men. The battalion was surely not unacquainted with the basic principle of tank tactics that tanks should only cross crests in a body and by rapid bounds, covered by fire — or detour round the crest. The legend of the "thick hide", the "invulnerability" and the "safety" of the Tiger which has sprung up in other arms of the service, as well as within the tank arm, must now be destroyed and dissipated. Hence, instruction in the usual principles of tank versus tank action becomes of specific importance for Tiger units.

'4. Reference para 7, though this train of

Captured somewhere in France by the US Army, this Tiger I has become the object of great interest to the local villagers.

thought is correct, three Tigers should not withdraw before five Stalins because three Tigers do not form a proper troop. Particularly with conditions as they are at the moment, circumstances may well arise when full troops will not be readily available. And it is precisely the tank versus tank action which is decided more by superior tactics than superior numbers. However, it is still true to say that single tanks invite destruction.

'5. It may be added that the Stalin tank will not only be penetrated in flanks and rear by Tigers and Panthers, but also by PzKpfw IV and assault guns.'

The fact that Tigers were no longer invulnerable was echoed in other German documents of the period, the following appearing in another captured report circulated by 21 Army Group in June 1944: 'When Tigers first appeared on the battlefield, they were in every respect proof against enemy weapons. They quickly won for themselves the title of

A lone 8th Army soldier, armed with a PIAT (Projector Infantry Anti-Tank), knocked out this Tiger single-handed. Note that the cupola is of the later type with built-in periscopes.

"unbeatable" and "undamageable". But in the meantime, the enemy has not been asleep. A/Tk guns, tanks and mines have been developed which can hit a Tiger hard and even knock it out. Now the Tiger, for a long time regarded as a "Life Insurance Policy", is relegated to the ranks of simply a "heavy tank"... No longer can the Tiger prance around oblivious of the laws of tank tactics. They must obey these laws, just as every other tank must. So remember you men who fight in Tiger tanks — DON'T demand the impossible from your Tiger DO just what your commanding officer orders. He knows the limitations of his vehicles and guns, and knows the best use to which they should be put...'

NORTH AFRICA

Small numbers of Tigers were sent to North Africa towards the end of 1942, after the TORCH landings and in time for the sub-

sequent battle for Tunisia. The first German Tiger unit to land was 501st *schwere Panzer Abteilung*, which then contained only two of its full establishment of three tank companies, each with four troops, with two Tigers and two PzKpfw IIIs in each troop. The leading elements crossed from Reggio di Calabria to Tunis on 20 November 1942 and the battalion was complete by early January 1943. Further reinforcements followed, with the arrival of part of the 504th *schwere Panzer Abteilung* in early March. The elements of the two battalions were combined into a single unit and then moved to the area of the Maknassy Pass, where they accounted for between 40 and 50 Allied tanks. They then moved to the area around Medjez-el-Bab at the end of March 1943.

'... on the night of 20–21 April, a force of the *Hermann Göring Jäger Regiment* together with four Tigers and five PzKpfw III and IV tanks of the 504th and 501st Heavy Tank Battalions put in a spoiling attack against the British 1st Infantry and 4th Mixed Divisions. One of these Tigers, with the turret number 131, of 3rd Troop, No 1 Company of 504th Heavy Tank Battalion, is now in the Bovington Tank Museum.' So

wrote Major Peter Gudgin in an article on the Bovington Tiger. He goes on to explain how the Germans, after achieving some success with their attack, retired to defensive positions to wait for the British counterattack. This took place during the afternoon of 21 April, with 48th RTR, a unit of 21st Army Tank Brigade equipped with Churchill tanks, supporting 1st/6th East Surreys. The leading troops of A Squadron 48th RTR attacked on one axis, the infantry on a completely separate axis '... a classic example of how not to carry out an infantry/tank attack'. The Tiger and its supporting IIIs and IVs quickly knocked out the leading Churchills and the battle was definitely going the German way, when a lucky shot from one of the Churchill's 6 pdrs struck the lower edge of the gun mantlet of the Tiger and was deflected into the turret ring, jamming the turret completely. The next shot hit the left hand lifting boss on the side of the turret and splinters wounded the tank commander. Inexplicably, the crew baled out and left their virtually intact Panzer, as did the crews of the other German tanks which had been in support. Thus when the battlefield was examined

The first Tiger I to be knocked out by an American Pershing, serving with 3rd Armored Division in North-West Europe. Sergeant Nick Mashlonik (on right) was the commander of the Pershing that did the damage. Pershing really came into the war far too late to have much effect on the situation, but it was probably the only gun tank the Allies had that could match up with Tiger's basic firepower, protection and mobility, until the Russians produced their JS I, II and III (Author's collection).

the next day it was found that '. . . at last, a virtually intact and relatively undamaged Tiger had fallen into British hands'.

The capture of the first complete Tiger was a significant event and, after preliminary examination by Tech Int, an initial report was signalled to MI 10 in London. The tank was then recovered from the battlefield by 21st Army Tank Brigade Workshops who, after the end of the North African campaign, began to replace damaged components from captured many stocks or by cannibalising other knocked out vehicles. These repairs and replacements were only minor, but did include freeing the turret and replacing turret hatches, one smoke grenade discharger cap and some of the roadwheels. Before it was shipped back to the UK it was inspected in Tunis by many famous people, including HM King George VI and Prime Minister Winston Churchill on 23 June 1943.

It arrived in the UK in October 1943 and was sent to the School of Tank Technology (STT), then part of the Military College of Science, located at Chertsey, Surrey. It was then, as has already been explained, the subject of an extremely detailed examination from which a series of reports were written covering every aspect of the tank's armour,

automotive equipment, gunnery and optical, stowage and layout, etc. Amazingly, Peter Gudgin, now serving at STT, was a member of the inspection team and was responsible for writing various parts of the report on the tank that had knocked him out. Unfortunately, in the interests of finding out everything that could be discovered about the Tiger, the tank was virtually taken to pieces and has never been put back into running order — this is now impossible as so much of the interior has been removed. It has, so the popular press is wont to remind us from time to time, inherited a ghost known locally as 'Hermann the German', but I have yet to see him myself, although one never knows what can be seen in the dark corners of the Museum on a cold winter's night.

ITALY

The Italian campaign saw its share of Tigers, a few even being supplied to the Italian Army, but hastily removed when Germany's Axis partner decided to sue for a separate peace. A number of reports on Tiger have survived from the Italian campaign, such as the following account of operations of Tigers from 508 Heavy Tank Battalion, which was included in a comprehensive report based upon the interrogation of prisoners of war, and appeared in an RAC Liaison Letter in August 1944: '*Tiger tank in action: First major reverse of 3 Sqn 508 Hy Tk Bn.* As an illustration of the difficulties encountered in the employment of Tiger tanks it is interesting to reconstruct one of the two mobile engagements on a Sqn basis

which the Bn fought in Italy, when it won a victory and yet lost almost all its tanks. The action took place between 23 and 25 May 1944 in the general area of Cisterna. 3 Sqn, which had brought down 14 Tiger tanks from France, lost two burnt out at the end of Feb 44 — one through carelessness on the part of the crew and another by Allied A/Tk action. It had received four of the latest pattern AFVs during May 44 and was two tanks over war establishment strength on 23 May 44, ie, 16 instead of 14. The Sqn formed up behind a railway embankment between the Mussolini Canal and the level crossing at G 063299 and engaged troop concentrations with HE. It then crossed the embankment and put three AFVs out of action in the attempt (one with gearbox trouble and two with tracks riding over the sprocket teeth). The remaining 13 crews had all to stop on open ground because the guns had dug into the earth as the tanks came down the embankment and needed pulling through. The Allied troops were driven back about three km and a number of Sherman tanks surprised and knocked out.

'The first loss sustained in action was a Tiger which had one radiator destroyed by an artillery round and had to limp back towards Cori in stages. Twelve Tigers were thus left in action during the night 23/24 May 44. On the morning of 24 May 44 a retreat was ordered to everyone's surprise and A/Tk fire accounted for one Tiger (hit on the right reduction gear and subsequently blown up by the crew). Eleven Tigers withdrew to the embankment and the OC Sqn ordered five to continue to hold the enemy whilst the other six were to tow away the three tanks which had failed to cross. Four of the six towing tanks experienced gearbox trouble and the OC Sqn then ordered the three towed tanks to be destroyed and two out of the five fighting tanks to assist in towing away the breakdowns. These eight AFVs were got back to the assembly point near Cori, leaving four Tigers only in fighting order. Of these four, one was hit by A/Tk gun fire and two more experienced gearbox trouble (all three were blown up), so that only one runner was left.

'Two converted Sherman tanks came down from Rome during the night 24/25 May and extricated the one runner which had also become U/S meanwhile, by towing it in tandem along the railway tracks. By 25 May 44, the situation had so deteriorated that it was manifestly impossible to get towing vehicles through and the OC ordered the blowing up of the nine Tigers which had reached the assembly area. Although a good many of the crews had gone back to Rome with the one runner, the OC and 45 men

A burning Russian farmhouse provides a dramatic background to this photograph of a Tiger I advancing.

The Bovington Tiger seen here with its original German crew, photographed in Tunisia in 1943, shortly before the action in which it was captured. Note the unofficial 'step' on the right side under the belly which can be seen on each of the other photos in this sequence (Major Peter Gudgin archive).

were left near Cori. They had to march to Rome and came under fire several times in the process, arriving in an exhausted condition. PW states categorically that this action had a profound effect upon the Sqn's morale and also decided against the mass use of Tiger tanks. Of 16 tanks put out of action, not one would have been lost had adequate recovery facilities been provided. Although the OC Sqn's personal courage was not in doubt, it was generally thought that he had not appreciated the situation and had created the disaster by attempting to salvage the three AFVs that jibbed at the embankment. Had he not done so, he might have saved 10 out of the original 16. "Penny wise, pound foolish" was the criticism made of him. 3 Sqn also took a poor view of the fact that almost at once a new troop was formed from tanks drawn from 1 and 2 Sqns, crews put in, the former crews going back to their Sqn pools.'

It is interesting to note that, while the problems the Tigers had encountered were not uncommon, it is clear that they had not followed the correct, laid-down procedure which another POW outlined in the same report under the heading 'Tiger tanks as towing vehicles'. It read: 'If a Tiger tank has gearbox trouble it is customary to dismantle the flexible couplings in the half-shaft drives and to tow it out of the immediate battle area by another Tiger, using two tow ropes secured in an 'X' formation to correct the tendency of the towed tank to sway. Should, however, the track on a Tiger have ridden up over the sprocket teeth, the tractive effort required to move it is so great that two Tigers must pull in tandem, each towing with crossed ropes.'

Another report from Italy, issued in September 1944, concerned the experiences of the 2nd New Zealand Division with Tiger tanks in the battle for Florence, the first time they had made contact with Tigers in any significant numbers. It reads:

'**a. Employment** Tiger tanks were employed usually well sited and well camouflaged with foliage so as to be difficult to pick up as follows:

'1. In hull-down positions to delay infantry and to pick off our tanks.

'2. From pre-selected positions which were reached via covered routes. From these positions the enemy would fire a few harassing rounds, withdraw and occupy an alternative position.

'3. As close support to enemy infantry, to thicken up artillery concentrations and to engage buildings occupied by our troops.

'4. With, almost invariably, the support of at least one other tank or SP gun, which remained silent until or unless needed.

'5. Sometimes with infantry accompanying it. These troops, who might only be six to twelve in number, deployed on the flanks up to fifty yards from the tank.

'**b. Vulnerability**

'1. The heavy front and rear armour of the tank make the likelihood of it being knocked out by hits on these parts remote. The side armour is definitely vulnerable to 17 pdr fire. The back hole of the tank over the engines is also a weak spot and a large exhaust hole just over the left centre of the back provides another weak point. HE is considered by some to be the most effective ammo to use against these parts.

'2. The Tiger was usually well enough sited to make deployment of a sniping anti-tank gun, M10 or towed gun for stalking purposes difficult. Unless very careful recce is carried out to site the gun to the best advantage and to locate supporting tanks or SP guns, the effort may be useless. The maximum time for recce and the maximum information appear, therefore, essential for a troop commander who is called upon to engage a Tiger.

'3. The gun and tank seem to be slow to manoeuvre and fire. It can also be effectively blinded by 75 mm American smoke ammunition. On one occasion two smoke rounds, followed by AP, were enough to force a Tiger to withdraw. This is a method of attack recommended by our own tank commanders.

'**c. Overconfidence** Tigers were sometimes used almost recklessly, their crews taking risks to a degree which indicated that they have the utmost confidence in the vehicle. This can render them vulnerable to tank hunting squads armed with PIAT or other close range anti-tank weapons. The Tiger when closed down and attacking on its own at some distance from its supporting gun is definitely vulnerable to such weapons.

'**d. The concentration of field artillery to counter Tigers is effective.**

'1. Even if a brew-up does not result, the tank has invariably withdrawn. It appears obvious that tank crews do not like the shellfire, as the possibility of damage to vital parts (tracks, suspension, bogies, wireless aerials, outside fixtures, electrical equipment, etc) is always present.

'2. Medium artillery has been incorporated in several of our concentrations. Medium artillery is ideal if sufficiently large concentration is brought to bear, but owing to dispersion of rounds, it is preferable to include a good concentration of field guns to thicken up.

'3. We have no experience of heavy artillery engaging Tigers although it is known

they have done so. It is hard for our tanks to locate a well camouflaged Tiger, sited in a defensive role and stationary. Artillery OPs, if given a suspected area, can be used to advantage. A case did occur when a suspected object was located in an area reported to contain a Tiger and the OP commenced to range. A round falling in the vicinity of the suspect completely blasted away all camouflage and the Tiger beat a hasty retreat.

'**e. The following are some experiences of our anti-tank gunners in contact with Tigers:**

'1. A Tiger observed 3,000 yards away was engaging three Shermans. It brewed up one Sherman while the other two withdrew over a crest. A 17 pdr was brought up to within 2,000 yards and engaged Tiger side on. When the Tiger realised that it was being engaged by a high velocity gun it swung round to 90° so that its frontal armour was towards the gun. In the ensuing duel one shot hit the turret, another the suspension, while two near misses probably ricocheted into the tank. The tank was not put out of action. The range was too great to expect a kill, but our tactics were to make the Tiger expose its flank to the Shermans at a range of about 500 yards by swinging round to the anti-tank gun. This he did, and on being engaged by the Shermans, withdrew. The infantry protection of some 6–12 men was engaged by our MGs.[73]

'2. One Tiger was just off the road at a road and track junction engaging our forward troops in buildings, another Tiger about 50 yards up the side road supporting the firing tank. A field artillery concentration which appeared to be from one battery was called for and, although no hits were observed, both tanks withdrew.

'3. A Tiger on a ridge was engaged by what appeared to be a battery of mediums. After the first few rounds had fallen the crew baled out (it is not known why) and shortly afterwards while still being shelled, one man returned to the tank and drove it off. The remainder of the tank crew made off in the direction of their tank some ten minutes later.

'4. A tank was located in the garage of a two-storey house from which it was driven 20 yards, fired a few harassing rounds, and returned to its hideout. Many hits were recorded on the building by our 4.2 inch mortars, firing cap-on, but little damage was visible. The tank was withdrawn from the area each night even though it was in an excellent concealed position and protected by infantry. The house was examined later and although it was considerably damaged and there were several dead Germans about,

Interesting Tiger I with additional armour plate bolted on to front glacis.

there was nothing to indicate that damage had been done to the tank.'

NORTH-WEST EUROPE

Tiger made a considerable impact upon the Allied armies landing in Normandy. None was greater, of course, than the much-recorded annihilation of the advance guard of 7th Armoured Division at Villers-Bocage, where the redoubtable SS Obersturmführer Michael Wittmann, and his small band of Tigers, carved a special niche in the history of tank warfare. This is how the battle was remembered by Major I.B. Aird, DSO, of 4th CLY in the Royal Armoured Corps Journal. 'On the afternoon of 12 June 1944, the Cromwells of the 4th County of London Yeomanry were dispersed in the open fields to the north of Tilly-sur-Seulles, one squadron keeping a look-out, the others resting after the bitter fighting before that village. It was very hot and comparatively quiet. The Colonel, Lord Cranley, was away and there was vague speculation among the squadron leaders as to what fresh orders he would bring back with him. They did not have long to wonder, for he was soon back and jumping out of his scout car, with orders to move immediately. We were in for a long march along a complicated route and an attack which the Regiment was to lead, and in which surprise was to be the most important factor. The objective was the township of Villers-Bocage. Maps were marked and orders given, and in a short time the tanks were marshalled, the men glad to leave the uncomfortable and unpromising area north of Tilly, though a little dubious of the advance along a centre line so tenuous and thin on the map and with so much at stake at its end.

'The axis of the advance was a narrow road along the extreme western flank of the British Army running parallel to the Americans. After 15 miles [24 km] of jolting and dust the head of the column reached the main lateral road from Caumont to Caen and away to the right could be seen the fires and smoke where the American First Infantry Division were fighting to hold the ground they had made in their rapid advance of the last few days. On the left the 8th Hussars had had a tank "bazooka'd" and the leading Honey of the Regiment had been fired on by an anti-tank gun from the east. As it was now dusk it was decided not to push on and the Regiment leaguered for the night in a field to the north of the crossroads.

Close-up of a completely destroyed Tiger I shows how the turret was made of one large horseshoe-shaped plate.

'Early the next morning the advance continued, "A" Squadron leading, followed by some Honeys of the Recce troop and "A" company of the 1st Battalion, The Rifle Brigade. Then came RHQ, followed by "B" and "C" Squadrons, followed by Tac brigade. The orders were to push on as fast as possible, there being no further opposition from the crossroad area. The country was very close, the road wandering over switchback hills, gradually swinging east towards Villers. Within a few hours, the leading elements, moving fast, were in sight of the small town. From Brigade came the information that the place was clear of the enemy and the cheering villagers on the side of the road seemed to confirm it. In consequence, "A" Squadron galloped through the town, seeing no sign of Germans, and reached their objective on the farther side, a hill which commanded the road to Caen. True, before that a troop leader had reported a German aroured car observing from a hill north of the town, but others had disputed this and the sign was disregarded. With "A"

A badly damaged Tiger I which was put on show in June 1943 at the Moscow War Trophy Exhibition, being examined by some American officers.

Squadron on the objective and all seemingly quiet, RHQ moved over the River Seulles and into the main square of the town. Recce sent a patrol to the south on the road to Aunay, perhaps the deepest penetration into France that had been made up to that time. The patrol shot up a German car and captured the occupants, which included an officer who volunteered the information that he was billeting!

'Colonel Cranley now decided to go in his scout car to see how "A" Squadron and the infantry company were getting on and he left his headquarters with all its appendages covered by a troop of the Recce and some Greenjackets, instructing them to move into the main street towards the eastern exists.

'For a short time all seemed quiet, and then the most indescribable confusion broke out. Up in the street in front, Lt Ingram's Honeys and a dozen half-tracks of the Rifle Brigade were burning. The RHQ tanks started to move backwards down the narrow street. As they did so, Spandaus opened up from the windows above and the street began to fill with smoke and the noise of falling slates, punctuated by the sharp crack of an 88 mm. Out of the smoke trundled slowly a German Tiger tank. Major Carr, the Second-in-Command, fired at it with his 75 mm but, heartbreaking and frightening, the shots failed to penetrate the side armour even at this ridiculous range. Almost immediately his tank was on fire, he himself seriously wounded and other members of the crew killed or wounded also.

'The Tiger went on to shoot up the Shermans of the OPs with their poor wooden guns, the IO's scout car and the MO's half-track. The other three tanks of RHQ managed to shuffle into various turnings, but soon the troop leader's tank was on fire and also the RSM's. Captain Dyas, Assistant Adjutant, commanding the remaining Cromwell, watched the Tiger pass him and began to trail it in his tank, hoping to get it from the rear, but by now it had encountered the more formidable obstacle of "B" Squadron and decided to beat a retreat. Therefore once more it was head on and there was no escape. The last remaining tank was set on fire.

'Captain Dyas managed to escape and, finding the RSM's tank which, although on fire, still contained a functioning wireless with a microphone hanging out of the turret, spoke to Major Aird, commanding "B" Squadron, telling him what had befallen the troops in the eastern end of the town. As communication still existed between "B" and "A" Squadrons, Major Aird decided to take over control. He appreciated that the German tanks must have come in behind the tail of "A", along the road from Evrecy, and that they now stood firmly between "A" and the rest of the Regiment. "A" Squadron with some of the Rifle Brigade's half-tracks and anti-tank guns, therefore, was cut off. The Colonel, who was with them, decided to make a reconnaissance down towards the railway with a view to sorting out the situation and possibly finding a way back.

'As Brigadier Hinde had been up in his scout car and had said that the town must be held at all costs, Major Aird set about organising the defence. Some of the Queen's infantry had arrived with anti-tank guns and these, with tank troops, were dispersed round the roads leading into the square. To the south Lt Simons, in charge of a troop of Honeys, had had his tank knocked out by a mortar, so his patrol was drawn in. Simons himself had his wounds dressed by French peasants, who looked after him until he was recovered enough to escape, but he had little fresh information to give on his return. "C" Squadron remained on the high ground to the east of the town.

Only three Tiger Is were ever converted to the ARV role. This photograph shows the small crane and winch which were mounted on top of the turret after the main armament had been removed.

'This was the position in the afternoon when "A" Squadron were attacked by Tiger tanks and infantry. The squadron leader, Major P.M.R. Scott, MC, and his officers were conferring in a ditch with Major Wright of the Rifle Brigade when the attack was launched. The Tigers swept up the road from Villers in their rear, "brewing" a few Cromwells on the way: the German infantry attacked from prepared positions to the east. Major Scott was killed almost immediately, most of the Cromwells were knocked out, and the officers and men trying to escape were killed or taken prisoner by the infantry. At that time too, Colonel Cranley went off the air and it was presumed that he had been killed or taken prisoner. One survivor alone from the troops on Hill 213, Captain Milner of the Rifle Brigade, succeeded in getting back under cover of darkness.

'The Germans must have been heartened by their successes and they prepared to attack the town. During the next four hours a curious battle developed in there, a battle which became a duel between Lieutenant Cotton, MM, commanding a troop of three Cromwells and a Firefly, with some infantry and anti-tank guns from the Queen's, on one side, and three Tigers and a Mark IV on the other. Cotton's own tank was a 95 mm, not much use against armour, so he put it into a garage and conducted most of the battle on his feet, merely using its wireless to give occasional orders. At intervals there was torrential rain, so he carried an umbrella as well as a blanket, soaked in petrol, with which to burn any tanks knocked out.

'The first Tiger was "killed" by a 6 pdr which Cotton directed on it. Sergeant Bramall had a duel with another and eventually finished it off by drilling a hole through the side of a house with 17 pdr HE until he could see it, then administered the *coup de grâce* with AP. Sergeant Lockwood and Corporal Horne played hide and seek with the last Tiger and the Mark IV, until they had set both on fire. The French fire brigade was an additional and surprising enemy, who could only with the greatest difficulty be prevented from putting out the fires in the burning tanks. This minor victory was something paid back of the heavy score which the Panzers had run up against the Regiment, and it put new heart into the survivors.

'After this reverse, the Germans must have given up the idea of further attack with tanks, for they now started to shell all they could see and the infantry in the houses and hedges became more active. A few hours before dark the order came to withdraw from the town to the village of Amaye-sur-Seulles, some 4,000 yards to the west along the

A few *Elefants* were also converted to the recovery role as the photo shows.

The heavy assault rocket mortar 38 cm RW61 auf *Sturmmörser* Tiger was a formidable weapon system. Eighteen were converted from Tiger Is. This one is being towed by a *Bergepanther* after capture.

main axis, where Tac Brigade had been for most of the day. This was not easy, as part of the road was exposed to anti-tank and machine-gun fire, while the sunken portions of the road were too narrow to allow a Cromwell to turn. Eventually, under a heavy barrage of smoke and HE by the American 155 mms and British 25 pdrs laid just before dark, the Queen's infantry and the two surviving squadrons were extricated to leaguer in the village of Amaye. Tanks of 8th Hussars were there, helping to remove an uncomfortable feeling of loneliness, and the L of C [lines of communication] was being protected by 1st Royal Tanks. Fortunately the night was quiet, as there was much reorganisation for Major Aird and his new Adjutant. The Regiment had lost its RHQ and one squadron complete — 14 officers and a hundred men. The Rifle Brigade and the 5th RHA had also suffered severely.'

Michael Wittman, who had caused all this chaos, had enrolled into the *Leibrstandarte SS Adolf Hitler* in 1937 and by the time war started he was an SS Unterscharführer. He commanded an armoured car in the campaigns in Poland and France. He was later awarded the Iron Cross 2nd Class, while commanding an assault gun in the Balkans in 1941, and the Iron Cross 1st Class, during the German advance on Rostov, having

knocked out six Russian tanks in his first action in Russia. He first commanded a Tiger in 13 Kompanie of SS Panzer Regiment 1, in early 1943, after being commissioned the previous December. From then on his tally of 'kills' mounted rapidly, 66 tanks on 9 January 1944 alone, while only a few days later (the day before he received his Knights Cross) he knocked out 19 tanks and 3 heavy assault guns. By 20 January, when he was promoted to Obersturmführer, he had been credited with 117 kills. He was awarded the Swords to his Knights Cross on 22 June 1944. Michael Wittman was himself killed on 8 August, only eight weeks after the Villers-Bocage battle, when his incredible total of 'kills' stood at 138 tanks and assault guns, plus 132 anti-tank guns — all destroyed by him and his tank crews — in less than two years.[74]

THE AMERICAN TIGER TAMER

Tiger was more than a match for most of the opposition, so it took a very brave man to take one on, even when hull-down in a Sherman Firefly with its high velocity 17 pdr. The normal 75 mm Sherman, or even the later model with the 76 mm, were simply no match for it, unless they were very lucky. It was not until almost the end of the

nearly three years before Pershing so perhaps the comparison is a little unfair.

Tiger went on knocking out the enemy tanks right up to the end of the war. It was overtaken on the production line by Tiger II (see later), but some of the Tigers which survived the war saw service in the French Army and then ended up being used as targets on French gunnery ranges. Adolf Hitler is supposed to have said that each battalion of Tigers was worth a normal Panzer division, and certainly its formidable reputation still exists today.

Variants

Bergepanzer Tiger A very small number of Tiger Es were converted into *ad hoc* armoured recovery vehicles and used mainly for towing damaged Tigers out of the immediate battle area. This was not a factory-built variant, like the *Bergepanther*, but rather the result of a field workshop modification. The main armament was removed, the mantlet sealed up and a small hand-operated winch mounted on the rear of the turret, with a tubular guide to take the wire winch rope over the front. An equally small number of the Porsche-built Tiger (P) were converted into *Bergepanzer*, this time the conversion being very similar to the work undertaken to produce the *Elefant* heavy assault gun. However, instead of the large turret mounting the PaK 43/2 L/71 gun, a smaller built-up superstructure was constructed at the rear of the hull, which had a ball-mounted MG 34 as the only weapon. There was in addition a small crane plus some associated lifting gear, but no sophisticated recovery equipment.

Panzerbefehlswagen Tiger An indeterminate number of Tiger Es were adapted to the command role, by the addition of extra radio sets. There was no loss of main armament, instead the co-axial MG, plus its ammunition, tools and spares were removed, together with 26 main armament rounds and 1,500 rounds of MG ammo. The crew of the PzBefWg Tiger Ausf E was still five, their main tasks being: commander, wireless officer (vice gunner), wireless operator 1 (vice loader), wireless operator 2 (vice hull gunner), and driver. There were two versions of the command tank, the SdKfz 267 which was fitted with Fu 5 and Fu 8 radios, and the SdKfz 268 with Fu 5 and Fu 7, the former

war that the Americans at last fielded a tank of comparable status. This was the M26 Pershing. The 41 tonne (40.3 UK/45.2 US tons) Pershing had armour up to 112.5 mm thick and was armed with a formidable 90 mm gun. The first Pershings to see action were a handful that had arrived in Antwerp docks in January 1945. They were split between 3rd and 9th Armored Divisions, the former being the first into action. Rather in the same way in which Tiger had been used in 'penny packets' with disastrous results, so this first action reflected little credit on the new 'Tiger Tamer'. A Pershing, with the name of *Fireball*, was located in a bad position, silhouetted in the darkness by a nearby fire. A Tiger, concealed behind the corner of a building only some 100 yards [60 m] away, fired three shots — the first entered the Pershing's turret through the co-axial machine-gun port and killed the gunner and loader instantly. The second shot hit the muzzle brake and the resulting shock waves set off the round in the chamber of the 90 mm M3 gun. Even though this round finally cleared the muzzle, it caused the barrel to swell about halfway down its length. The third and final shot glanced off the right-hand side of the turret and in doing so took away the upper cupola hatch which had been left open. Unfortunately for the Tiger, while it was backing to avoid retaliatory fire, it reversed into a large pile of debris and became so entangled that the crew had to abandon it.

Not long after this engagement *Fireball* was avenged by the crew of another of the Pershings assigned to 3rd Armored Division. The tank commander, Sergeant Nick Mashlonik told me: 'Our first exposure to

the enemy with the new M26 was very fruitful. We were hit hard by the Germans from Elsdorf. The enemy appeared to have much armor as we received a lot of direct fire and this kept us pinned down. Our casualties kept mounting and the Company Commander asked me if I thought I could knock the Tiger out that was almost destroying us. The Company Commander and I did some investigating by crawling out to a position where we could see from ground level, a sight to behold. The German Tiger had slightly dug in and this meant it would be more difficult to destroy. I decided that I could take on this Tiger with my 90 mm. Our M26 was in defilade position, more or less hidden in a little valley. I detailed by driver Cade and my gunner Gormick to accompany me on this mission. I would be the gunner and have Gormick load. I instructed them both that once we had fired three shots — two armor piercing and one HE point detonating — we would immediately back up so as not to expose ourselves too long on the top of the hill.

'Just as we started our tank and moved slowly forward (creeping) I noticed that the German Tiger was moving out of the position and exposed his belly to us. I immediately put a shot into its belly and knocked it off. The second shot was fired at his track and knocked his right track off. The third shot was fired at the turret with HE point detonating and destroyed the escaping crew.'

Clearly Pershing and Tiger were very much on a par, so it depended far more on the circumstances of the engagement as to which was the winner in a single tank versus tank clash. However, what is well worth remembering is that Tiger was in service

set being, in each case, fitted in the turret, while the latter was mounted in the hull.

Sturmmörser Tiger Under 20 of these enormous 65-ton heavy assault mortars were built in the latter half of 1944. They were based on the Tiger E chassis and mounted a 38 cm mortar, plus one MG 34 in a separate ball mounting. The *SturmTiger* came about as a result of a stated operational requirement from the infantry, after fighting in built-up areas in Russian cities such as Stalingrad, for a heavy SP howitzer to provide high angle support during street fighting. The original requirement was for a mortar of about 20 cm calibre, but nothing was available. It was eventually decided to adapt the massive 38 cm rocket-assisted RW 61 (*Raketenwerfer 61*) developed by Rheinmetall-Borsig for the German Navy for use in anti-submarine warfare. The Tiger chassis was used, with a large box-like superstructure fitted on to the hull and running gear. Armour was up to 150 mm thick on the steeply angled (45°) front plate, while the sides and rear were 80 mm and the top plate 40 mm. The breech-loaded mortar was slightly offset to the right of the fighting compartment. The projector could traverse 10° either side of centre and elevate from 0° to 85°. Captured range tables showed its maximum range varying considerably with charge temperature, from 5,900 m (6,450 yd) at + 50°C to 5,150 m (5,630 yd) at O°C and down to 4,200 m (4,590 yd) at −40°C. The 38 cm RW 61 *auf Sturmmörser Tiger*, to give its proper nomenclature, was produced by Alkett in their Berlin factory. Its crew was seven — a tank commander, a forward observer and five men to operate the vehicle and man the mortar.

Tiger II (SdKfz 182)

After their salutary lesson with T-34, the *Heereswaffenamt* were clearly never going to allow themselves to be upstaged again and were therefore determined only to accept designs for tanks that would be bigger and better than anything the Allies could possibly produce. Hitler also appears to have been obsessed with the idea of superheavy tanks, while the Panzertruppe, like any other tankmen, although wanting a proper balance of the three basic characteristics of firepower, protection and mobility, were always prepared to accept anything that would give

them an edge on the battlefield. This was particularly relevant since by then it was becoming clear that the tide was turning against Germany, so the need for fast-moving, mobile forces with which to conquer new territories had passed. Instead the requirement was for slower, better-armed and armoured AFVs to protect the Fatherland and the conquered territories surrounding it, from the inevitable invasions that were to come from both east and west. The result of all this combined determination was the largest tank to see combat service during the war, Tiger II, the *Königstiger* (King Tiger), also called Tiger B, Royal Tiger (the name favoured by the Americans), or to give its full correct nomenclature: PzKpfw VI Ausf B (SdKfz 182). Under 500 of these streamlined 68 tonne (66.9 UK/75 US tons) monsters were produced, all being built by Henschel between January 1944 and March 1945. Design work began two years earlier in the autumn of 1942, following a specification from the *Heereswaffenamt* issued that August. By then the T-34 had made its debut and the Panther had been designed, so the new Tiger II reflected their streamlined shape rather than the more angular lines of Tiger I.

As with Tiger I, both Henschel and Porsche were invited to submit designs for the new tank, which was to mount the new, long-barrelled 8.8 cm L/71 gun. Porsche merely revamped their VK 4501(P), producing a heavier version, but this was rejected in favour of a second design, the VK 4502(P), which had a larger turret set well back on the hull, with a forward-mounted engine and electric transmission. It was the manufacture of this transmission which proved to be its eventual downfall, because the sea blockade of Germany was so effective that there was a

great shortage of the copper needed in quantity for that type of transmission. The Porsche project was therefore cancelled, although some 50 turrets which had been produced were subsequently fitted to the early production Tiger IIs. The Porsche turret can be distinguished by its use of bent plates, giving the front a more rounded appearance. The Henschel turret which replaced it had a single flat front plate and a redesigned mantlet which was the same as the one designed for the Panther II.

PZKPFW VI AUSF B (SDKFZ 182)		
Date of origin 1944		
Weight (tonnes) 68		
Overall dimensions (m)	**Length**	10.3
	Height	3.08
	Width	3.76
Armament/Ammunition carried		
Main 1 × 8.8 cm KwK 43 L/71		
72 rounds		
Secondary 2 × 7.92 mm MG 34		
Armour thickness (mm)	Max.	180
	Min.	25
Engine **Type** Maybach HL 230 P30		
bhp/rpm 700/3,000		
Crew 5		
Max. speed (km/h) 35		
Range (km) 170		
Remarks The heaviest German tank in operational service		

It was the Henschel design VK 4503(H) which was finally accepted for production, after an earlier design from them had also been rejected by the *Heereswaffenamt*. Tiger II was officially ordered in January 1943, and the first prototype appeared nine months later in October. This was three

months later than planned, the delay having been caused by attempts to standardise and simplify production between the new tank and the new Panther II design.

As will be seen from the report on the Henschel factory (Appendix 'A'), the production of the Tiger II took place in tandem with that of the Tiger I for a number of months, but from mid-1944, the firm's main production effort was switched over to the new tank. The planned output for Tiger II was 140 a month, but actual production fell well short of that figure. The final build appears to vary slightly between 485 and 489 — the factory report estimates 487. Clearly it was well below what Hitler had hoped for and not really sufficient to have much effect on the strategic outcome of operations, although tactically there was nothing on the Allied side that could compare with its massive firepower and high level of protection.

A good view of the PzKpfw VI Ausf B, the Tiger II, or *Königstiger* (King Tiger) as it was popularly called. There were two versions; the one shown in the photograph above has the Porsche turret fitted.

Below and overleaf.
Two more views of Tiger II, this time fitted with the Henschel turret. The long-barrelled 8.8 cm gun could deal with any tank then in service with consummate ease. Fortunately for Allied tankmen only 498 Tiger IIs were ever built!

General description

Tiger II was an impressive-looking tank of advanced design, but its basic layout followed standard German practice, being designed to be operated by a five-man crew, three of whom manned the centrally placed turret, while the engine was mounted at the rear, the drive being taken through the tank to the gearbox and thence to front-mounted sprockets. Armour was up to 180 mm thick and well angled, the turret and hull construction having been achieved using the minimum number of plates[75] and a limited number of plate thicknesses — six in all, ranging from 180 mm down to 25 mm. For example, the turret front plate was 180 mm at 10°, glacis plate 150 mm at 50°, turret sides and pannier sides 80 mm, top and belly 40 mm, (which made the latter thicker than the front glacis of the early Panzer IIIs and IVs). The whole of the hull and turret construction was effected by the German system of welding and plate interlocking, which added to its strength as is evidenced from the detailed Allied investigations of Tiger II which showed that they had stood up satisfactorily to all systems of attack. The later type of mantlet used on the Henschel turret had distinct advantages, being designed to prevent strikes being deflected down into the hull roof, as had been the case with the Porsche turret. Automotively, the layout and equipment fitted was very similar to Tiger I and Panther. This was probably the main weakness of the new tank, as it was underpowered and difficult to handle, being fitted with the Maybach HL 230 P 30 700 bhp engine as per later production Panthers, so there was a considerable difference in the power-to-weight ratios:

Type of tank	Power to weight ratio (hp/ton)
Panther Ausf G	15.6
Tiger I	12.3
Tiger II	10.1

Despite having a top speed on roads of 38 km/h (23.75 mph) and cross-country of 17 km/h (10.6 mph), comparing favourably with Tiger I's, the big tank was cumbersome to manoeuvre, difficult to steer and suffered from a very high fuel consumption, giving it a limited operational range — although, to be fair, this was not much worse than Tiger I. Tiger II carried 795 L (175 gal) of fuel, giving it an operational road range of about 160 km (100 miles), but on cross-country work it guzzled fuel at the rate of 7 L/km (2.48 gal per mile). Steering and transmission were as for the Tiger I, but as has been mentioned already, the steering had become even more delicate. The

suspension was also similar to that of the Tiger I, except that the bogies were overlapped only and not interleaved as had been the case with both Tiger I and Panther. Steel-tyred resilient wheels were used instead of the rubber-tyred pattern. Tracks were extremely wide — 80 cm (32 in) as compared with the 72.5 cm (28.5 in) tracks of the Tiger I.

A British War Office report[76] on Tiger II made some interesting observations on the AFV which, although they are valid, were perhaps overstated deliberately so that the battleworthiness of the new tank was played down. For example, it has this to say about the armoured protection: 'The armour, particularly that carried on the front of the vehicle, is the thickest to be employed on a tank to date, nevertheless the flanks are vulnerable and particularly so, because of the very large silhouette area (approx 24 ft long by 10 ft high) which has been incurred through certain characteristics in German design... Generally speaking the armour is arranged to offer a high standard of protection, but this is offset by reason of the bulk of the vehicle, which in turn is a function of general design.' It goes on to say the following about the suspension: 'The general assembly of suspension units is similar to that employed in Tiger I and the only important departure in suspension design is the use of overlapping bogie wheels as distinct from the overlapped and interleaved system found in Panther and Tiger I. It is assumed that interleaving has been abandoned on this vehicle by reason of the difficulties encountered in suspension maintenance and further through the problems of wheel jamming in shingle or boggy country. There can be little doubt that the tyre

loading, particularly with synthetic rubber, would have been prohibitive in a vehicle this size and the steel-tyred, resilient wheels have offered the best solution to the problem... Never-the-less captured German documents indicate that the resilient wheel has been designed in order to conserve rubber.' Both these statements are undoubtedly true, as we have already discussed the problems which Tiger I faced in Russia with snow and ice jamming the suspension, while the steel disc wheels certainly did save precious rubber.

Of course, the major improvement in Tiger II was the 8.8 cm KwK 43 L/71 tank gun, which at 6.3 m (20 ft 8 in) had the longest barrel and the largest calibre of any tank gun employed operationally by the Germans. It was also considered by many on both sides to be the best all-round tank gun of the war. Fitted with a double baffle muzzle brake and a semi-automatic falling-block type breech, the enormous gun needed a chassis wide enough to accept a 1.85 m (6 ft 1 in) turret ring (internal diameter). The front of the turret had to be built out to allow room for the trunnions to be mounted well forward and to allow space for the loader to load the long, heavy rounds into the breech. (An APCBC round for Tiger I weighed 12.5 kg (27.5 lb), while one for Tiger II weighed 16.4 kg (36.25 lb).) All this extra frontal weight meant that the turret needed a rear bustle, which provided stowage room for 22 rounds and thus made a very effective counter-weight. However, it added considerably to turret weight (Tiger II with the Porsche turret was 68.43 tons and this went up to 69.75 tons with the Henschel), making the turret very slow to traverse. The gun could elevate to +15°, depress to −8°, the gunner having to turn

the handwheel 13 times for every 10° of elevation or depression. Traverse was either by hand or power, using a similar two-speed power traverse system to the one already described on Tiger I, all round traverse taking 19 seconds at high ratio at 2,000 rpm and 77 seconds in low ratio at 1,000 rpm. The poor old gunner had to turn his handwheel through 700 complete revolutions to achieve 360° traverse, although there was an auxiliary handwheel for the loader which was marginally faster. No wonder they used to say that more Tiger II crews died of overwork than through enemy action! The gunner had a TFZ 9d monocular sighting telescope with either × 3 or × 6 magnification, while the commander had a rudimentary type of blade vane sight with which he could approximately line up the gun. Ammunition stowage varied between the two types of turret, 78 for the Porsche and 84 for the Henschel. The main armament rounds were either AP (APCBC or AP/CR) or HE (HE/AT or HE) as for the L/56 gun of Tiger I, but the muzzle velocity of the APCBC was much higher at 1,018 m/s (3,340 fps) (compared with 809 m/s

(2,657 fps) for the L/56). The gun's performance was formidable, a captured German report giving the following table of shoots against homogeneous armour plate:

A Tiger burns. American troops entering La Gleize, Belgium, pass a burning King Tiger, one of some 70-plus tanks to be destroyed east of Malmedy in December 1944, during the Ardennes offensive.

Range	Penetration at normal	Penetration at 30°
100 m (109 yd)	250 mm (9.8 in)	203 mm (8 in)
1,000 m (1,094 yd)	215 mm (8.5 in)	165 mm (6.5 in)
1,500 m (1,640 yd)	160 mm (6.3 in)	148 mm (5.8 in)
4,000 m (4,374 yd)	80 mm (3.1 in)	not given

Three machine-guns were fitted: MG 34 as co-axial, MG 34 hull in a ball mounting and MG 42 on the cupola for AA defence; a total of 39 × 150-round belts of MG ammunition was stowed. The commander had seven fixed episcopes (not vision blocks) in his cupola, one of which was sighted directly ahead, the loader had a fixed episcope also sighted directly forward, while the driver had a single periscope with movement ±15° in azimuth and ±5° in elevation. Finally, the hull gunner had a fixed episcope sighted 15° to the right-hand side, plus his standard Kfz 2 telescope for the MG 34. The escape

hatches on the tank comprised irregular shaped doors in the hull roof for the driver and hull gunner and a rectangular hatch in the turret roof for the loader, while the commander and gunner both used the commander's hatch which had a circular door in the top. In addition to these hatches there was a large door 52 cm × 47.6 cm (20.5 in × 18.75 in) in the bulge at the rear of the turret which could be used for escape purposes as well as getting rid of empty cases and for bombing up. It was fitted with a wedge-shaped pistol port, closed by a plug attached by a chain. Finally, there was a

The gigantic 70-ton *Jagdtiger*, the heaviest tank destroyer to see action during World War 2. Its 12.8 cm gun and 250 mm thick armour plate made it a fearsome weapon. It was underpowered, however, having only the same engine as the Panther.

JAGDTIGER (SDKFZ 186)
Date of origin 1944
Weight (tonnes) 70 [Porsche turret*]
Overall dimensions (m) **Length** 10.65
  Height 2.95
  Width 3.63
Armament/Ammunition carried
  Main 1 × 12.8 cm PaK 44 L/55
    40 rounds
  Secondary 1 × 7.92 mm MG 34 &
    1 × 7.92 mm MG 42
Armour thickness (mm) Max. 250
    Min. 25
Engine Type Maybach HL 230 P30
  bhp/rpm 700/3,000
Crew 6
Max. speed (km/h) 38
Range (km) 170
Remarks Heaviest tank destroyer in
    service in World War Two;
    *2 tonnes heavier with
    Henschel turret

circular aperture 23 cm (9 in) in diameter over the breech of the gun, fitted with a hinged cover, to provide extra ventilation during heavy firing.

Command tanks A number of Tiger IIs were converted to the command role in the normal way. The PzBefWg mit 8.8 cm KwK 43 L/71, as it was known, was only able to carry 63 rounds of main armament ammunition, the loss of the other 17 rounds being the penalty paid in order to install the extra radio equipment.

The Tiger II made its debut on the Eastern front in May 1944, while the first specimen the British inspected (mounting a Porsche turret) was knocked out in Normandy in August 1944. Only small numbers were used in Normandy, so they had to take a hammering and were mainly knocked out by the sheer weight of Allied numbers. Tiger IIs were used in many subsequent actions, for example in the Ardennes offensive, but were present only in small numbers as all three heavy tank units which took part in the attack were under-strength. However, the Tiger's reputation was such as to completely outweigh all other reports. As Charles Whiting explains in his book *The Battle of the Bulge*, 'Although reports from American soldiers would indicate that the Tiger was omnipresent, only about 150[77] of them were to fight in the Ardennes... A Tiger advancing with machine-guns blazing or 88 blasting was a near paralyzing sight.'

Jagdtiger (SdKfz 186)

As a very young officer, newly commissioned in the summer of 1948, I remember vividly being taken to visit the battlefields in the Ardennes area and coming across what seemed to be an entire regiment of Sherman tanks which had been completely annihilated. There were Shermans lying in heaps everywhere one looked, turrets blown off, hulls ripped apart, most had clearly been brewed up — not for nothing was Sherman known as the 'Tommy Cooker'. They had been advancing with the grain of the country and had clearly been taken by surprise from a flank. The follow-up echelon had then turned right-handed towards their tormentor, but had found little cover along their new line of advance. The author of all this carnage was one single *Jagdtiger*, whose immense bulk still occupied a perfect fire position in a farmyard at the top of a commanding hill feature. The *Jagdtiger* itself had been burnt out either by air attack, or perhaps by its own crew when they ran out of ammunition. The memory of the scene has remained with me for nearly 40 years, a perfect example of a tank destroyer doing its deadly work. *Jagdtiger*, of course, had the firepower and protection it needed to get the job done, with its 12.8 cm PaK 44 L/55 gun and armour 250 mm thick on its front plate.

Jagdtiger came into existence as the result of a *Heereswaffenamt* decision to produce a limited-traverse version of Tiger II. At over 70 tons it was the heaviest German AFV to go into service, the prototype appearing in April 1944. The chassis was about 25 cm (10 in) longer than the Tiger II's, with the superstructure built up to form a vast, fixed turret, with sloping sides, in which the 12.8 cm gun, turret crew of four (commander, gunner and two loaders) and 38 rounds of ammunition (separate projectile and charge) were located. The rest of the crew, driver and hull gunner/radio operator, were in their normal positions in the front of the tank destroyer. The enormous cast, bell-shaped gunshield allowed for a normal amount of elevation but very limited traverse (elevation $-7\frac{1}{2}°$ to $+15°$, traverse only $10°$ left and right of centre). The *Jagdtiger* was initially armed with the Pak 44 L/55 version of the 12.8 cm gun, but later models mounted the Pak 80L/55 although, when there was a shortage of 12.8 cm guns, some had to be fitted with the same 8.8 cm PaK 43/3 as the *Jagdpanther*. Of 150 *Jagdtigers* ordered, only some 70–80 were actually built. Sole manufacturer was Nibelungen-Werk (Steyr-Daimler-Puch) of St Valentin. Just two were built with a special suspension designed by Dr Porsche, but this proved unsatisfactory. *Jagdtiger* must have been difficult to manoeuvre, although its top speed was not much below that of the Tiger II and it had a range of 160 km (100 miles) on roads and 82 (75) cross-country. *Jagdtiger* was only issued to two combat units and saw action in the Ardennes offensive and later in the defence of Germany.

10
Superheavies, specialised vehicles and captured tanks

The superheavies

Hitler's obsession with heavy tanks reached its zenith with the production of the superheavies of which only two[78] models were actually ever built — *Maus* and the E 100 — although a number of others were talked about and some even reached the design stage. Clearly certain influential members of the German armaments industry shared Hitler's enthusiasm for superheavy tanks, initially anyway, and foremost among them was Dr Porsche, President of the Panzer Kommission and confidante of the Führer. Whether his ideas were widely approved among the other tank designers is unclear — they were certainly highly critical after the war — but Dr Porsche must have had limited support at least in the early days or nothing would have ever materialised. What is clear, is that the time and effort spent on designing and producing these behemoths wasted a vast amount of precious design and production effort, which Germany could ill afford to spare.

Maus on trial, with a 55 ton weight on the superstructure instead of the turret.

MAUS

'This gigantic offspring of the fantasy of Hitler and his advisers' is how Guderian described *Maus*, which started life under the more appropriate codename of *Mammut* (Mammoth). A British War Office Technical Intelligence summary dated 11 October 1945 gave details of the development of *Maus*, as obtained from examination of documents and the interrogation of staff at the Porsche establishments of Zell-am-See and Gmud. It told how Dr Porsche was interviewed in Berlin on 8 June 1942, by Adolf Hitler and Albert Speer, Reich Minister for armaments and war production in the Nazi government. They spoke first about the fitting of the 8.8 cm L/71 gun on to Tiger (P) (the *Ferdinand/Elefant* project as explained in the last chapter) and then Dr Porsche was asked to start work on a chassis to mount a 12.8 cm or 15 cm gun in a revolving turret as a self-propelled gun. A co-axial 7.5 cm gun was also to be included, while the basic armour was to be of the following thicknesses: front 200 mm; sides 180 mm; track guards 100 mm; turret front 240 mm; and turret sides and roof 200 mm. Porsche suggested that he should design an

air-cooled diesel engine for the vehicle, but Speer over-ruled him, saying that there was insufficient time, so it was decided to use a

MAUS		
Date of origin 1943		
Weight (tonnes) 188		
Overall dimensions (m)	**Length**	10.09
	Height	3.66
	Width	3.67
Armament/Ammunition carried		
Main 1 × 12.8 cm KwK 44 L/55 32 rounds		
Secondary 1 × 7.5 cm KwK 44 L/36.5 200 rounds		
Armour thickness (mm)	Max.	240
	Min.	40
Engine Type DB 509 V12 petrol or MB 517 diesel		
bhp/rpm N/A		
Crew 5		
Max. speed (km/h) 20		
Range (km) 186		
Remarks Two only constructed; never entered service		

Daimler-Benz aircraft engine instead. No stipulations were given as to the size, weight or performance of the new tank (known then as Type 205) and Porsche was given far more latitude than ever before, perhaps to make up for his disappointment on losing the Tiger competition to Henschel.

Porsche decided to use electric transmission again, despite the inevitable problems this would raise due to shortage of copper. However, as the report says: 'He states, however that he would have used it in any case as he considered it by far the most practical method of obtaining light steering of an ultra-heavy vehicle'. He did decide to redesign the Tiger (P) system, the basic differences between the two being as follows. Firstly, as a single engine was to be used, it was necessary for Zadnik (Porsche's electrical specialist) to redesign the generator layout, using a duplex generator instead of two separate ones. Secondly, a completely different electrical circuit was needed. When both Porsche and Zadnik were questioned as to why they had decided to alter a perfectly workable system, they both said it was because of their desire to produce an electrical transmission which would present no difficulties to a driver who was used to conventional designs. The Tiger system had the disadvantage that every time the driver lifted his foot and left both control levers in the forward position, he would feel as though he was 'free wheeling' in neutral, whereas the *Maus* system gave the same feel as a solid mechanical drive.

Towards the end of 1942, the *Heereswaffenamt* appointed a Colonel Haenel, as a 'chaser' to all the firms concerned in the project, his directive being to pay continual visits, threatening them with serious penalties if they fell behind schedule! Porsche was annoyed and Colonel Haenel was treated as something of a joke — certainly his first directive when he visited Stuttgart on 18 December 1942, that Maus should be ready for trials by the following May, was 'considered as being more humorous than anything else and no notice was taken'.

Just before Haenel's appointment a major hitch had occurred, as Daimler-Benz said that they could not supply the diesel engine which Porsche had proposed to use. The only available engine was the DB 509 petrol engine, so this had to be used instead, despite Porsche's desire for a compression ignition engine. Then it was found that the engine could only be installed in an inverted position, which necessitated the provision of a vertical gear train to bring the drive to the level of the generator shaft. Another minor design point was that the gear ratio had to be made very slightly different in order to re-move the possibility of excessive wear due to gearing a 12-cylinder engine to a 6-pole generator.

Dr Porsche went to Berlin on 4 January 1943 to show Hitler a model of the new tank; the Führer was very interested and no amendments were made at that stage. Later in the month members of the *Heereswaffenamt* came to Stuttgart and allocated the construction work on an official basis, as follows: hull and turret — Krupp; electrical — Siemens-Schuckert; engine — Daimler-Benz; suspension, tracks and gearing — Skoda; assembly — Alkett. After another conference in Berlin on 21 Janaury, it was decided to push on with the project as fast as possible. 'The only discordant voice appears to have been Kniekamp[79] (representing Wa Pruf 6) who was positive that the vehicle would prove quite unsteerable.'

Dr Porsche's next summons to Berlin was on 2 February 1943, when he was told by Colonel Haenel that it had been decided to incorporate a flamethrower with 1,000 l (220 gal) of fuel. Dr Porsche protested that this could not be done, but he was over-ruled and told that it was considered essential. Yet another meeting took place at Stuttgart on 10 February between the *Heereswaffenamt* and representatives of the contracting firms, to discuss the flamethrower. At that time, in early 1943, there appears to have been considerable urgency to get the project completed, so all the contractors protested that the flamethrower would impose more delays, but they were all over-ruled. No firm production dates were agreed, although the firms did say they would do their utmost to complete the work as quickly as possible. The decision to fit the flamethrower was, however, the cause of a major design change, namely the alteration from torsion bar to volute spring suspension. The original intention had been to use complete Tiger (P) suspension units. The first detailed estimate of weight had come out at 179.3 tons, but this had now to be increased with the addition of the flamethrower and fuel (4,900 kg/10,800 lb), the total increase being more than $5\frac{1}{2}$ per cent. The only way to cater for this extra weight was to include one more suspension unit on either side, but there was no room. It was therefore decided, in co-operation with Skoda, to change to a simple volute suspension in view of the timescale. Dr Porsche had thus to depart from his favourite form of suspension as he felt that there was not time for him to design and test a new torsion bar layout.

The War Office report states that Speer paid an unexpected visit to the Stuttgart offices on 6 April 1943 and stayed for half an hour inspecting a full scale wooden model of Maus. Four days later, orders were received to take the model to Berchtesgaden, presumably as a result of Speer's visit, so it was dismantled, packed up and got ready for the journey. However, the order was then cancelled, so it was reassembled. On 6 May the order came a second time and the model was finally seen by Hitler at Rastenberg on 14 May. Apparently he complained that the size of the tank made the 12.8 cm gun 'look like a child's toy' so Krupp were ordered to build a new turret containing a 15 cm gun, but with the 7.5 cm co-axial still retained.

The *Heereswaffenamt* now began to complain, as anticipated, about the amount of copper being used and Porsche's chief engineer, Herr Rabe, was sent to Zahnradfabrik of Friedrichshaven, to discuss plans for using the ZF electro-magnetic box which had been originally developed by ZF before the war and now further developed to provide seven ratios. Herr Wiedman, a director of ZF, refused to do anything without an OKH contract, and as this was not forthcoming the matter was dropped and the manufacture of the electric drive continued.

On 16 July, the DB 509 engine arrived at Stuttgart where it was put through trials in conjunction with the cooling system, under a Professor Kamm, at the Technical Institute. The modifications necessary to convert the engine from aircraft to tank use had been minor and were concerned with the need to allow free operation in the inverted position and for a lower grade of fuel to be used, by lowering the compression ratio and boosting pressure. It passed all its tests with flying colours. However, it was later decided to construct a second prototype *Maus*, because Daimler-Benz could now provide a diesel engine, modified from the MG 517 motor boat engine.

Alkett started to assemble the first prototype on 1 August, but Krupp had been unable to keep to their schedule for the hull and turret construction, because of constant Allied air raids. Perhaps the most significant date in this whole saga was 27 October 1943, when Porsche and Rabe met Speer in Berlin and were told that, although construction of both prototypes (*Maus* I with the DB 509 petrol engine and *Maus* II with the MB 517 diesel) could continue, no arrangements were going to be made for its eventual production. This must have made them wonder if all their hard work was really to be in vain, but it did not stop progress, as later a further nine *Maus* were known to be under construction, while the total anticipated production figure was set at 150. Krupp supplied the first hull in the middle of September, and *Maus* I, completed as far as possible, made its first test run at Alkett's on

23 December, with a 55 tonne (54 UK/60.6 US tons) weight in place of a turret. The short trial run was most satisfactory and the tank was then sent to the nearby testing grounds at Böblingen for further trials, with a Herr Zadnik as driver. Remarkably these trials were also trouble-free, with the exception of some cases of spring failure meaning that these would have to be stiffened slightly if *Maus* went into production. There was also a bearing failure in the auxiliary gearbox which had not occurred before — the only three troubles which had been experienced during rig testing had been overheating of the vertical gear train between the engine and generator; reversal of polarity on the 48 v independent exciter in the electrical system; and severe rusting of the manifold due to use of low grade material. The first two were both cured satisfactorily, but nothing could be done about the rusting, as no other material was available. The driver found the steering excellent, reporting that it was possible to turn the tank on its own axis. It was tested on snow, ice, grass, mud and hard surfaces and as the report explains: 'independent observers, who had witnessed earlier tests of different vehicles, are reputed to have told Zadnik that the *Maus* did everything that the Panther did'. Maximum speed achieved on hard surfaces was 13 km/h (8 mph) with full motor field, and by weakening the field to the minimum, a top speed of 22 km/h (13.75 mph) was achieved.

About the time of this testing, Porsche was given instructions that Hitler wanted the complete tank, including turret and weaponry, to be ready by June 1944. *Maus* II arrived at Böblingen on 20 March, but was put on one side, awaiting delivery of its diesel engine. The first Krupp turret arrived on 3 May, but with no fittings, to be followed

by the guns, power traverse and other turret items a few days later. By 9 June the Krupp's fitters, who had come with it, had fitted the complete turret on to the tank and it was then ready for further trials. Once again these proved most satisfactory, in fact it was recorded that the performance of *Maus* I was even better than before, doubtless because the actual turret weighed less (the turret complete with ammunition weighed 50.5 tonnes (49.7 Uk/55.7 US tons) instead of the expected 55 tonnes (54 UK/60.6 US tons). Orders were received to send *Maus* I to the Kummersdorf testing ground in October and shortly afterwards the diesel engine for *Maus* II arrived at Böblingen. It had already proved superior to the petrol engine during earlier trials, so was immediately installed in *Maus* II, which was sent to Kummersdorf without further testing. This was at the beginning of November and was done on orders from the OKH. On arrival the engine started, but immediately broke its crankshaft — due to faulty alignment between the engine and the generator.

They had to wait until the middle of March 1945 before another diesel engine could be delivered to Kummersdorf and Porsche sent a team of fitters to install it. This was done successfully, but no testing took place before the war ended, so the final situation seems to have been: *Maus* I — complete with DB 509 petrol engine, 12.8 cm and 7.5 cm guns, fully tested; *Maus* II — with MB 517 diesel engine, no turret, untested. Both were located at Kummersdorf, where they were supposedly blown up in order to prevent their capture by the Russians. However, since the war there have been reports that one *Maus* still exists in a museum somewhere in Russia. I have recently been able to confirm this claim

Maus I complete with its turret fitted with the main armament — 12.8 cm KwK 44 L/55 gun. It then weighed 189 tons.

as I have seen it 'alive and well' on a video taken in a military museum just outside Moscow.

So ends the *Maus* story. The tank would certainly have been a remarkable sight on the battlefield, being over 9 m (30 ft) long with the gun front and over 11.5 m (38.5 ft) long with the gun rear (due to the fact that the turret was much nearer the rear of the hull). It was over 3.6 m (12 ft) wide, nearly the same in height and, combat-ready, weighed 189 tonnes (180 UK/208 US tons). Its tracks were over 109 cm (43 in) wide and it had a ground clearance of 54 cm (1 ft 9.25 in). Sixty-one rounds of 12.8 cm and 200 rounds of 7.5 cm ammunition were carried, together with 2,650 l (583 gal) of fuel (1,000 l/220 gal in a jettison tank), while it had a crew of five men. It is said that, despite its great size, the interior of the tank was almost completely filled with masses of complicated machinery, so it is doubtful whether it could ever have remained battle-worthy for very long periods. However, it had a good performance on test, with a top speed of over 20 km/h (12.5 mph). It could also deal with a 30° slope, a 76 cm (2.5 ft) vertical obstacle and ford to a depth of 2 m (6 ft 7 in) (it was also intended to be sub-mersible to a depth of 8 m (26 ft)). It had a radius of action, with the jettison tank, of 160 km (100 miles) on roads.

E 100

An ETO Ordnance Technical Intelligence Report issued on 24 May 1945, by Headquarters Communications Zone, ETOUSA, deals with the examination of the Henschel tank proving ground and development

centre near Kassel, where an experimental heavy tank and a gun motor carriage were discovered. The latter was *Grille*, which is described in Note [78]; the former was known simply as the E 100, and the American report stated that it was 'a tank estimated to weigh approximately one hundred and ten tons', that its external features 'resemble the Tiger Model B tank, with the following new features: (1) increased length and width, (2) heavier armor plate throughout, (3) wider track, (4) new suspension. The torsion bar is not used. A search is being made for coil springs for use in conjunction with mechanical hydraulic shock absorbers. (5) spaced armor plate, made in three sections is bolted to the side plates of the tank, giving a rounded surface at the sponsons... Major items lacking for the complete assembly are the gun, turret ring, suspension springs and drive sprocket.'

The E 100 heavy tank which the Americans had found was the most advanced of an entirely new series of tanks which the weapons Department had initiated in mid-1943, to be known as the 'E-series'.[80] The aim was to endeavour to draw upon the potential of these firms in the automobile industry who were not then engaged in AFV production. Development projects were sent to such firms as Klockner-Humbolt-Deutz and Magirus, Argus and Adler. The following types of AFVs were planned:

E 5 — light tank of 5 tonne (4.9 UK/5.5 US tons) class, also as basis of an APC, radio-controlled or recce tank.

E 10 — light tank destroyer, weapons carrier or APC in the 10 ton (9.8 UK/11 US tons) class.

E 25 — medium tank destroyer, recce tank or heavy weapons carrier in 25 tonne (24.6 UK/27.6 US tons) class.

E 50 — a 50 to 65 tonne (49–64 UK/55–72 US tons) 'light' battle tank to replace Panther.

E 75 — a 75 to 80 tonne (74–79 UK/83–88 US tons) 'medium' battle tank as the replacement for Tiger.

E 100 — heavy tank in the 140 tonne (138 UK/154 US tons) class.

In an interrogation held at 27 Grosvenor Square, London, on 31 August 1945, Dipl Ing Heinrich Ernst Kniekamp, Chief Engineer of *Waffenprüfamt* 6, had this to say in answer to the question 'What was the reason for embarking on the design of the "E" series tanks and what were the general design considerations?' He said 'The reasons were: (1) That to achieve a very strong front plate all possible weight had to be moved to

the rear of the tank. (2) Unit motor and power train was desired because of the simplified manufacturing and service. (3) It was planned, by using two types of engine and power train, to produce four vehicles, the E 10, E 25, E 50, and E 100... This programme was first conceived by Herr Kniekamp in May 1942 and was submitted and approved as a project in April 1943. (4) All suspensions should be attached from the outside and no fighting space should be encumbered by through torsion rods. (5) In case the front idler or any of the bogie wheels were destroyed by mines, the vehicle must be capable of proceeding by adjusting the track around the remaining wheels. The

The enormous 100 cm wide tracks of the E-100, outside the Henschel factory at Paderborn, where one E-100 was partly completed.

technical superiority of forward drive was recognised, but the military advantage of having the drive at the rear where it was not endangered by mines or gunfire, influenced the choice of rear drive. The rear drive was also favoured because of the clean fighting compartment achieved thereby.'[81]

The E 100 was to have been armed with the same weapons as *Maus* in the same Krupp turret, although one was never fitted. The tank was to have been powered by a Maybach 12-cylinder 'V' type engine, developing 700 hp at 3,000 rpm; since this was the same engine intended for the E 50 and E 75 models, the E 100 would have had a very low power-to-weight ratio of just over 5 hp/ton. A modified engine was built later, which had fuel injection and supercharging and could have developed some 1,000–1,200 hp, but this still meant that the power-to-weight ratio was raised to only about 8.5 hp/ton. For initial testing a normal Tiger B H1 230 P30 engine was fitted. With tracks nearly 102 cm (40 in) wide, the E 100 had a ground pressure of nearly 1.4 kg/cm² (20 psi), while its suspension comprised a series of overlapping steel road wheels, with MAN disc springs, so it looked very like the Tiger B. Despite what Ing Kniekamp said about the desirability for rear drive on the E series, the E 100 (the only model to be built) had front drive.

VK 7001

Another superheavy tank to be partially designed during the war was the VK 7001 (K), which resulted from the *Heereswaffen-amt* giving Krupp a development contract to study a series of superheavies between 100 and 170 tons, presumably because they were somewhat put out by Hitler dealing direct with Porsche. It was also known by a number of other names, including 'Lion' and 'Tiger-Mouse'. It came to nothing. Finally, some passing consideration was even given to a 1,500-ton tank, which was to be driven by four submarine diesel engines, with armour 250 mm thick and armed with dual 11.5 cm guns in rear-mounted turrets, plus an 8 cm cannon at the front! Fortunately for the German armament industry at least sanity prevailed to some degree and this project never left the drawing board. However, as has already been stated, much valuable effort was undoubtedly wasted on the design of these superheavies.

Specialised vehicles

Although the vehicles in this section are not strictly tanks, they are tracked vehicles and because of their small size, do form an interesting comparison with the super-heavies, so I feel they are well worth covering. They were all so similar in purpose as to be allocated the same prefix letter in the OKH vocabulary, namely 'B', but were actually of two distinct varieties: *Minenraumwagen* (mine clearing vehicles) and *Ladungsträger* (explosives carriers).

The SdKfz 300 *Minenraumwagen* was an expendable, remotely-controlled mine-clearing vehicle, built by Borgward in 1939–40. There were two versions, known as BI and BII, the earlier towing a number of rollers intended to detonate mines. They

Earliest of the expendable mine clearing vehicles were the SdKfz 300 *Minenraumwagen* B1 which had three roadwheels, and the B2 (seen here) which had four roadwheels.

weighed about 1,500 kg (3,300 lb), and had no crew. There was also an experimental amphibious version called *Ente* (Duck), based upon the BII. Some 50 were produced in all, but none saw any combat service and they were later replaced by *Goliath*.

GOLIATH

There were two versions of the *leichter Ladungsträger* Goliath, the first being the SdKfz

The first Goliath (SdKfz 302) was powered by two electric motors. The photograph shows it being manhandled by soldiers using a small wheeled trailer.

302, about 1.5 m (6 ft) long by 0.6 m (2 ft) high and weighing 370 kg (816 lb). It was powered by two electric motors, one to run each track, could move at speeds up to 10 km/h (6 mph) and had a range of 1½ km (1 mile) before the batteries ran down. Goliath was guided by means of a three-strand cable, two strands for steering and one for detonating the 60 kg (132 lb) charge of explosive which the little rhomboidal vehicle carried in its belly. Over 2,600 were built in 1942–43, but they lacked range and carrying capacity.

The second model, the SdKfz 303,

The second Goliath (SdKfz 303) was powered by a two-cylinder motor cycle engine which gave it a better performance. It could also hold more explosive.

weighed slightly more (430 kg/948 lb) and carried up to 100 kg (220 lb) of explosive. It was powered by a two-cylinder 703 cc motor cycle engine and could travel at speeds up to 12 km/h (7.5 mph). With a range of 12 km (7.5 miles), it was a great improvement on the earlier Goliath. Over 4,900 were built between April 1943 and January 1945.

SPRINGER

Built by NSU, some 50 SdKfz 304 *mittlerer Ladungsträger* were produced between late 1944 and early 1945. It was designed to replace both the earlier light and heavy demolition vehicles and weighed 2.4 tonnes (2.35 UK/2.65 US tons). The 3.2 m (10 ft 6in) long vehicle had a crew of one and was powered by a 1.5 litre Opel Olympia engine, which gave it a top speed of 42 km/h (26 mph) and a range of 200 km (125 miles). It could carry 330 kg (728 lb) of explosive and the technique used was for the *Springer* to be driven as near as possible to the target, when the driver then dismounted and closed down the turret so as to protect the radio receiver, which was used to guide the vehicle to its target and then to set off the explosive charge.

SONDERSCHLEPPER B IV

Heaviest of the three types was the *schwerer Ladungsträger*, the SdKfz 301, of which there were three versions, Ausf A, B and C. Just over 570 were built by Borgward between 1942 and 1944, the Ausf C being the most numerous and powered by a slightly more powerful Borgward engine than the other two (3.8 litre instead of 2.31 litre). All could carry 500 kg (1,100 lb) of explosive, had a crew of one, a top speed of 38–40 km/h (24–25 mph) and a range of 212 km (132 miles). The Ausf C weighed 4.9 tonnes (4.8 UK/5.4 US tons) and was just over 4 m (13 ft) long, while the smaller previous models weighed 3.5 tonnes (3.4 UK/3.86 US tons)

The *Springer* was built by NSU and had a crew of one man who had to drive it as near to the intended target as possible. It was then guided the rest of the way by radio.

There were three types of heavy tracked demolition vehicle and the photograph shows the first of these, the *Sonderschlepper* BIV Ausf A. The explosive was carried in the wedge-shaped bin on the front of the vehicle.

Borgward produced 305 of the Ausf C version of the BIV. It had better protection and improved performance, but it still must have been a great test of nerve to drive one, full of explosive, in the battle area.

and were 3.6 m (11 ft 10 in) long. They were all radio-controlled and worked in much the same way as already described for *Springer*. The explosive was carried in a wedge-shaped bin on the front of the vehicle.

Operational use

'*Beetle Tanks' used against the bridgehead:* that was the headline in the London *Evening News* of 1 March 1944, reporting that the Germans were using wire-controlled 'beetle tanks' against the Allied bridgehead at Anzio, south of Rome. The report explained that the new weapon had been used for the first time a month or two previously on the

Russian front and was the latest secret weapon referred to by Hitler in one of his recent speeches. Another newspaper report of the same period included a diagram showing how the weapon was used and mentioned the existence of a 'Beetle Mark II' which was radio-controlled instead of wire controlled. A contemporary American article on the same subject talked about the Goliath as being nick-named the 'Doodle bug' by GIs and explained that: 'in Italy the Goliaths got stuck in the mud and on hills and sometimes exploded before reaching our lines, wounding German troops. The Goliath was also vulnerable to small-arms fire. Neither radio nor cable control made it effective. The Goliath was first committed against our positions on the Anzio beachhead in February. Fourteen were knocked out by artillery and none reached our positions.'

The same article goes on to explain a second type of radio-controlled demolition tank, called the B4, which was stopped by a British mine near the beachhead positions in April 1944. The writer, Major James H. Quello, had this to say about the tactical use of the weapon: 'The B4 is used to clear paths through barbed wire and destroy roadblocks and pillboxes. The operator drives it as far toward the target as he can. Then he switches the vehicle over to remote control and leaves by a side door. A stationary control unit, carried by the driver or in a nearby tank, assault gun or other vehicle, then directs the B4 in zigzag fashion to its objective. There the explosive is dropped and the tank is moved to a safe distance before a time fuze sets off the demolition. The vehicle, unlike the Goliath, is recoverable. But if there is the danger of capture, the operator can set off a self-destroying device in the tank. The driver of the B4 has a dangerous job. German soldiers call it the "death trap" or the "living coffin".'

Another British report[82], talks about specimens of Goliath being captured in France, after having been concealed in small dugouts facing the beaches, but in dead ground behind a slight rise. It goes on to say that: 'The vehicles were almost identical with the electrically-driven Goliath captured in Italy, escept that the front driving gear and sprocket were enclosed in an oil-bath. An attempt to make the vehicle waterproof appears to have been made and it is possible that it could travel under water for a limited period.' The amphibious capability is again mentioned in another Tech Int Bulletin, which talks about Goliath as being capable of 'moving under water (presumably along the bottom) and to be intended for use against landing craft or large boats'. No reports appear to exist of Goliath actually

being used in this role, but a slightly earlier report from the Mediterranean area claims the origin of the Goliath concept as being French: 'It is interesting to note how closely the conception and design has followed that of our own "Metrovick Beetle", which was developed early in the war and subsequently dropped. The reason may be found, perhaps, in a common origin for the two — the French "Machine K" of which particulars were made available to us and also, doubtless, to the Boche at a later date.'

Captured equipment

Prior to the outbreak of the war, the *Heereswaffenamt* had instituted a system for listing all foreign equipment and weapons, giving details in a series of illustrated books known as the *Kennblatter Fremdgerät*.[83] Each item was recorded in some detail with, where available, photographs and drawings. Group series numbers were allocated, tanks for example being 700 and self-propelled guns 800, while armoured cars were 200. To this figure was added a letter in brackets which denoted the country of origin, so (e) stood for *englisch* (British), (r) for *russisch* (Russian), (a) for *amerikanisch* (American), and so on.

Germany, like all the other combatants of World War 2, made full use of captured enemy equipment, as the photographs in this section show. They did, however, do this to a far greater degree than the Allies, and in particular took into service all the French tanks which were captured when France surrendered in 1940. With typical German thoroughness, these were 'taken on charge' by the Army and given full German names and designations. So, for example, the main infantry tank in the French Army, the Renault R 35, became the PzKpfw 35 R 731(f): the Somua S 35 medium tank became the PzKpfw 35 S 739(f) and the main medium

This assault version of the KVI, armed with a 152 mm howitzer, was captured in Russia and pressed into German service. It is seen here leaving a hangar with its German crew/Oberst Helmut Ritgen.

Probably the oldest tanks in service with the German Army were these World War 1 vintage French Renault FT17s (Rudolf Wulff).

tank, the Char B I *bis*, was known as the PzKpfw B 2 740(f). There were a number of others, many original tank chassis being converted into self-propelled guns, using a mixture of German, French and Russian guns. Even the ancient Renault FT 17 of World War 1 vintage was captured in large numbers and pressed into service. These French AFVs were able to be kept running from the existing stocks of spare parts held by the French Army on capitulation, and of course as the Germans took over all the tank factories when they occupied France, production could continue. We have seen how this happened in Czechoslovakia and it was repeated in France.

The Germans also took over a fair number of Italian tanks, when their erstwhile ally made a separate peace in September 1943. These included the *Carro Armato* M13/40 and M 15/42 which were known as the PzKpfw M 13/40 735(i) and PzKpfw M 15/42 738(i) respectively.

Annexia

Date of visit 19–24 Apr 45

I. Introduction

Henschel & Sohn consists of three general engineering works in Kassel.

Werk I — Kassel proper was devoted to locomotive assembly and gun production.

Werk II — Rothenditmold, comprising a large foundry, boiler, and other locomotive component shops.

Werk III — Mittelfeld, was largely devoted to tank assembly and component manufacture.

Leading personalities of the Henschel concern are as follows:
Chairman Herr Oscar Henschel *Welfare Director* Herr Robert Henschel *Managing Director* Dr Stieler von Heydekampf *Financial Director* Herr Fleischer *Production Manager* Dr Pertus *Tank Designer* Dr Aders

This report is restricted to the Mittelfeld plant as being the only one engaged on tank assembly.

Werk III sustained considerable damage in the past two years from air attacks, thus necessitating a certain amount of re-organisation of the manufacturing facilities. When examined, however, the plant was still capable of producing a substantial number of tanks a month. Layout of the plant is included as Appendix A.

II. Historical background

Originally established as long ago as 1810 at Kassel on the site of the present Werk I, Henschel built up a world wide reputation as a designer and builder of locomotives and were, during the present war, the largest single producer in Germany. In 1871 the Company expanded its productive capacity considerably by the erection of Werk II for locomotive component manufacture. During World War I, Henschel undertook armament manufacture, producing both tanks and artillery and had by the end of the war built a further works (Werk III).

In the interim period between 1918 and the resumption of land armaments production in 1935, Henschel extended their activities to include the manufacture of MT, diesel engines and aircraft; in the case of aircraft, new works were erected at Berlin-Johannisthal (1933), Berlin-Schönefeld (1935) and Kassel-Altenbauna (1938).

A great deal of development has gone on in recent years, particularly at Werk III, and at the time of the occupation this large concern was making an extremely valuable contribution to the German war effort in the shape of aircraft, locomotive, tank and gun production; MT manufacture was suspended early in the war.

Some indication of Henschel's importance in fields other than tank manufacture, which is dealt with in more detail below, may be gained from the following production figures, based on deliveries, which exclude components and/or spare parts: —

	1942	1943	1944
Locomotives	620	820	590
Medium artillery	220	216	95
8.8 cm Pak 43/41	} 120	} 1,182	251
8.8 cm Pak 43			1,341
2 cm Flak 38	1,588	1,292	72

III. Armament production

1935 — Henschel started to make the PzKpfw I, Model B. The parent concern of this tank was given as Krupp although documentary evidence has shown the 'Lieferfirma' to be Henschel. It appeared to have made prototypes in 1933 and 34.

1937 — Assembly of the PzKpfw II was commenced.

1938 — Henschel experimented with 30-ton tanks called the DW I and DW II incorporating 50 mm frontal armour, interleaved wheels, torsion bar suspension adapted from half-tracks and had also a regenerative steering system designed by them and following the same general principle as that employed later in the Tiger tank. The main armament was to be a 7.5 cm KwK (short barrel) and the tank was powered by a Maybach HL 116 six-cylinder in-line engine. Later a 36- and 65-ton tank were designed.

1939–40 — Henschel began large scale production of the PzKpfw III.

1941 — In response to a German General Staff requirement, the project for the 'Tiger I' was first discussed in the summer of 1941. It was designed to have as many basic features of the DW I as possible. This tank went into production in November 1941 and a prototype was presented to Hitler on his birthday on 20 April 1942. Considerable development ensued particularly in regard to the steering gear which was designed to provide for three radii of turn in each gear as on the DW I, but afterwards two radii were found to be adequate and the design was accordingly simplified.

1942 — In the autumn of this year, the 'Tiger II' was conceived. The specification provided for thicker frontal armour, sloping plates similar to the "Panther" and the 8.8 cm KwK 43. It was first produced in November 1943 and has been Henschel's sole product since June 1944

1945 — at the time of the occupation Henschel was developing an improved steering mechanism using the same general design as the previous one, but bringing about considerable simplification in production and having a greater torque capacity. This was necessitated by the parallel development of a new engine of greater output. This Maybach power unit is alleged to be of the same swept volume, this is, 23 litres, but was to be supercharged giving a maximum hp of 1,000.

Development was also stated to be proceeding on alternative power units of greater output by Steyr-Daimler-Puch, Argus, and Klockner-Humboldt-Deutz. The Steyr-Daimler unit was of double 'V' form, the Argus of 'H' form and the Klockner-Humboldt-Deutz was a diesel. Yet another engine development had been envisaged, namely a BMW radial but this was abandoned because of considerations of space. Further development was stated to have begun in December 1944 on a steam power unit under the Doble license. Work on this was at the drawing office stage at the time of the occupation. It was stated that the greater bulk of this installation would preclude its use as a fighting vehicle and therefore development was proceeding with a view to providing a fully tracked armoured recovery vehicle. Considerations of weight and speed, however, were thought to necessitate a reduction in armour thickness. This steam project was intended to be used in adaptations of both the 'Tiger II' and 'Panther'.

In 1943 some exploratory research work was embarked upon in connection with fluid transmissions for the 'Tiger II'. The 'Foettinger' torque converter was tried in this machine but the scheme was abandoned as a power loss of some 15–20% was considered too high in view of the limited power the Maybach engine made available. Work on this torque converter was stated to have been undertaken by Voith of Heddernheim, Maybach of Friedrich-shafen and AEG presumably of Berlin.

Another interesting development project which had been tried was the electro magnetic operation of the dog clutches used in ZF gearboxes (employing the Aphon principle) as an alternative to the hydraulic operation known as the Olvar (Oel-Variorex). This project was abandoned owing to the excessive generation of heat.

IV. Wartime organisation
8,000 workers were engaged on tank production, working in two shifts each of 12 hours. The night shift was stated to have only 50% of the output of the day shift. A pure 'Takt' system was employed in the assembly shop and this consisted of nine 'takte', each of six

hours. The total time estimated to complete a tank, including the various machining processes, was said to be 14 days. An average of 18–22 tanks were carried in the hull assembly shop and ten on the final assembly line.

At the beginning of 1943, the 'Tiger I' was being produced at the rate of 20 a month but a total of approximately 650 were completed within that year. In 1944, 623 'Tiger I' were assembled (work on this tank stopped in August 1944) and 377 'Tiger II'. In 1945 planned output for the 'Tiger II' was 140 a month, but actual production was 40 in January, 42 in February, and 25 in March. Monthly output figures are given in Appendix B.

A large number of components arrived in semi-finished or finished condition. A list of the main suppliers is included as Appendix C.

V. Processes and plant layout
The part of the Mittelfeld plant on the left-hand side of the main railway line, looking north, was concerned with truck re-work (see layout in Appendix A) including engines, and the manufacture of locomotive components. The main tank components' stores were located here as well as sheds containing tank turrets and hulls. The second part of the Mittelfeld works (ie, to the right of the main railway line looking north) consisted of four shops numbers 1, 2, 3 and 5. Number 4 shop, which was supposed to be constructed some time ago, was in fact never built. Shop Number 1 was a general machine shop mainly concerned with locomotive components. Shop Number 2 was the same. Shop Number 3 was concerned with machining of various tank components such as suspension arms, steering mechanism, hatch cover plates, etc, and hull assembly. Shop Number 5 was divided into two parts. On the left (looking north), it was engaged in locomotive work and on the right, with final assembly of tanks, ie, fitting of the turrets (received in a finished condition from Wegmann) to the already completed hulls.

The hull assembly line
There were two hull assembly lines fitted in shop Number 3, one on each side of the two large bays. The remainder of each bay was devoted to the machining of suspension arms, hatch cover plates, steering mechanism, top decks, and assembly of the resilient bogey wheels (see diagram in Appendix

A). The hull arrived as a welded unit with holes for suspension arms, final drive, rear idler, etc, rough bored. It then went to an eight-spindle horizontal borer (in fact only six were being used) where the holes in the hull sides for the suspension arms were finish bored. The next process is the four-spindle borer which finished the holes, both front and rear, for the final drives and idlers. The hull then goes to a vertical lathe for machining the face on the superstructure roof for the turret ring. Simultaneously with this process, the milling of the hull sides to receive the final drive casing is carried out. The hull then moves on to an assembly line so that the various components can be added.

Significant differences between the two hull machining lines lies in the fact that, whereas in the one case the hull is straight away mounted on to bogeys running on rails (so that accurate alignment is thereby maintained with the help of adjustable jacks for each operation), in the other case (the older line), the hulls have to be craned from one drill jig to the next which necessitates accurate alignment before each operation. In this case, the hull moved sideways whereas in the former case, they were positioned nose to tail. The machining of the superstructure top plate to receive the turret ring, and the end milling of the hull side plates to receive the final drive casing, are taken as data for all subsequent machining operations. This process must therefore be carried out first on the newer machining line if satisfactory results are to be obtained, because the hull is only adjusted for alignment once. On both assembly lines, the hulls move nose to tail and were carried on bogies mounted on rails.

VI. Machine tools
(a) A vertical two-tool lathe with a double horizontal end milling machine carries out simultaneously the surfacing of the superstructure top plate to receive the turret ring and the milling of the hull side plates to receive the final drive housing. The vertical two-cutter planer manufactured by Maschinenfabrik Turner of Frankfurt a/M is generally similar to the one used at Wegmann's for the same process on the turret ring (see Wegmann report). The two horizontal end millers (one each side) travel on a rack but are provided with no vertical adjustment. The setting up of this machine is essentially

achieved by mounting the hull to be worked on two four-wheeled bogies which are on rails set into a rigid concrete bed. Final adjustment for locating the hull is provided by adjustable jacks at various points. The hull is firmly anchored by stretching bolts secured to the shop floor.

(b) Eight-spindle horizontal borer for suspension arms and torsion bar borings in the hull side plates is manufactured by Berninghaus of Velbert Rhld. This tool is understood to be commonly referred to as 'Acht-spindelbohrwerk' which infers that four horizontal boring machines are installed on each side. In this instance, however, only three on each side were in fact present. The hull to be worked is secured in exactly the same manner as in (a) and each boring bar is a completely separate motorized unit capable of traverse by means of a rack but without any vertical adjustment. It is understood that the datum is taken from the machine surface of the superstructure top plate as referred to in Section V above.

Various adaptations of this machine are used in the various processes concerned with finishing the hull sides. Whilst there is nothing unconventional in the borer when considered as an individual machine, the univeral manner in which they are employed as multiple units for varying purposes is of considerable interest.

(c) Twin pillar radial drills by Raboma (Borsigwald-Berlin) are used for boring the holes in the superstructure top plate for the turret ring. Simultaneously two horizontal drilling machines of the same pattern as those described in para (b) above, bore the small holes in the hull side plates required for the suspension assembly. The horizontal drill unit traverses on a rack but has no provision for vertical adjustment.

(d) A further machine tool worthy of note is the rather ingenious double end mill capable of machining the end faces of 12 suspension arms at one time.

The suspension arms call for a large number of machining operations and many adaptations to orthodox tools have been employed, notably in one case where the home product of the 'Tiger I' final drive has been incorporated to achieve a suitable reduction.

(e) A somewhat unusual cluster type side mill incorporating five cutters in one tool was used to machine the faces

of the steering mechanism half-cases as opposed to the more usual method of end milling the flanges.

(f) The assembly of resilient bogey wheels is laid out for quantity production and a 15-ton hydraulic press is employed.

(g) A section of the shop was laid out for the assembly of steering units which were then bolted up to the gearbox (received at the plant complete) and the whole transmission unit was passed on to the test bay which comprised two beds with dynamometers. The control panel, however, was provided for three test units. A rectification bay was situated alongside to deal with rejects.

(h) Various machine shops in the Henschel plant covered most phases of machining processes used in general mechanical engineering. Gear grinding is almost exclusively by the Maag process. A number of the tools soon were of Somua (French) manufacture.

As this firm receives turrets complete and hulls completely fabricated, they have no plant for handling heavy armour plate bending or welding. Their locomotive activities, however, involved the profiling and welding of lighter sections.

Tec. Int. Sec.
G-2 Division.
Supreme HQ AEF.

Attached:
Appendix A — Layout of plant
Appendix B — Production data
Appendix C — List of main suppliers

Appendix A — Layout of Plant

See line diagrams on page. 154–155.

Appendix B — Production data (Henschel)

I. PzKpfw 'Tiger' Model E ('Tiger I')

	1942	1943	1944
Jan	—	35	93
Feb	—	32	95
Mar	—	41	86
Apr	1	46	104
May	—	50	100
Jun	—	60	75
Jul	—	65	64
Aug	12	60	6
Sep	15	85	—
Oct	15	50	—
Nov	17	60	—
Dec	23 +	65	—
Total	83	649	623

+ Estimated figure.

II. PzKpfw 'Tiger' Model B ('Tiger II')

	1943	1944	1945
Jan	—	3	40
Feb	—	5	42
Mar	—	6	25
Apr	—	6	—
May	—	15	—
Jun	—	32	—
Jul	—	45	—
Aug	—	84	—
Sep	—	49 +	—
Oct	1	29 +	—
Nov	—	56 +	—
Dec	2	47	—
Total	3	377	107

+ Estimated figures.

III. PzKpfw 'Panther'

	1943
Jan	—
Feb	—
Mar	10
Apr	26
May	25
Jun	25
Jul	30
Aug	30
Sep	30
Oct	17
Nov	7
Dec	—
Total	200

Appendix C — List of main suppliers of parts and equipments for Tiger II

Hull Dortmund-Hoerder Huettenverein, Dortmund Fr Krupp, Essen Skoda, Pilsen, Factory Koeniggraet

Gearbox Zahnradfabrik Friedrichshafen Waldwerke, Passau

Engines Maybach, Friedrichshafen Auto-Union, Chemnitz

Tracks Aug Engels, Velbert

Turret Wegmann & Co, Kassel

Fuel Tank I. Arnold, Friedensdorf/Lahn

Hand and foot pedal movement Berg Achsenfabrik, Wiehl (near Cologne)

Exhaust installation Karl Born, Aschersleben

Periscope Maschinenfbk Dorst AG, Oberlind-Sonneberg Sylbe u Ponndorf, Schmoelln

Accelerator & starter rods Hermann Fesel, Zwiesel

Gear valve Hermann fesel, Zwiesel

Track guard Gotthardt u Kuehne, Lommatzsch (near Dresden) Wilh Lenze, Neheim-Huesten

Ventilation installation Maschinenfabrik Imperial GmbH Meissen

Ammunition stowage frames Richard Krahmer, Chemnitz Schneider u Korb, Bernsbach

Driver seats Wilh Lenze, Neheim-Huesten

Ball mounting for MG Luftfahrtgeräte-bau Arno Mueller, Leipzig

Crank starter Jos Muench, Brotterode

Hatch Cover O.D. Werk Willy Ostner, Branderbisdorf/Sachsen

Shock Absorber Cover Scheidt & Bachmann, Rheydt (later Pirna)

Bogie wheels Diana Maschinenfabrik, Kassel-Bettenhausen

Driving sprocket (rough) Bochumer Verein, Bochum Berg Stahlindustrie, Remscheid Ruhrstahl AG, Witten-Annen Eisenwerke, Oberdonau, Linz

Idler Dingler, Karcher & Co, Worms Ruhrstahl AG, Annen Van Tongelsche Stahlwerke, Guestrow, Mecklenburg Wittmann AG, Hagen-Haspe Knorrbbremse AG, Volmarstein Deutsche Eisenwerke, Muehlheim

Final Drive Housing Dingler, Karcher & Co, Worms Van Tongelsche Stahlwerke, Guestrow, Mecklenburg Deutsche Eisenwerke, Muehlheim Lindener Eisen-u Stahlwerke, Hannover-Linden Pleissner GmbH Herzberg/Harz

Gearbox housing Dingler, Karcher & Co, Worms Meier & Weichelt, Leipzig Deutsche Eisenwerke, Muehlheim

Safety clamp Ruhrstahl AG, Witten-Annen Vereinigte Oberschleisische Huettenwerke, Gleiwitz, Werk Malapane

Grille (louvres) Dingler, Karcher & Co, Worms Meier u Weichelt, Leipzig Ruhrstahl AG, Witten-Annen

Torsion bars Hoesch AG, Hohenlimburg Roechling GmbH, Wetzlar

Sprocket in rough condition Vereinigte Stahlwerke Charlottenhuette, Niederschelden/Sieg Kioeckner-Werke AG, Osnabrueck

Steering brake Sueddeutsche Arguswerke, Karlsruhe

Fan assembly Ehrlich, Gotha

Turret mechanism Ehrlich, Gotha

Electrical equipment Bosch, Stuttgart

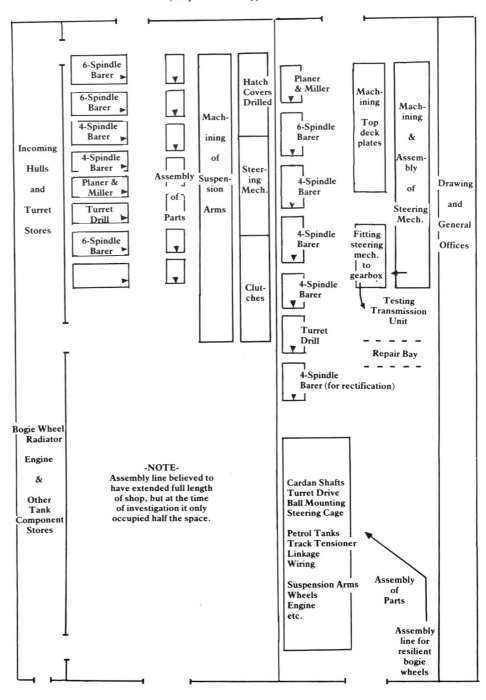

DIAGRAMMATIC LAYOUT OF HULL ASSEMBLY SHOP

(Shop No.3 – see Appendix A/1

HENSCHEL & SON
KASSEL-MITTELFIELD PLANT
SCALE - 1/6,000

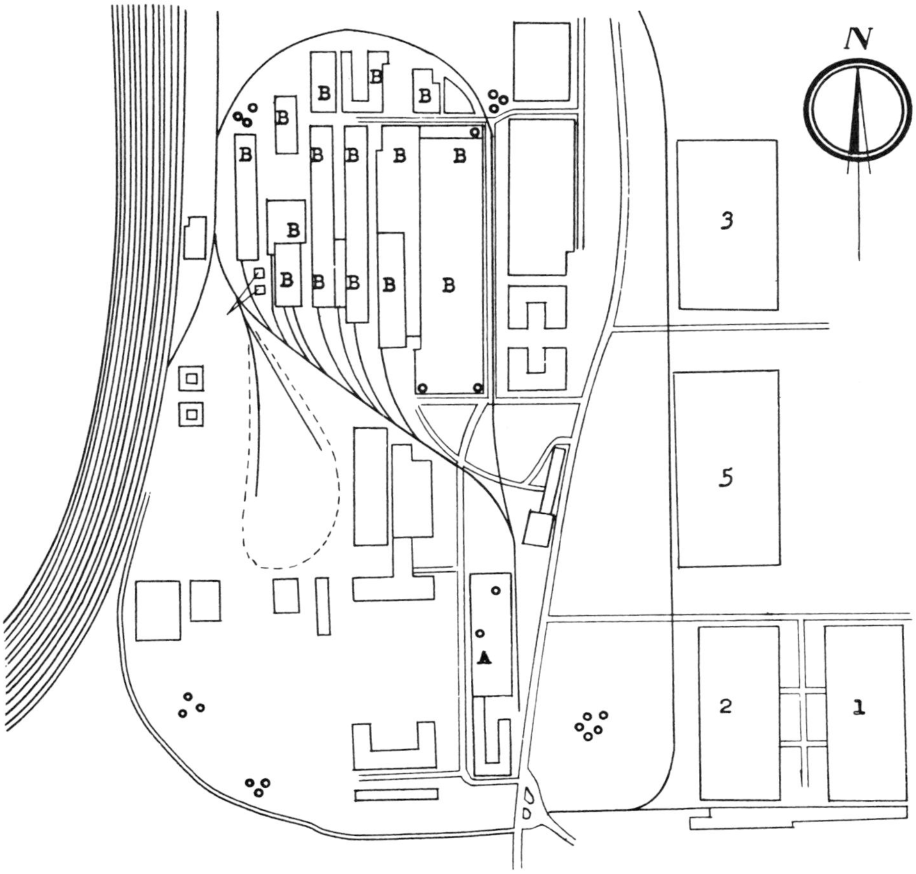

N

3

5

2   1

A Tiger I under construction at the Hensehel Tiger factory at Mittelfeld, which is the adject of Annex A. See also the photograph on page 15.

LEGEND

3. **Hull machining and Assembly**
5. **Final Tank Assembly**
1. **General Machine Shop (spare parts and gears)**
2. **General Machine Shop (locomotive parts)**
A. **Repair Shop**
B. **General Shops engaged on locomotives
   and spare parts for trucks.**

Endnotes

Introduction

1. Sadly, Albert von Boxberg is now deceased.

Chapter 1

2. All A7Vs were collected and scrapped by the Inter-Allied Control Commission with the exception of one model, taken as a trophy of war by the AIF and still in existence and on display in the Australian War Memorial Museum.

3. The *Truppenamt* was the organisation formed after the abolition of the German General Staff, to oversee the affairs of the *Reichswehr*.

4. The *Grosstraktors* finished up as parade monuments at various Panzer regimental headquarters.

5. *Covert German Re-armament 1919–1939*.

6. Figures as given in *Armour, the development of mechanised forces and their equipment*, by Richard Ogorkiewicz.

7. Report of the *Heereswaffenampt*, pt IV H 15/40.

Chapter 2

8. As quoted by Brigadier H.B.C. Watkins in *Panzer Divisions of WW2* from Seeckt's book *Thoughts of a Soldier*, 1928.

9. General-Oberst (Colonel-General) Heinz Guderian became head of the Panzer arm in 1938 after over two years' commanding 2nd Panzer Division.

10. Most AFV crews also took steps to carry useful spare parts with them. For example, tank crews in the Middle East and Russia carried up to eight spare bogie wheels, fixed to the sides of the superstructure or fore and aft on the hull. Six to twelve spare track plates were also draped fore and aft, together with two steel tow ropes. Extra fuel cans were carried and, in some cases, a special two-wheeled trailer was towed behind the tank (see photograph later). A large ration box, stoves, buckets, camouflage nets, poles, tank bivouacs, sleeping bags and blankets — the amount of kit needed to enable the crew to survive under all conditions was legion.

Chapter 3

11. *A German Panzerwaffe 1920–1939* by R. Burke.

12. The MG 13K (Dreyse) machine-gun weighed 10.84 kg (23.9 lb), had a cyclic rate of fire between 500 and 625 rpm and a muzzle velocity of 770 m/s (2,525 fps). Ammunition was in 25- or 100-round boxes.

13. Fu = *Funkgerät* (wireless equipment).

14. 'It could be seen that Spain would serve as the "European Aldershot". I was in command of all the German ground troops in Spain during the war... They were used to train Franco's tank force — and to get battle experience themselves... The first batch of German tanks arrived in September, followed by a larger batch in October. They were the Pz I. Russian tanks began to arrive on the other side even quicker — at the end of July. They were of a heavier type than ours, which were armed only with machine-guns, and I offered a reward of 500 pesetas for every one that was captured, as I was only too glad to convert them to my own use.' Quote from a conversation between von Thoma and Liddell Hart, taken from *The Other Side of the Hill*.

Chapter 4

15. Belt bags were made of canvas, with a metal mouth and hinged metal lid fitted with a quick-release fastening. To prevent dirt and sand getting inside the bag, a pad of greaseproof paper was inserted into each between the top of the container and the lid. The belt bags were highly effective, even in the very dusty conditions of North Africa.

16. The 20 mm cannon shell was too small to produce an effective high explosive round, but its armour-piercing capability was quite good.

17. *German Tanks of World War II*, by FM von Senger und Etterlin.

18. The KwK 30 was fed by a flat box magazine which held ten rounds, because the standard magazine of the 2 cm Flak 30 gun (which held 20 rounds) was too large for use in tanks. It was recoil-operated and, when mounted in the PzKpfw II, could only be fired on automatic.

19. Taken from *So lebten und so starben sie*.

Chapter 5

20. (t) stood for 'tschech', ie, 'Czech' in German — see end of Chapter X for further examples of nomenclature for captured vehicles.

21. *Czechoslovak AFVs 1918–1945* by Charles Kliment and Hilary Doyle.

22. *The 6th Panzer Division 1937–45* by Oberst aD Helmut Ritgen.

23. Quote provided by Hilary Doyle.

24. *The 6th Panzer Division 1937–45* by Oberst aD Helmut Ritgen.

25. *Czechoslovak AFVs 1918–1945* by Charles Kliment and Hilary Doyle.

26. Comment provided by Hilary Doyle.

27. *Czechoslovak AFVs 1918–1945* by Charles Kliment and Hilary Doyle.

28. Quote provided by Hilary Doyle.

Chapter 6

29. *German Tanks of World War II* by FM von Senger und Etterlin.

30. *The Ordnance Department on Beachhead and Battlefront*, pages 23 et seq.

31. *ibid*.

32. *ibid*.

33. Taken from a report on PW OS/95 who had been a member of *schwere* Panzer Abteilung 5, 25th Panzergrenadier Division, CSDIC (UK) SIR 1364.

34. Intelligence Bulletin Vol II No 11 of July 1944, published by the War Department, Washington, DC.

35. The use of *Ostketten* was essential, as this quote from Department of the Army Pamphlet No 20–291 of February 1952 entitled *Effects of Climate in Combat in*

European Russia shows: 'The principal shortcoming of German tanks was the narrow width of their tracks. Tanks sank deep in the snow and, because of their limited ground clearance, ultimately became stuck. Russian tanks, particularly the T-34, KV 1 and KV 2, were able to drive through deep snow because of their good ground clearance and wide tracks, and therein lay their special effectiveness in winter warfare. After the first winter of the war, Germans started to use wide, removable tracks. These solved the problems of snow mobility, but tanks so equipped could not be moved on German railroad cars and were too wide to cross the standard German military bridge. Russian wide tank tracks were factory equipment; the broad gauge of Russian railroads with their correspondingly wide flatcars eliminated the transportation problem. In December 1942 a German armoured division, diverted from the abortive relief thrust on Stalingrad to consolidate an extremely critical situation on the Chir River front, was delayed 12 hours because the snow tracks of its tanks were too wide for a military bridge over the Don. The tracks of more than 150 tanks and assault guns had be removed in total darkness and remounted on the far shore.'

Chapter 7

36. Kummersdorf was where, in early 1934, Adolf Hitler had his first viewing of the new Panzer force's equipment, Guderian demonstrating to him the basic elements of the Panzer division — a motor cycle platoon, an anti-tank platoon, a platoon of PzKpfw I light tanks and some reconnaissance cars.

37. Quoted by FM von Senger und Etterlin in *German Tanks of World War II*, page 44.

38. The Brinell (sometimes misspelt 'Brinnel') hardness method was devised in 1900 and involves pressing a hardened steel ball into the surface of the material to be measured, causing an indentation. The hardness number of the material is then calculated by dividing the applied load by the surface area of the indentation.

39. It is doubtful if the command tank described in this story was based on a PzKpfw IV, because the *Panzerbefehlswagen* converted from the Mk IV was not produced until 1944. It is far more likely that this was a *Panzerbefehlswagen* III Ausf D₁ — see previous chapter for details.

40. 24th Panzer Division, which was destroyed at Stalingrad a few months later.

41. US Army Intelligence Bulletin, *GI comments on German use of firepower*.

42. *The Battle of the Bulge*, page 202.

Chapter 8

43. There had been a VK 3001 produced in October 1941 as a logical development of the proposed *Durchbruchswagen* (breakthrough vehicle) of 1937, which was intended to replace the PzKpfw IV/BW series then in prototype. While the VK 3001 had an effect on the design of the Panther, it is more germane to the Tiger's development, so is dealt with in the next chapter.

44. He was a key figure in German AFV design at that time, had been with *Waffenprüfamt* 6 since 1936 and remained as its chief engineer for the rest of the war. He was responsible for many innovative features such as the interleaved roadwheels.

45. Guderian also mentions in his diary that he 'Spent 15 June worrying about our problem child, the Panther; the track suspension and drive were not right and the optics were also not yet satisfactory'. The following day he told Hitler that he still did not think the Panther was ready.

46. First action was in Operation ZITADELLE (the German offensive at Kursk), which had been delayed so as to allow the new tanks to take part.

47. As quoted in *The Ordnance Department Planning Munitions for War*. However, I would personally question the accuracy of this claim. It is far more likely to be 1,900 yd (1,737 m) or even 2,900 yd (2,650 m) as 7,900 yd is quite out of the question.

48. The *Nahverteidigungswaffe* (close-in defence weapon) was a short-barrelled grenade projector firing smoke grenades (*Nebelkerzen*) or HE grenades.

49. Projector Infantry Anti-Tank, the British equivalent of the *Panzerfaust*. It fired a 3 lb (1.36 kg) hollow-charge grenade and had a combat range of 100 yd (90 m).

50. Department of Trade Design, Materials Division, Armour Branch Report AT No 232 dated 12 January 1945.

51. M1 10A/BM/4049 PANTHER, GS1 (Tech) 21 Army Group.

52. Most of the original information on Panther F was obtained by the British from Ing Kunze, of Daimler-Benz, Berlin, who had been concerned with its design. He gave them the facts from memory, as his file and drawings had been removed by the Russians!

53. Foremost among the new 'assault rifles', it had a cyclic rate of fire of 500 rpm.

54. A prerequisite of their design had been the need to simplify production and reduce production costs. Leaving aside the gun sight, rangefinder and armament, there was a 30 to 40 per cent saving in man hours in production time.

55. Extract from Appendix D to War Office Tech Int Summary dated 9 August 1945.

56. As quoted in *German Tanks of World War 2* by FM von Senger und Etterlin.

57. Extract from DRAC Tech Int Digest No 3 Appendix E.

58. Extract from War Office Tech Int Summary No 146.

59. On later models there were usually two distinct boxes rather than just one. The upper box structure measured 11 ft × 9 ft × 3 ft (3.35 × 2.74 × 0.91 m) and the lower 11 ft × 9 ft × 6 ft 6 in (2 m), with three compartments in it (one for accommodation, one for stores and the third to provide access to the upper box). Both upper and lower structures were fitted with access hatches which coincided when the two structures were fitted together.

60. Extracted from a PW report circulated my MI 10A on 6 September 1944. The covering letter commented that the PW was 'well informed and fairly reliable'.

61. The T-43 was the up-armoured version of the T-34/76B, built during the winter of 1942/43 before the Russians decided upon the 85 mm. It had thicker armour, an improved mantlet and a hexagonal turret.

62. Taken from *So lebten und so starben sie* by Hans Schaufler and quoted here by kind permission of the *Kameradschaft Ehem Panzer-Regiment 35 eV*.

63. See *Effects of Climate on Combat in European Russia*, US Army Pamphlet No 20–291 or February 1952.

64. In 1939 the Iron Cross was divided into four degrees, the second highest being that of the Knights Cross of the Iron Cross, a decoration which was itself during the course of the war divided into five degrees — plain, with oakleaves, with oakleaves and swords, with oakleaves, swords and diamonds and with golden oakleaves, swords and diamonds.

65. The VW166 *Schwimmwagen* was the amphibious version of the famous Volkswagen Typ 82 *Kubelwagen* developed from the prewar 'People's Car', or 'Beetle'.

66. Presumably they were the 122 mm Field Gun Model 1931/37 (A-19) which was later mounted on the KV heavy tank

chassis to form the SU 122 heavy anti-tank SP.

Chapter 9

67. This was a name which also applied to the NbFz at one stage, while both the British 'Independent' and the French *Char de Rupture* were classed as heavy breakthrough tanks.

68. The report itself plus other British material on the Tiger has been made the subject of a fascinating book called *Tiger: The British View*, published in 1986 by HMSO. The book was edited by David Fletcher, Librarian of the Tank Museum.

69. The report has been altered in pen to read 'Ausf E'. Also, of course, the SdKfz quoted is wrong, 182 being that of the Tiger II, 181 being the correct *SonderKraftfahrzeug* (special purpose vehicle) number for the Tiger I.

70. Taken from *Report on PzKw VI (Tiger) Model E*, Part 1, *General Description*, published in January 1944 by the Military College of Science, School of Tank Technology, Chobham Lane, Chertsey.

71. As the first Panthers did not go into action until July 1943 in the Kursk area,

either this is a misprint for 'Panzers' — or the source has got his facts sadly awry!

72. As quoted in *Panzers at War* by A.J. Barker.

73. There is an interesting pencilled note in the margin alongside this sub-paragraph which reads: 'Not to be passed on to troops. CO.'

74. Figures are taken from *Panzers in Normandy Then and Now* by Eric Lefevre.

75. This was done both for strength and for ease of production.

76. Technical Intelligence Summary dated 7 February 1945.

77. This figure covered both Tiger I and II.

Chapter 10

78. To be strictly accurate, there were two other AFVs built in the superheavy class, although these were really self-propelled artillery pieces and not tanks. The first was called *Grille* (Cricket) and was designed to mount either a 17 cm gun or a 21 cm howitzer on a lengthened Tiger II chassis. Only one pilot model was built but it was not completed before the war ended. The other was an enormous self-propelled mortar called *Karl*, originally designed for work

against the Maginot Line, which mounted a 60 cm mortar (later replaced on some vehicles by a 54 cm mortar). Six 60 cm *Mörser* (*Gerät 040*) were completed and saw service from 1939 onwards. Towards the middle of the war some were re-equipped with the new 54 cm weapon. Although *Karl* was self-propelled, its sheer size and weight (125 tons, rising to 132 tons when the new mortar was fitted) made any long moves extremely difficult, so they had to go either by rail or on special trailers. The PzKpfw IV Ausf F chassis was used as the basis of a *Munitionspanzer* specifically designed for use with *Karl*, to handle the enormous mortar shells with a special 2.5 ton (2.46 UK/2.76 US tons) crane. It also carried three extra rounds of ammunition.

79. See Panther chapter and later for more about this brilliant engineer.

80. 'E' stands for *Entwicklung* (development).

81. The interrogation report is held by the Tank Museum Library.

82. Technical Intelligence Summary No 132 dated 30 June 1944.

83. Loose-leaf books of foreign equipment.

Select Bibliography

Published works

Bender, R. James and Odegard: *Uniforms, Organisation and History of the Panzertruppe*, R. James Bender Publishing Co, 1980.

Burke, R.: *A German Panzerwaffe 1920–1939*, University Microfilms Inc, 1975.

Carell, Paul: *Hitler's War in Russia*, Harrap, 1964.

Chamberlain, Peter, Doyle, Hilary and Jentz, Tom: *Encyclopaedia of German Tanks of World War Two*, Arms and Armour Press, 1978.

Crow, Duncan (Ed): *AFVs of Germany*, Barrie & Jenkins, 1973.

Green, Constance, Thomson, Harry and Roots, Peter: *The Ordnance Department: Procurement and Supply*, Office of the Chief of Military History, US Army, 1955.

Guderian, Heinz: *Panzer Leader*, Michael Joseph, 1952.

Hauschild, Reinhard: *Der springende Reiter. 1 Kavallerie Division-24 Panzer Division im Bild*, Ernst J. Dohany, 1984.

Howe, George F.: *The Battle History of 1st Armored Division*, Combat Forces Press, 1954.

Kleine, Egon, and Kühn, Volkmar: *Tiger — Die Geschichte einer legendären Waffe 1942–44*, Motorbuch Verlag, 1976.

Kliment, Charles, and Doyle, Hilary: *Czechoslovak AFVs 1918–1945*, Argus Books, 1979.

Liddell-Hart, Basil: *The Other Side of the Hill*, Cassell, 1948.

Mayo, Lida: *The Ordnance Department: On Beachhead and Battlefront*, Office of the Chief of Military History, US Army, 1968.

Manchester, William: *The Arms of Krupp*, Michael Joseph, 1969.

Macdonald, Charles B.: *Battle of the Bulge*, Weidenfeld & Nicholson, 1984.

Oechelhauser, Justus Wilhelm von: *Wir zogen in das Feld*, Harald Boldt Verlag, 1983; and *Udelheit es ist soweit*, Moewag Books, 1984.

Ogorkiewicz, Richard: *Armour, the development of mechanised forces and their equipment*, Atlantic Books, 1960.

Perrett, Bryan: *The Tiger Tanks*, Osprey/Vanguard, 1980; and *The PanzerKampfwagen III*, Osprey/Vanguard, 1980.

Rebentisch, Ernst: *Zum Kaukasus und zu den Tauren, Die Geschichte der 23 Panzer Division*, Verband ehem Angehöriger der 23 Pz Div, 1963.

Ritgen, Oberst aD Helmut: *The 6th Panzer Division 1937–45*, Osprey/Vanguard, 1982.

Schaufler, Heinrich: *So lebten und so starben sie. Das Buch von Panzer Regiment 35*, Kameradschaft ehem Pz Regt 35 eV, 1983.

Schroeder, Gerd: *Die 1(H) 14 Pz im Westen 1940*, published privately.

Spielburger, Walter J.: *Die Panzer-Kampfwagen I und II und ihre Abseiten*,

Motorbuch Verlag, 1984.

Spielburger, Walter J.: *Die Panzer-Kampfwagen 35(t) und 38(t)*. Motorbuch Verlag, 1980.

Thomson, Harry C. and Mayo, Lida: *The Ordnance Department: On Beachhead and Battlefront*, Office of the Chief of Military History, US Army, 1960.

Watkins, Brigadier H.B.C. and others: *Panzer Divisions of World War 2*, Profile Publications, date unknown.

Weidmann, Gert-Axel: *Unser Regiment, Reiter Regiment 2-Panzer Regiment 24*, Ernst J. Dohany, 1984.

Whalley, Bart: *Covert German Re-armament 1919–1939*, University Publications of America, 1984.

Reports, pamphlets and similar material

Economic Survey of Germany, Section K — Armaments and Munitions; Foreign Office and Ministry of Economic Warfare, May 1945.

Glossary of Tank Terms; prepared by the School of Tank Technology, March 1943.

Report on German Armoured Vehicle Production; Foreign Office and Ministry of Economic Warfare, June 1944.

Illustrated Record of German Army Equipment 1939–45, Vol III — AFVs; DMI War Office.

Summary of German Tanks; Office of AC of S G-2 SHAEF, October 1944.

Preliminary Survey of German AFV Plants; SHAEF, May 1945.

Report by War Mechanisation Board on Praga Light Tank, March 1939.

Report on Trial of Praga Light Tank at Lulworth, March 1939.

School of Tank Technology wartime reports on enemy AFVs as follows:

No 5 on PzKw III of September 1942;
No 6 on PzKw II of October 1942;
No 9 on PzKw I (Commander's model) of March 1943;
No 10 on PzKw I Ausf B of April 1943;
No 16 on StuG III dated October 1943;
No 23 on BIV demolition vehicle of October 1944;
Report on PzKw VI Tiger of January 1944 together with other similar reports on the same AFV.

Report by the Associated Equipment Co Ltd on PzKw III of January 1942.

Report on Turret and Armament of PzKw III by Merz and McLannan of August 1942.

Report by Research Department, Leyland Motors, on PzKw IV, of January 1942.

Report on Turret and Armament of PzKw IV by Dept of Tank Design, Ministry of Supply of October 1943.

Miscellaneous Technical Intelligence Summaries, from UK and USA (see text for full details).

Miscellaneous RAC Liaison Letters (see text for full details).

US Department of the Army pamphlets, Small Unit Actions — German Campaign in Russia 1941–1945 as follows:

No 20-261A German Campaigns in Russia;
No 20-290 Terrain Factors in Russian Campaign;
No 20-291 Effects of Climate in European Russia;
No 20-255 German Campaign in Poland (1939);
No 20-233 German Defence Tactics against Russian Breakthroughs.

Index